Plato: Dramatist of the Life of Reason

PLATO

DRAMATIST OF THE
LIFE OF REASON

✦ ✦ ✦

John Herman Randall, Jr.

FREDERICK J. E. WOODBRIDGE PROFESSOR EMERITUS
OF PHILOSOPHY, COLUMBIA UNIVERSITY

Columbia University Press

NEW YORK AND LONDON · 1970

For Frank Tannenbaum
Philosopher, Teacher, and Friend
and
Lifelong Lover of Plato

FOREWORD

"Just before he died, we are told, Plato dreamed that he was changed into a swan, and, flying from tree to tree, caused much trouble for the bird-catchers who vainly tried to take him. Simmias, the companion of Socrates, interpreted the dream to signify that all men would desire to catch the spirit of Plato, but none would succeed, for each would interpret him in his own fashion. It was a true dream, repeatedly fulfilled by admirers of Plato." [1]

All interpretations of "the spirit of Plato" are very personal, and the present small volume is no exception. A few years ago I began a brief account of Aristotle by saying, "This little book attempts to set forth what one man has found to be the significance for the present day of the thought of the second of the two major philosophers our so-called 'Western' civilization has managed to produce." I also there confessed, "No student of the human achievement can forswear the hope of eventually commenting on the literary and philosophic genius of Plato."

In yielding to the temptation there hinted at to write upon the first of those two major philosophers, I am here offering a very personal statement of what I have found to be not merely the significance for the present day, but the eternal and ever-renewed significance of Plato. Such a perspective upon Plato will inevitably exhibit a rather different tone and temper than one on Aristotle. The Stagirite is straightforward and forthright, and measurably

[1] Frederick J. E. Woodbridge, *The Son of Apollo* (Boston, 1929), p. 31.

succeeded in getting into words, into bald prose, what he had seen and wanted to say. But Plato is a poet, whose writing is extremely subtle and suggestive rather than literal, and contains so many levels of meaning that each rereading reveals something not seen the last time. Plato needs to be read with sensitivity and imagination. And to such reading each man brings, and must bring, his own personal store of such qualities.

My own acquaintance with Plato began by hearing of him from a scholar of just such sensitivity and imagination, Frederick J. E. Woodbridge. All those privileged to enjoy the experience of studying under him can recall, I think, some particular moment when the power of his discourse touched us most profoundly. Dean Woodbridge was master of the spoken word. With him discourse was once more what it had been for his beloved Greeks—a thing to rejoice and delight in, to play with and manipulate, to ponder and to use. In the end, it became for him the very voice of Nature herself, transmuting her articulation and her ways into human speech, and teaching her lessons to him who had the wit to coöperate with her and to experience what she is. Listening to the Dean, one found credible the doctrine of the Word as the instrument of creation. For there was nothing he could not effect with his words, nothing he could not evoke by their power.

Woodbridge was himself philosophically an Aristotelian, a careful scholar and a profound philosophical interpreter of Aristotelian thinking, who taught me how to find all I think I have come to learn from Aristotle. But Woodbridge was at the same time a poet of insight and vision, and he taught me also to see and recognize what Plato had to offer. The power of his discourse presided over an hour I still recall as the most moving intellectual experience of my student years. It was that unforgettable morning when, speaking of Plato's theory of ideas, he carried us, as on the tones of a great organ, to that Platonic heaven which is above the heavens, and then, suddenly altering the stops, burst in like Alcibiades at the feast with a humorous and realistic comment on the idealism bred of fine words. In that dramatic confrontation of vision with experience he made one auditor "see"—and conceive a lasting devotion to Plato. I should like to think that my personal interpretation of Plato is not merely personal, that it was shared by Woodbridge.

Woodbridge wrote a book about Plato, *The Son of Apollo*. The title has been rather blind to those unfamiliar with the legend of Plato's ancestry. Woodbridge was a learned critical scholar of the Greeks, and he had reams of careful notes on Plato and the Platonic dialogues. But he disliked controversy, and when he came to write his book he put all those impedimenta of the classical scholar aside and concentrated on Plato himself, directly and with inspired vision. His book, though the product of erudition and critical scholarship, has never greatly impressed schol ars. Paul Shorey, dean of American Platonic scholars of that generation, dismissed the chapter on "Death" as "mortuary meditations." Only Raymond Weaver,[2] of those who wrote of *The Son of Apollo,* had the critical insight and the imagination to see what Woodbridge was doing, and its originality and achievement. But I have never had the slightest reservation in recommending the book as by far the best writing on Plato, almost the only one that is as interesting and valuable as reading further in Plato himself.

[2] Raymond M. Weaver is best known for his *Herman Melville* (1921). In addition to his Melville studies, he is remembered as an inspired teacher in Columbia College.

As a student, I also learned from another great interpreter of Plato, Wendell T. Bush. Bush had studied Plato
at Harvard under Santayana. At Columbia he gave an inspired course on the Platonic dialogues, a fresh and imaginative reading of the text, which revealed to the full what his
slender writings merely suggest, his gifts for unconventional
insights and turns of thought and for simple, concrete, yet
unhackneyed illustrations. He brought out tersely the functional theory of knowledge that Plato's dialogues elaborate.
All his thinking was fresh, imaginative, and perceptive;
and I should like to imagine that my own reading of Plato
reflects something of his insights. He originally suggested
to me the viewing of the *Republic* against the background
of the social experience of the immediate audience for whom
it was written, who had lived through the Spartan victory
over Athens and many of whom were tempted to collabo-
rate with the conqueror. This suggestion has ever since led
me to see in Plato's masterpiece an ironical commentary on
the Spartan ideal of military efficiency and a glorious defense of the ideals of the earlier Athens.

In my student days we had to submit to an oral examination on four philosophers we could choose. Naturally,
everyone chose Plato as one figure. I diligently prepared on
all the dialogues. Bush took charge of my interrogation,
and proceeded to devote the whole time to questioning me
about the unwritten *Philosopher* dialogue, the third in that
trilogy announced to begin with the *Sophist* and the *Statesman*. If anyone other than Plato himself could have made
the *Philosopher* a masterpiece, it was surely Wendell T.
Bush.

John Herman Randall, Jr.

Columbia University
February 14, 1969

ACKNOWLEDGMENTS

I am deeply grateful to those scholars and philosophers who have gone carefully over the first draft of this volume, and contributed immensely to it by their considered comments and suggestions. Charles H. Kahn, of the University of Pennsylvania, a former valued colleague at Columbia, made clear to me just how a trained and penetrating classical scholar would welcome this rather unconventional interpretation of Plato's life and philosophy. Paul O. Kristeller, a present colleague, gave me the comments of one who has been a lifelong student of the tradition of Platonism. Herbert W. Schneider, now of Claremont College, spent hours suggesting changes in some of the more colloquial passages, echoes of lectures these many years. As a fellow student of Woodbridge, Schneider did not violently disagree with most of my emphases in interpreting Plato's philosophy. My son Francis B. Randall, historian at Sarah Lawrence College, corrected my most glaring historical errors and endeavored to tone down some of my polemical zeal.

Most of all, perhaps, I am indebted to Gilbert Ryle (without his knowledge, to be sure), whose scholarly and genuinely philosophic and imaginative article on Plato in the *Encyclopedia of Philosophy,* and whose suggestive volume, *Plato's Progress,* have stimulated Platonic scholarship to reconsider problems recently taken as settled, and made a fresh examination imperative. I have not avoided the temptation to bring Ryle's evidence and cogent arguments to bear on those points where it supports my own judgment in Platonic interpretation.

Once more I am deeply aware of the invaluable assistance of Joan McQuary of the Columbia University Press. This time I am especially grateful for her unrelenting war against capitalism, which she hates as bitterly as e.e. cummings. But for discerning editorial revision I am as usual most indebted to the patient and indefatigable labors of my wife Mercedes, who has fully lived up to the traditional role of severest and most constructive critic.

It is to me especially gratifying that the swan, the bird of Apollo, that appears on this volume was drawn by Frederick J. Woodbridge, the architect. For he is responsible for the drawings adapted from the Greek that served as symbols in his father's book on Plato. This swan is taken from a coin of Klazomenai. It is an Attic four-drachma piece, and dates from the period 360 to 300 B.C. On the obverse appears a head of Apollo. Thus the Platonic symbolism is wholly appropriate.

J. H. R., Jr.

CONTENTS

	Foreword	vii
	Acknowledgments	xi
I.	The Dialogues as Dramatic Vision	1
II.	Plato the Man	6
III.	The Platonic Corpus	30
IV.	The Greek Heritage of Plato	36
V.	Plato's Heritage from the Early Greek Philosophers	55
VI.	Plato's Immediate Background: The Sophists	80
VII.	The Historical and the Platonic Socrates	93
VIII.	Plato's Circle and Audience	103
IX.	Plato the Artist-Philosopher	122
X.	The Philosophy of the Artist and the Artistic Experience	133
XI.	The Theme of the Good Life	146

Contents

XII. The Efficiently Organized City:
      The Republic   161

XIII. The Good Life: "Later" Treatment   172

XIV. Plato's "Ideas"   188

XV.   Platonic Idealism   201

XVI. Platonic Immortality   211

XVII. Plato's "Later" Philosophy   220

XVIII. Plato's Mathematical Cosmology:
       His "Unwritten Philosophy"   238

XIX. Plato's Ethical Cosmology:
      The Timaeus   247

XX.   Epilogue: Plato and the
      Tradition of "Platonism"   257

      Index   265

Plato: Dramatist of the Life of Reason

The Dialogues as Dramatic Vision

THE first and greatest of the two major philosophers our Western civilization has managed to produce is Plato. This Plato, whom every succeeding generation has been able to call "our Plato," is not the man who walked the streets of Athens, however interesting that figure might be if we only had some certain knowledge about him, which we probably do not. He is not even the teacher who set up a school in the Academy grove, a school which was the first of the many teaching institutions that have played so central a role in the long tradition of Western culture.

Plato the historical figure, the citizen of ancient Athens, has nothing to do with our Plato. Our Plato is the Platonic dialogues. They stand alone. Their author, whoever he was, never founded an Academy; these dialogues are quite irrelevant to the report, which may well be true, that the author of some of them had become a schoolmaster.

The author of the dialogues which have been the most influential philosophical literature produced in the Western world observed human life, and managed to transfigure it. He held it up and looked at it, clearly and in a spirit of detachment, and made it the object of _nous,_ of imaginative vision, of _theōria_. The dialogues are, in fact, pictures of men, what the Greeks called "θεωρίαι," pictures of men talking, discussing, arguing, sometimes even thinking. They are objective and universal, as true, as relevant to human life today as when they were written. To be sure, a knowledge of the intellectual atmosphere in which they were written, could we ascertain it, might throw light on just who is talking, and just what issues they are talking about. But who the characters are, and what they are talking about, is not the important thing about the dialogues. The important thing is the way they talk. Wherever they may be found, men, intelligent, cultivated men, talk like that. The dialogues are the picture of what we today call "intellectuals"—of intellectuals in any age. In Plato's own language, they exhibit the "Idea" of the Intellectual himself, the pure intellectual, *autos ho dialektikos,* the Talker himself—as Jowett would put it, of the Absolute Talker.

Men discuss endlessly the ideal state—though it could not possibly exist, and would be intolerable if it could. They come out always with a utopia in which every institution is perfectly perfect, and every man perfectly miserable —for they always arrive at what we today call a closed society. They know, if philosophers were only kings—that is, if only wise experts were running the government—there would be none of our troubles. This means, give them a chance, and they would show us how to do it.

They know, if you could only begin with children young enough, you could iron out all their human failings, and bring them up to be what children ought to be. They sometimes even try it. Parents and teachers meet together and discuss education. They get so interested in pointing out just what is wrong with education as it is, in lecturing on their pet ideas as to what education might be and ought to be, that they often completely forget to teach their children anything at all.

Those old enough to have children—especially if they have not any—discuss education interminably. The rest of us talk about love. It is an eternal theme, the most fascinating in the world. Nine-tenths of our literature is about it. And we always get slightly drunk on the talk about love: we end by thinking it is the most important and wonderful and divine thing in the world, the gateway to Heaven. But when we have sobered up from our talk the next morning, we realize it probably is not like that at all.

Plato, in other words, is a poet and a dramatist. And this does not mean, besides being a philosopher. There is no "besides" about it. Plato is a philosopher *because* he is a poet. True philosophy is poetry—poetic insight and vision, the imaginative enhancement of life. At least, we are so convinced while we are reading Plato.

Aeschylus, Sophocles, and Euripides depicted the dramatic qualities of man's emotions, the play and conflict of his passions. They held them up for contemplation, as a spectacle for *theoria.* Plato, it can be said, depicts the dramatic qualities of man's thinking, the play and conflict of his ideas, the spectacle of his mind. Plato raised the Greek passion for seeing life as it is to the level of philosophy, to the vision of the realm of ideas—which has its abode, not in some impossible Heaven, but in the discourse of men—in man talking—in the drama of the Life of Reason.

Platonic dialectic is no method or theory of logic—it is the soul of discussion. And it does not tell us anything about the world, about "reality," or "what is." We never acquire any such factual knowledge by discussing, in the sense in which Plato is constantly contrasting true knowledge, *epistēmē,* with mere opinion, *doxa.* Discussing things can never lead to more than better opinion. Francis Bacon was right enough in insisting that only hard grubbing among facts can yield genuine knowledge. And Aristotle's constantly recurring disparaging remarks contrasting the discusser, the talker, the intellectual, *ho logikos* and *ho dialektikos,* most unfavorably with the *physikos,* the inquirer and investigator, the scientist, we should say, are probably quite justified. Discussion never even proves anything. But it can convert men's souls. It does not make men wiser. Only experience can do that, and even experience accomplishes this miracle but rarely.

You may sit up all night discussing God and politics and art and women. You do not know any more in the morning than when you started. Indeed, you probably know rather less; for when intoxicated with talk you find yourself saying things you would never even think of when sober. As the discussion goes on you grow more and more foolish. We have all done it. It does not make you any wiser, but somehow it does succeed in making you fall in love with wisdom.

Young people read Plato, and at once start applauding Socrates the hero and hissing the villain. They soon get caught in the toils of the discussion, and begin searching for truth, like Socrates and the other characters. When they have grown older and developed more sense, they read Plato again, and find the truth—about men and human nature.

Were the Athenians actually like that? Were they indeed as they appear in the pages of Plato? There has grown up the myth of the God-like citizens of Athens, sometimes actually believed by literal-minded scholars and scientists. Sir Francis Galton, the cousin of Charles Darwin, even tried to calculate the cranial capacity of the average Athenian, which he was convinced must have been superior to that of Englishmen, even Cambridge and Oxford men.

Were the Athenians actually supermen? Of course not. But they would have liked to be. Did anyone ever actually love like Romeo? or was anyone ever actually so grandly tragic as Lear? Did anyone, any intellectual, ever really lead the Life of Reason? We would all like to think we could. But we are probably very lucky we cannot.

The dialogues, in a word, are the very "Idea" of the Life of Reason, of Talk—Talk itself, Absolute Talk. Human discourse is such that it can be so perfected in imagination.

II

Plato the Man

PLATO means to us the dialogues—the ancient documents that have come down to us and have never got lost.
We read and reread them. They stand alone. We do not
need to know Greece to understand them; in fact, our understanding of Greece, such as it is, owes much to them.
They have been a major factor in making the Greece we
believe we know.

Who was Plato? We ask such a question out of curiosity about an author who could produce such an impact
upon us, and upon pretty much every intervening generation and culture. We receive no enlightenment, nothing
that could be called an explanation of the Platonic documents themselves. A comparison with Shakespeare is at this
point inevitable. Nothing we know about Shakespeare the
man can be said to explain the plays. Hence we work out
theories proving that they were really written by someone
else we do know something about—by Francis Bacon, for
example, or by the Earl of Southampton.

Plato's personality is hardly revealed in the dialogues.
Do they contain Plato's "doctrines"? On this score there has
been a great division of opinion, even in antiquity. Even
Diogenes Laertius, the one ancient historian of Greek phi-

losophy whose account has come down to us, the heir of centuries of textbook writing, painfully anxious to reduce every thinker to a neat pigeon-holed set of opinions or *doxai,* admits the disagreement on this fundamental point: "Some assert," he writes, "that in the dialogues Plato dogmatizes [or teaches] in a positive manner; others vigorously deny it." And it is well to remember that this latter opinion was held for some two centuries at least by the Platonic School, by the Academy, as its orthodox position—during this period they were the stronghold of philosophical skepticism, which they held to have been the teaching of their founder, Plato. Certainly in the writings that have come down to us under the name of Plato there is not one personal touch—save the selective hand of a great artist.

Plato the man, in fact, has been idealized. From an early day he became a great tradition. Gradually there grew up what we can call "the romance of Plato's life." In terms of actual facts, we know as much—and as little—about the life of Plato as we know about the life of Shakespeare—enough to write long accounts of his times, but not enough to understand a single force that made him what he was. We have, to be sure, several "Lives" of Plato written in antiquity. But they were written centuries after Plato's death, when he had long become a mythical figure, when there was a great school of Platonists who had to have a worthy founder.[1] As literal or factual history they are very dubious. They contain the stories accumulated about the reputation

[1] There are very few contemporary references to Plato. Ryle points out that Isocrates failed to mention Plato or the Academy, Xenophon mentions him only once, and Demosthenes only twice, "but quite uninformatively." Gilbert Ryle, article "Plato" in *Encyclopedia of Philosophy,* ed. Paul Edwards (New York, 1967), VI, 314–15.

of Plato for some ten centuries, the rags and tags of anecdote molded into a beautiful Platonic myth. We strongly suspect that appropriate incidents had over the centuries been invented to illustrate passages in the dialogues.

In the nineteenth century, the higher criticism got busy upon the life of Plato. Scholars set out in the fashionable quest for the "real"—that is, the historical—Plato, forgetting that the "real" Plato is and always has been the dialogues. In the manuscripts there are included thirteen letters purporting to be from Plato's own hand. The tradition had it that Plato wrote thirteen letters: certainly thirteen letters have been preserved. Suspicions begin to arise. The scholars in the second half of the nineteenth century asked, are all of these letters genuine? If not all of them—and that all were written by Plato has always been very hard to accept—then which? The scholars proceeded to disagree, and have disagreed ever since. Some said, "Only a supreme master of fourth-century Attic style could have written them." Others rejoined, "They are abominably written, in a miserable style, and are full of solecisms and errors." The latter opinion has some justification. This school held, the Platonic Epistles are obvious forgeries.

The Letters certainly reveal a man concerned with trivialities, petulant, complaining, above all, with an overweaning self-esteem. The nineteenth-century scholars were inclined to judge, they are all spurious. They cast reflections on Plato's character, and that will never do. Plato must have been endowed with true Christian humility. Besides, it is notorious that the overwhelming mass of so-called letters of the ancient writers are either outright forgeries, or else literary productions, written in character—like the speeches in Thucydides.

Then, in the twentieth century, some scholars began to realize that the Seventh and Eighth Letters are the only real source we can claim to possess for any knowledge of Plato's life, and felt that it was necessary to bolster up a dubious tradition. Early in the century, when men had all become disillusioned by the excesses, especially by the predominantly negative results of the higher criticism, scholars on the whole were apt calmly to accept the Letters as an integral part of the tradition. Yet those same scholars continued to disregard in them what conflicted with their own interpretation of Plato. Thus, a recurrent theme in the Epistles runs: "I shall never attempt to put my doctrines into writing." "There is not and never will be any written work of Plato's own. What are now called his are the work of a Socrates grown beautiful and young." Of course, such statements were not to be taken seriously, and certainly not literally. What would then become of Platonic doctrine?

It is true that the Seventh and Eighth Epistles are the only source of the legend about Plato's attempt to set up a philosopher-king in Syracuse. Plutarch, who is usually cited as a source, seems to have based his account mainly on them. Even cautious scholars insist, Plutarch "must have had" some other sources, in lost works by historians of Sicily. That "must have had" is unfortunately typical of a good deal of our scholarly arguments concerning Plato's life. Yet recently a number of critical scholars have begun to suspect that the whole story is probably inspired by the *Republic,* and that the Letters are furnished with apt quotations from the dialogues.[2] Indeed, the only plausible reason

[2] Cf. George Boas (and Harold Cherniss), "Fact and Legend in the Biography of Plato," *Philosophical Review,* LVII (1948), 439–57. Boas and Cherniss are now joined by Ludwig Edelstein, in his *Plato's Seventh Letter* (Leiden, 1966). Edelstein came to have grave doubts as to the authenticity and reliability of that essential document.

Gilbert Ryle has now joined the doubters. He writes: "There have come down to us thirteen letters reputedly written by Plato.

for accepting these letters as genuine is stated frankly by A. E. Taylor: "If we reject them, then we know nothing about Plato's life." It is curious to see Taylor's tremendous scholarship arriving at such critical wisdom. He is obviously quite unable to contemplate the possibility that perhaps we do *not* know anything about Plato's life. How, in that case, could you write a book about it? No scholar can resist such an argument.

Then, too, Plato's life was furnished with conventional dates. According to the scheme invented by the Alexandrian librarian Apollodorus, on which nearly all the chronology of the early Greek writers is based, which assigned every man an *akmē* at the age of forty (translated into Latin as "floruit"), Greeks lived four periods of twenty years each. And so we find that Plato met Socrates at the age of twenty, established his Academy at the age of forty, went to Syracuse at the age of sixty, and died at the age of eighty—fourscore was the appointed lot of men in Greece; the ten extra years were granted them to make up for the absence of the divine inspiration accorded the He-

---

Most of these letters are unanimously rejected by scholars as forgeries or imitations. There remain Letters III, VII, VIII, and XIII, some or all of which are accepted as authentic by most, though not by all scholars. . . . There exists, however, the skeptical minority view that [Letter VII] is also a forgery. It is unmentioned by Aristotle, even in any of the many passages in which he criticizes the Theory of Forms. Nor do all latter-day philosophers find the letter's exposition of the Theory of Forms genuinely Platonic either in doctrine or in argumentation. According to one variant of the skeptical view, this letter is, with Letters III, VIII, and XIII, a contemporary political forgery intended to misrepresent, for Sicilian political purposes, Plato's relations with Dion and Dionysius. It needs to represent Plato as the confidant and supporter of Dion and the critic and opponent of Dionysius, just in order to put Dion's political actions and policies in a good light and those of Dionysius in a bad light." Ryle, "Plato," *E. of P.,* VI, 314.

brews. The whole chronology of Plato's life, one comes to
suspect, comes from the scheme of Apollodorus.

There is, in fact, no real evidence that Plato ever established an Academy, or that there was one until later times.3
There is no mention of Plato's supposed school by any
contemporary. There is, in fact, hardly a word about Plato
himself. The Academy is mentioned once in the dialogues
themselves—as a country race-track. It is mentioned by
one or two other writers, in the same terms Xenophon
refers to it as a place where troops were quartered. Aristotle
is completely silent about the Academy.4 Not till much
later do we find evidence of a flourishing school—though
the traditional site, where later writers refer to it as having
enjoyed an unbroken existence since Plato's day, we know
was leveled to the ground at least twice by the first century.

Modern "Lives" of Plato, produced by our able classical
scholars, appear all to be written by a regular formula. We
do know a little about Athens in the latter part of the fifth

---

3 Cf. Harold Cherniss, *The Riddle of the Early Academy* (Los
Angeles, 1945). Plato's will, given in Diogenes Laertius's *Life of
Plato,* fails to mention any Academy at all.

4 Ryle puts it: "In [Aristotle's] voluminous writings that have
come down to us there is next to no personal information about
Plato. Aristotle constantly draws examples from Plato's dialogues
and frequently criticizes Plato's doctrines, especially his Theory
of Forms, but about Plato's character or the course of his life we
learn next to nothing from Aristotle.

"Even our natural supposition that the young Aristotle and his
fellow students had been taught philosophy by Plato has been at-
tacked. Nowhere does Aristotle indisputably mention anything
taught by Plato that could not have been learned from Plato's
writings or else from the lecture (or lectures) on the Good that
Plato on one occasion gave but did not transmit in writing to
posterity. . . . Hardly one whisper of the tutorial voice of Plato
is relayed to us by Aristotle, even on philosophical matters." "Plato,"
E. of P., VI, 314-15.

century B.C. and the first half of the fourth. Think what Plato "must have learned" from it, and how its bitter experience "must have" influenced him. So we proceed by writing: "We must suppose" that so and so. There are some fifteen "we must supposes" in three pages of Zeller.

Eduard Zeller is the great pioneering student of Greek philosophy of the second half of the nineteenth century. His immense five-volume history of Greek philosophy was epoch-making, and since his death has been expanded into some nine volumes by subsequent German scholars. How does this eminent and unquestioned authority write his chapter on "Plato's Life"?

There is hardly another philosopher of antiquity with whose life we are so intimately acquainted as with Plato's; yet even in his case, tradition is often uncertain and still more often incomplete.[5] Born some years after the commencement of the Peloponnesian War, the son of an ancient aristocratic house, favored also by wealth no less than birth, he *must have found* in his education and surroundings abundant intellectual food; and even *without* the express testimony of history, we might conclude that he profited by these advantages to the fullest expansion of his brilliant genius. Among the *few further particulars* that have descended to us respecting his earlier years, our attention is principally drawn to three points, important in their influence on his mental development.

Of these we may notice first the general condition of his country, and the political position of his family.

Plato's youth coincided with that unhappy period succeeding the Sicilian defeat when all the faults of the previous Athenian government were so terribly avenged, all the disadvantages of unlimited democracy so nakedly exposed, all

[5] Zeller is one of those conscientious scholars whose pages consist of a single line of text at the top, and a long double column of fine print of references filling the rest of the page.

the pernicious results of the self-seeking ethics and sophistical culture of the time so unreservedly displayed. . . . It is *easy to see* how a noble, high-minded youth, in the midst of such experiences and influences, *might be disgusted,* not only with democracy, but with existing State systems in general, and take refuge in political Utopias, which would further tend to draw off his mind from the actual towards the ideal.

Again, there were other circumstances simultaneously working in the same direction. We know that Plato in his youth occupied himself with poetical attempts, and the artistic ability already evinced by some of his earliest writings, coupled with the poetical character of his whole system, *would lead us to suppose* that these studies went far beyond the superficiality of a fashionable pursuit. There is, therefore, *little reason to doubt* (however *untrustworthy* may be our *more precise information* on the subject) that he was intimate with the great poets of his country. [Plato had probably heard of Homer and Hesiod, and may even have read them!]

Lastly, he had, even before his acquaintance with Socrates, turned his attention to philosophy, and through Cratylus the Heraclitean had become acquainted with a doctrine which in combination with other elements essentially contributed to his later system.

All these influences, however, appear as of little importance by the side of Plato's acquaintance with Socrates. . . . Whether at that time he directed his attention to other teachers of philosophy, and if so, to what extent, *we do not know;* but it is *scarcely credible* that a youth so highly educated, and so eager for knowledge—whose first impulse, moreover, towards philosophy had not come from Socrates—should have made no attempt until his thirtieth year to inform himself as to the achievements of the earlier philosophers. . . . It is nevertheless *probable* that the overpowering influence of the Socratic teaching *may have* temporarily weakened his interest in the earlier natural philosophies, and that close and repeated study *may* afterwards have given him a deeper insight into their doctrines. Similarly, his own imaginative nature, under the restraining influence of his master's dialectic, was *probably* habituated to severer thought and more cautious investigation; *perhaps,* indeed, his idealistic tendencies received at first an absolute check.

The tragic end of his aged master, a consummation which he *seems* at the outset to have thought wholly impossible, *must have been* a fearful blow to Plato [This sounds plausible!]; and one consequence of this shock, which still *seems* long years afterwards to vibrate so sensibly in the thrilling description of the Phaedo, *may have been* perhaps the illness which prevented the faithful disciple from attending his master at the last. We are, however, more immediately concerned with the enquiry as to the effect of the fate of Socrates on Plato's philosophic development and view of the world; and if for this enquiry we are thrown upon *conjectures,* these are not entirely devoid of *probability.*6

This is the approved way in which the most conservative scholars write—and in the nature of the case *have* to write —the life of Plato.

Probably the best of these modern scholarly lives of Plato is that by Ulrich von Wilamowitz-Moellendorff.7 Wilamowitz at least knows the real Plato is the dialogues, and he knows what is in them. Yet even Wilamowitz tells us, "We may confidently *assume* generalities *without being*

6 Eduard Zeller, *Plato and the Older Academy,* translated by S. F. Alleyne and Alfred Goodwin (London, 1876), pp. 1–13. Emphasis throughout mine.

7 Ulrich von Wilamowitz-Moellendorff, *Platon,* 2 vols. (Berlin, 1919). Cf. also Paul Friedländer, *Platon: Seinswahrheit und Lebenswirklichkeit,* 3 vols. (Berlin, 1928; 2d ed., 1954), of which two have appeared in Eng. tr., the present "standard" German work on Plato. Cf. also Constantin Ritter, *Platon: Sein Leben* (in 162 pages of "we must supposes"), *Seine Schriften, Seine Lehre* (Munich, 1910, 1923).

informed about particulars." And he proceeds to do so, with a vengeance. It is no wonder that Paul Shorey, reviewing Wilamowitz's large opus, calls it ironically a fine "historical novel." Shorey at least confined himself to "what Plato said." [8]

The scholar who for a generation dominated Platonic scholarship in the English-speaking world, John Burnet,[9] was an erudite Scotsman, learned, master of the Greek tongue. Unfortunately, on every point where several different views are possible, Burnet manages to plump for one which seems hard to accept. Accordingly we find him saying, "We know more about Plato's life than of any other ancient philosopher." And Burnet proceeded to develop a novel theory about Plato's philosophy. It is not to be found in the dialogues at all; the Socratic dialogues are recordings of actual conversations with Socrates. Plato's own philosophy is very different: it is not in the dialogues, but somewhere else, mainly in the reports of the Aristotelian commentators. Now, this view is rather like holding that Shakespeare is not to be found in his plays at all: he was really a Catholic who wrote polemics against Calvin, polemics which unfortunately are all lost.

The greatest English student of Plato's philosophy in the last generation, A. E. Taylor,[10] wrote probably the most useful popular commentary on the dialogues in English in recent times, which ranks with Paul Shorey's *What Plato*

[8] Cf. Paul Shorey, *What Plato Said* (Chicago, 1933).

[9] John Burnet edited the Oxford text (still the best) of Plato (1899–1906), and wrote *Greek Philosophy: Thales to Plato* (London, 1914), in which he developed his views on Plato, as well as his still more famous *Early Greek Philosophy* (London, 1892).

[10] A. E. Taylor, *Plato: The Man and His Work* (New York, 1926).

Said. It is a very helpful book. Taylor had written articles in support of Burnet's theory.[11] "We have to discover," he put it, "Plato's ultimate metaphysical positions indirectly, from reference to them elsewhere." But he was sobered at the thought of a book about the dialogues. It is a commentary on the dialogues, with often wise common sense. Taylor does lose his caution occasionally: Plato says so and so, he admits; but from what we know he believed, it is clear he must have meant the opposite. It is reassuring that this Burnet–Taylor theory, that the dialogues are stenographic transcriptions of historical encounters with Socrates, and do not reveal Plato's own philosophy, has met with only amazement from other scholars, in England, Germany, and France.

Taylor's ultimate purpose, he made clear, was to show that Plato, rightly understood, proves the soundness of the Christian faith. Such an enterprise is, in fact, quite the usual thing for an interpreter of Plato to undertake. Paul Natorp, leader of the Marburg School, wrote a big book to show that Plato was really a Neo-Kantian.[12] Several learned works were written in the old days to prove that Plato was a Social Democrat attacking the capitalistic system. Raphael Demos, who long taught Greek philosophy at Harvard, wrote a large book arguing that Plato was a disciple of Whitehead.[13] Another Harvard man, John Wild, wrote one to show that Plato was a follower of St. Thomas.[14]

Is it any wonder that the Athenians accused Socrates of

[11] Collected in *Varia Socratica* (Oxford, 1911).
[12] Paul Natorp, *Platons Ideenlehre* (Leipzig, 1903).
[13] Raphael Demos, *The Philosophy of Plato* (New York, 1939).
[14] John Wild, *Plato's Theory of Man* (Cambridge, Mass., 1948).

corrupting the youth? If he could do things like that to professors of Greek, and Scotsmen, and even Harvard men —what could he not do to a simple-minded Athenian boy? For a time I myself lived in daily fear lest some instrumentalist would prove that Plato was really a disciple of John Dewey. Indeed, a student once started a paper to show just that. But fortunately he had to leave for the wars.

THE MYTH OF PLATO'S LIFE

In the light of all these cold facts about our lack of knowledge of the biography of Plato the man, let us nevertheless recount the traditional reports, what may be called "the Platonic myth." If Plato the man was not in historical fact actually what is depicted in it, he clearly ought to have been. In any event, it is a good story worth telling.

Plato, we are told, was born in 427 B.C., after having got his *akmē* fixed up—Greeks were always born just forty years before their *akmē*. He could not arrange to be alive in the successful Periclean Athens, which remained a memory for him—"we may suppose." He was twelve years old at the time of the Syracusan defeat, and twenty-three when the Spartans occupied Athens. His uncle Charmides and his cousin Critias, we are told, were killed fighting the democrats.[15] Plato thus lived during the most unhappy period of Athenian misfortune, in a time of civic and political disintegration. What "must he not have felt" in such degenerate times! His youth was spent during the sorrow and failure of his native city. How this experience "must have" influenced his whole attitude! These feelings and their influence

---

[15] Men were doing that even in those days.

on Plato's later development are clearly good for a whole chapter.

Now, out of a deep respect for the critical standards of the best classical scholarship, let us apply to this traditional story the methods of the higher criticism. We are also told that Plato was born on the birthday of Apollo himself. And this stands up under the most rigorous tests. There is some slight doubt as to just when Apollo's birthday was, however. In ancient times Apollo was born on the seventh of Thargelion, corresponding to our twenty-first of May. When the Platonic Academy was established in Renaissance Florence under Marsilio Ficino, however, Apollo's and Plato's birthday was celebrated on November seventh. This puzzles those who fail to realize that the birthday of an Italian saint—as Plato had become—is the day he enters eternal life—the day of his death.

Plato, we are assured, came of an aristocratic family with popular traditions. Hence every good English classical scholar at once remarks that the family was Whig, not Tory. It is also reported Plato was descended from kings, which is doubtful; that he came from a line of gods, which is more probable, and that he was in fact the son of Apollo himself.[16]

Plato was thus a young aristocrat—handsome, strong, broad-shouldered, broad-chested, broad-minded. His father called him "Aristocles," but he was nicknamed "Plato," which means "broad"—so he must have been "broad." It is interesting that the most famous philosopher of all time

[16] Cf. F. J. E. Woodbridge, *The Son of Apollo* (Boston, 1929), ch. 1. This circumstance is well-authenticated. It is actually the best-established fact in the whole life of Plato. For it comes from our very oldest source, Plato's nephew, Speusippos, who certainly ought to have known the truth about his own grandmother.

should have come down through the ages under the nickname of "Fatso."

Plato received the best education Athens had to offer, of course. He studied the poets, music, painting; he pursued science under Cratylus, the disciple of Heraclitus. He wrestled, we are told, at the Isthmian games, and won his contest. He had naturally, for an upper-class Athenian, intended to go in for politics, with hopes of a political career. But history fails to record any participation in political life. So he had a weak voice, a fatal drawback in those days of oral statesmanship. He hoped justice would come from the Thirty Tyrants—the regime set up to be collaborators with the Spartan victors. But he found the conservatives were worse than the democrats.[17]

The accounts tell us also that as a young fellow Plato wrote poetry. This fact stands up under criticism. He wrote dithyrambs, lyrics, even tragedies. There is a true story that he slept with the books of Epicharmus and Sophron under his pillow. These men were Sicilians who wrote "mimes," realistic skits or sketches; and the story is true because the dialogues in their dramatic form are "mimes."

At the age of twenty, Plato had to do something important. So he met Socrates—though in Athens Socrates must have been hard to avoid; men were always bumping into him. It is rather touching to think of Plato as conscientiously ducking around the corner whenever he saw Socrates coming, until he had reached the age of twenty. We are told that the night before this historic meeting, Socrates had a dream. He saw a swan, the bird of Apollo, who came toward him, uttering melodious song. The manuscripts bear this out.

[17] This fact is always true.

Plato went home, burnt his poems, and resolved thereafter to follow philosophy. But it was of no use, he still
wrote poems, from now on about Socrates and the other
Sophists, as an artistic enterprise. Socrates had become common literary property, and various men wrote dialogues
about him, including Xenophon, whose dialogues happen
to have come down to us, along with Plato's. The anecdote
is recorded that Socrates heard Plato's *Lysis* read, and exclaimed, "O Herakles! What lies this young man is telling
about me!"

One account states that Plato went into politics with the
democrats. But then came Socrates's incredible death. Plato
was convinced, "All governments are bad." [18] There can be
no hope for mankind until philosophers are kings, and real
experts run the government. Inspired by the worship of the
great man, Plato resolved to defend his memory. He fled to
the adjoining city of Megara, where Euclides, a fellow-
disciple of Socrates, was teaching. Some say this flight of
Plato was out of a sense of danger, which is false; others
out of sorrow, which is true. (It is necessary to account for
the absence of Plato himself from the *Phaedo*.)

Plato was now, we can figure, twenty-eight years old,
and had to wait for his *akmē* to arrive. So he engaged for
twelve years on what German scholars naturally call his
Wanderjahre. These supposed travels of Plato are not reflected in the dialogues at all. Marvelous tales are told. Plato
went to Cyprus, and on to Egypt, where he became familiar
with the mathematics and the art of the Egyptians. He
went to Judea, to Babylonia, to Persia, and even got as far
as India. He traveled also to the western part of the Greek
world, to Magna Graecia in southern Italy, where he met

---

[18] Criticism shows this to be absolutely true.

the Pythagoreans, and came to admire their fellowships. (Plato had certainly encountered the Pythagoreans somewhere.) During these twelve years, Plato fought in the wars, and it is reported he won a medal for bravery at the battle of Delium. This presents a problem. There is no evidence he was at Delium. But if he was, he certainly won a medal.

In 388, when he was thirty-nine years old and approaching his *akmē*, he appears at the court of the splendid tyrant Dionysius the Elder of Syracuse in Sicily. He soon won the friendship of Dionysius' son-in-law Dion. Dionysius had two daughters, Sophrosyne and Arete, "Temperance" and "Virtue," and Dion had chosen to marry Virtue. But at Syracuse Plato was seduced by luxurious living. He developed, the story goes, a passion for olives, which becomes a standing reproach to his good name. The saying ran (attributed to Diogenes the Cynic), "Plato was a proud philosopher, but he loved his olives!" It is difficult to decide, in the absence of an authoritative Freudian interpretation, whether this story is true or not. In any event, the Platonic Epistles make clear, Plato developed airs. When the episode was all over, a letter (II) was written, designed by its author—whoever he was, if not Plato himself—to explain why Plato got into trouble. This begins: "Be careful, Dionysius, what you say. Remember how posterity will discuss our relations!" It continues in the same vein: "I went to Sicily by far the greatest philosopher in the world. . . . You should be doing homage to me." These are all lies, of course; Plato must have been endowed with true modesty.

The trouble began when Plato started to speak too freely about the tyranny. Dionysius the Elder remarked, "Your words are those of an old dotard!" Plato rejoined with the rather obvious objection, "You are talking like a tyrant!" So Plato was given by Dionysius to the Spartan ambassador, Pollis, to be sold as a slave. Pollis took him to Aegina. The reputation of Athens at this time was such (men remembered Melos, as Thucydides recounts that episode in Athenian diplomacy, and Aegina had its own mistreatment to recall), that Aegina had a law that the first Athenian to appear on the island should be put to death. But the citizens of Aegina found out that Plato was a philosopher (this was, after all, Greece), and so instead they put him up for sale as a slave. He was bought by Annikeris, the Cyrenaic follower of Aristippos, and taken back to the adjoining Athens. Plato's friends there raised a sum to repay Annikeris, but the Cyrenaic (who taught friendliness and fellow-feeling as most conducive to pleasure) would not take the ransom. So Plato's friends bought him a house and garden near the Academy gymnasium or exercising field. The story concludes, appropriately, that Pollis on returning to Sparta was drowned by Apollo. This stands up. When it was all over, Dionysius wrote Plato a letter, urging him: "Please do not mention the quality of my hospitality." Plato is supposed to have replied: "Don't worry! I am far too busy to be thinking about you."

Now at last Plato was forty years, and had finally achieved his *akmē*. In 387 B.C. he could found his "Academy." This is reported to have been a kind of religious guild, like the Pythagorean brotherhoods. To it came, we are told, youths and scholars from all over the Greek world. Plato had, as the years went by and its reputation grew, very distinguished pupils, kings, and statesmen. This is certainly true—if Plato set up a school at all, which is doubtful. Plato taught science, true knowledge or *epistēmē,* and statesmanship. For some reason, it seems agreed that the

passage on education in the *Republic,* Book VII, is a kind
of college announcement. Plato, tradition has it, lectured to
his students, like Aristotle—the scholars love to think of
Plato as a professor. Harold Cherniss, however, has pointed
out that there is no real evidence that Plato ever did any
teaching. Ryle has his own doubts about the Academy, and
as to whether Plato himself ever taught there at all.[19]

We find allusions to only one public lecture, that on
"The Idea of the Good." One story indeed runs that Plato
read a "Treatise on the Soul." He did not hear the bell ring
for the closing of the hour, and went on for six full hours.
At the end, all had left except Aristotle, who remained
down in front busily taking notes. The difficulty in judging
this story is that while it is certainly false of Plato, it is
obviously true of Aristotle.

All this while, Plato is supposed to have been writing
dialogues. Before he set out on his *Wanderjahre,* he produced "early dialogues," in which the protagonist is Socrates. But after he had become a professor and schoolmaster,
he found he could write only "later dialogues."

Finally, after twenty years had duly elapsed, and Plato
was sixty, in 367, Dionysius the Elder died in Syracuse, and
Dion sent for Plato to come to Syracuse. Thus began the
most famous episode in the romance of Plato's life, the one
reflected in the Seventh and Eighth Epistles. Dion had
counted on the fruits of Virtue, and expected that their son
would inherit the rule. But Dionysius the Elder had a son
of his own, who had his plans for reigning. Dion figured
that his influence could be saved if he could only get the
philosopher Plato to educate the young tyrant. Plato, for his
part, realized that this was his great chance, to catch a king

[19] See Ryle, *E. of P.,* VI, 315, 318–19.

and make him a philosopher. It was clearly now or never! Plato saw it as his duty to go to Syracuse.

He arrived at the city in fitting splendor, in a three-banked ship. He was met by the royal chariot, all decked out with garlands. Dionysius, in his joy, was pulling the chariot himself. There were sacrifices, banquets at the palace. When the Herald prayed that the Tyranny might endure, the young Dionysius burst out, "Stop cursing us!" Dionysius the Younger had been kept away from all politics by his father, and had spent his time making toy wagons and dolls' furniture. Plato put him to work at once on the program of studies outlined in the *Republic*. The whole court, it is said, went to work studying geometry, until the sand—in which diagrams were drawn—fairly flew.

But Dionysius the Younger was too old: he was thirty, far past the age of ten, by which time the *Republic* says boys' miseducation is complete. He did not want to study geometry, he wanted to rule. And the other courtiers thought two could play at the same game. Deciding to fight philosophy with philosophy, they imported a philosopher of tyranny, a certain Philistos. Santayana's early play, *Philosophers at Court*,[20] exhibits this confrontation, with a fitting imaginative rearrangement of Plato's three legendary visits to Syracuse, since, as he explained in 1941, "When this play was written, in the years 1897–1901, the principal critics regarded Plato's *Letters* as apocryphal. This circumstance perhaps encouraged me to go too far in fusing the various visits of Plato to Sicily and in modifying the incidents to suit my intention." And he goes on with

[20] George Santayana, *Philosophers at Court,* in *The Poet's Testament* (New York, 1953; the play was written 1897–1901).

philosophic wisdom as to the life of Plato, "That the *Letters,* or most of them, would be genuine would not touch my guiding interests in this composition." [21]

In the end, the story goes, Dion was banished. War broke out between him and Dionysius the Younger, and Plato left Syracuse, a complete failure in practical politics. He was convinced that there can be no Perfect City or Ideal State—on earth. Education is the only way out, but they must be caught young.[22]

---

[21] *Ibid.,* Note to *Philosophers at Court,* p. 89.

[22] Ryle's more critical account of the second visit to Syracuse runs: "In 367 Plato sailed again to Syracuse, where he stayed as the guest of Dionysius the Younger for over a year. Letter XIII is or purports to be *inter alia,* Plato's thank-you letter. Its tone of voice towards Dionysius is quite incongruous with the story in Letter VII of a wide and deep breach between Plato and Dionysius over the young tyrant's maltreatment of Dion, whom, a few months after Plato's arrival, Dionysius had banished for treasonable correspondence with Carthage.

"The story given in Letters III, VII and XIII is that Plato came to Sicily on the joint invitation of Dion and Dionysius the Younger after the latter's accession to the tyranny. As the death of Dionysius the Elder cannot have occurred more than a couple of months before Plato left Athens and may have occurred only a few days before Plato reached Syracuse, this story cannot be true. Plato's invitation to Syracuse must have come, not from Dionysius the Younger, but from his father, during 368 or 369. If so, these three letters must be forgeries, since Plato himself could not have got wrong the identity of his inviter. It happens that we possess a letter from Isocrates to Dionysius the Elder, written in 368, regretting that he cannot risk the long journey to Sicily. As two other philosophers or sophists from Athens, Aristippus and Aeschines, were in Syracuse with Plato, it looks as if Dionysius the Elder had in 368 or 369 invited several Athenian luminaries, including Plato, to visit his court in 367. If so, then the so-called Platonic letters are in error not only about the source of Plato's invitation but also about the reasons for it, since these reasons would presumably be the reasons also for the invitations to Isocrates, Aristippus and Aeschines." *E. of P.,* VI, 315–16.

In 361 Plato is supposed to have undertaken a third journey to Syracuse, to reconcile Dionysius with his friend Dion. But Plato failed again. He was made prisoner once more, and was rescued this time by the Pythagorean Archytas.[23]

Plato's last years in Athens, some report, were embittered by the success of the school his star pupil Aristotle had set up as a rival to his own in the Lyceum—though the lives of Aristotle date the founding of the Lyceum well after Plato's death. Finally, in 347, having reached the appointed age of eighty, he had to die. And fittingly he did so at a marriage feast.

Is this account of Plato's life all true, as literal fact? Of course not. It is far too perfect a life, just what the conventional "author of the dialogues" should have lived. It is a Platonic myth; and it will remain such, even if some of the details should turn out to be facts.

There are, of course, other stories that come down to us, not quite so beautiful. We are told, especially by Athenaeus, that Plato was vain, ambitious, quarrelsome, cowardly, disloyal, licentious, intemperate, gluttonous, sensual. There appears another dream of Socrates, this time about a crow who came and started pecking Socrates' bald head. Socrates interpreted it as meaning, "Plato will say much that is false about my head." We are told that at the death of Socrates, Plato gave a great banquet, at which he proposed a toast to himself as the coming man, now that that old bore was out of the way. Aristodemus, Socrates' little admirer, burst out: "I had rather have taken the hemlock from Socrates than that pledge of wine from you!" Of course, all such stories can be explained away. But then, we can explain away all

[23] This story strikes one as an anticlimactic repetition.

the beautiful stories by the same method: they are to be found in much the same sources as the ones the tradition has preserved.

Frederick J. E. Woodbridge, whose general attitude toward this Platonic romance I have been elaborating, wisely concludes: "The life of Plato is not the biography of a man. . . . It is the imaginative tribute to a genius. . . . We cannot correlate [Plato's] writings with any confident knowledge of his life or with any assurance of his purposes beyond what we may gain from the writings themselves. For us he is well-nigh an anonymous author whose books fire the imagination and stimulate our curiosity. He is ours to enjoy and interpret." 24

APPENDIX

This somewhat skeptical appraisal of the extent of our actual knowledge of the facts of Plato's life, which the author originally absorbed from the critical attitude of his teacher Frederick J. E. Woodbridge, itself the conclusion of a lifetime of weighing the alleged evidence, is not likely to appeal to all scholars, among whom until recently the majority had come to take the tradition as fairly well but-

24 Woodbridge, pp. 28, 31. Woodbridge writes also: "That the life of Plato cannot now be written as the biography of a man, is the one solid conclusion to be drawn from our sources of information. The words of Grote written many years ago have lost none of their force in spite of the far superior and more elaborate work on the sources since his day. 'Though Plato lived eighty years, enjoying extensive celebrity—and though Diogenes Laertius employed peculiar care in collecting information about him—yet the number of facts recounted is very small and of these facts a considerable portion is poorly attested!'" (George Grote, *Plato* [London, 1886], I, 246).

tressed. What such scholars will object to most of all is the refusal to accept as established fact Plato's attempt to train Dionysius the Younger to set up a perfect state in the city of Syracuse. This depends on taking the Seventh and Eighth Epistles in the Platonic Corpus as genuine, or at least as relating historical facts.

As Santayana remarks, "In the years 1897–1901, the principal critics regarded Plato's *Letters* as apocryphal." This was the conclusion of nineteen-century Platonic schol-arship, which I am supporting once more—along with Ludwig Edelstein and certain other recent scholars, like Gilbert Ryle, as well as Woodbridge. Since those days the general scholarly opinion, to be sure, for a time came around to accepting them once more as authentic letters of Plato himself, without, however, bringing forth any new evidence. But today opinion seems to be reverting to nineteenth-century skepticism again.

It may well be that this point will never be definitively settled. The distinguished student of Greek philosophy, Emerson Buchanan, once spent a year under the direction of Woodbridge appraising all the evidence pro and con. His conclusion was that the evidence for and against the spuriousness of the Epistles, and of the Seventh in particular, was equally cogent on both sides. Perhaps we can never get farther than this unsatisfactory conclusion.

In this situation, the major *philosophic reason* for taking the Seventh Epistle as legendary is the influence a literal acceptance exerts on the interpretation of the *Republic*. If we take Plato as eager to set up in the city of Syracuse the kind of well-ordered city Socrates talks of in that dialogue, despite all the indications Plato gives in the *Republic* that the perfect city can have its abode only in the sky, we shall understand Plato's philosophy of politics in one fashion, as proffering a practical program of political reconstruction. Without being committed to that motive of the practical statesman, we are free to explore the *Republic* in its own terms, in the context within which it was written, and in the light of the audience for whom it was prepared. We shall then be free to come out with a version of Plato's philosophy of political discussion that can take account of all the nuances and levels of meaning and irony it actually reveals, as is here attempted in Chapter XII.

That the non-dramatic or "later" dialogues reveal a different controlling interest from that displayed in the *Republic,* seems beyond dispute. That leaves us with the perplexing question, could the same man who wrote the *Republic* possibly have written the *Statesman* and the *Laws?* The contention in this volume is that it may well have been the same man, but that he was writing in very different political circumstances. When the *Republic* was composed, or at least begun, Sparta was riding high in the Greek world. The *Laws* was set down after Sparta had been definitively defeated, in 362 B.C. at Mantineia.

III

The Platonic Corpus

A WORD is in order about the Corpus of Platonic writings.[1] These writings were first collected and printed in Greek in 1513, after wandering as the editor puts it, "for many centuries in dissevered members." None of our manuscripts of Plato is older than the ninth century. A few fragmentary texts have been found on ancient papyrus, in Egypt. We know nothing of the history of these texts. Diogenes Laertius tells us of a list of Plato's writings drawn up by a certain Thrasyllus, four hundred years after Plato's death—a list whose arrangement our manuscripts reflect. Thrasyllus' list was based upon an earlier and different list, itself made by the Alexandrian librarians after what Sir Gilbert Murray has called "two hundred years of carelessness" had gotten all the books of the Greeks into hopeless confusion, before the Alexandrian bibliographers went to work upon them.

In 1513 we had a dialogue to correspond to every name on the list of Thrasyllus. This is remarkable. For nothing comparable is true of any other Greek writer (save

[1] The best edition of the Platonic text is still *Platonis Opera* recognovit . . . Joannes Burnet, in *Scriptorum Classicorum Bibliotheca Oxoniensis*, 5 vols. (Oxford, 1899–1906).

"Homer"). It may suggest the extraordinary care given to the Platonic manuscripts, which is all the more remarkable, since the tradition is very fragmentary and careless. Or, again, it may suggest that the Platonic Canon was formed rather late, during the Alexandrian period, and was based upon the manuscripts then available, and not necessarily upon the works that Plato actually wrote. Yet we find a scholar like A. E. Taylor saying: "Plato is the one voluminous writer of classical antiquity whose works seem to have come down to us whole and entire. Nowhere in later antiquity do we come on any reference to a Platonic work which we do not still possess." [2] We can indeed go even further: the later we come, the more certain we are we have everything Plato wrote. There is no doubt whatever we still possess everything collected in 1513. But that we have everything Plato wrote, or that "Plato" wrote everything we have, seems a matter of sheer faith. As Woodbridge puts it, "The continuity and fidelity of the Platonic tradition is no guarantee of the completeness of our collection; it is rather an inference from the fact that we are supposed to have Plato 'whole and entire.'" [3]

There has been, to be sure, recurrent uncertainty as to Plato's authorship of this or that dialogue. The authenticity of three quarters of the Corpus has been assailed at one time or another, from the Alexandrian to the late nineteenth-century German scholars— often on very plausible grounds. It is possible to maintain the genuineness of all the dialogues only by an elaborate theory of Plato's philosophical and intellectual growth, which itself is founded on accepting all of them as genuine. You can arrange all the

[2] A. E. Taylor, *Plato: The Man and His Work* (New York, 1926), p. 10.

[3] F. J. E. Woodbridge, *The Son of Apollo* (Boston, 1929), p. 34.

dialogues in a certain order of differences, then infer a development to explain the vast divergencies, and then use this theory of development to prove the genuineness of any particular dialogue. But this procedure is unconvincing and raises many doubts. Only a scholar really committed to the higher criticism can actually believe that the genuineness of any dialogue is established by a system built on first supposing the dialogue genuine. Or else scholars argue: "If the *Epinomis* is spurious, we must deny the authenticity of the most important pronouncement on the philosophy of arithmetic to be found in the whole Platonic corpus." [4] But Plato has to have a philosophy of arithmetic; therefore the *Epinomis* cannot be spurious. This is, alas, typical of much Platonic criticism.

Now, on the face of it, it is difficult to believe that the same man wrote all the dialogues in the Corpus: the *Republic* and the *Timaeus,* for example, the *Symposium* and the *Laws,* the *Protagoras* and the *Sophist.* There are not only apparent conflicts of doctrine, not only glaring differences in style and literary power; some of them are profound, and some such as almost any reader of Plato could write by formula. These discrepancies are to be resolved only if one is already convinced they were all written by Plato. The dialogues are nearly all independent of each other. Save in a few special cases, themselves puzzling, like the *Theaetetus,* the *Sophist,* and the *Statesman,* or the *Timaeus,* which refers to the *Republic,* and the *Critias,* there are no cross-references between them. Each dialogue can be taken in its own terms, and does not cry for another to explain it.

Hence we are driven to conclude that we possess no sure

[4] A. E. Taylor, *Plato,* p. 14.

test of what Plato really wrote. Since the Socratic dialogue was at the time a literary convention, and we know of a large body written by different men, and possess those of Xenophon, we have no conclusive reason to believe that all the dialogues attributed by Thrasyllus to "Plato" were actually the product of one man. We possess no knowledge of Plato himself, of his intellectual growth—or degeneration—or of the history of his writings. Hence we are actually at liberty to choose those dialogues that seem to us to be profound, and to disregard the others; especially since the former are in no wise dependent upon the latter. Or, if we prefer, we can try to concoct an ingenious scheme, that will make them all consistent, and explain all the discrepancies. If we succeed—and it has been done often, in many different ways: establishing "the unity of Plato's thought" has been a familiar if varied enterprise in the long tradition of Platonic interpretation—that is no proof that all the dialogues are genuine, but only that the scheme is ingenious. Above all, there is no test of the genuineness or importance of any dialogue in anything not found in the dialogues themselves: in the belief that Plato was a Christian, and so must have written the *Gorgias* or the *Timaeus,* or that he was an activist political reformer, and so must have written the *Laws*. There is really nothing in the evidence, save where Aristotle explicitly mentions a dialogue as Plato's, to carry any weight against the impression and interpretation suggested by the dialogues themselves, taking each one as a unit.

Now, our lack of real certainty about the Platonic authorship of the entire Corpus is not being here emphasized in order to throw out any of the dialogues that have come down to us. They are all interesting, and well worth reading and studying—more so than most of the literature of philosophy. Rather, our uncertainty is being emphasized in the interest of flexibility and freedom of interpretation. This means, first, freedom *from* the distortion that comes from the attempt to fit all the dialogues into some preconceived scheme, even schemes hallowed in the long tradition of Platonism, schemes derived *from* but only dubiously maintained *in* the dialogues themselves. Secondly, it means freedom *to* explore the wealth of suggestion in the dialogues themselves, with a sensitivity to their dramatic implications and ironic nuances.

It is well to realize that the schemes of Plato's intellectual development, setting the dialogues in chronological order, are all extremely dubious. It is well to remember that it was never imagined the chronological order of the dialogues had any relevance at all, until the dominance of the idea of evolution and development in the nineteenth century. There is no trace of any such scheme in the manuscripts, which group the dialogues into tetralogies or groups of four, according to theme, not order. Such schemes are based on assumptions hard to defend in theory, and in application nearly always distorting and misinterpreting the Platonic text.

The most ingenious scheme of all, invented by German scholars in the second half of the last century, and elaborated with indefatigable patience but rather curious logic by the Polish scholar W. Lutoslawski, divides the dialogues into three groups, "early," "middle," and "later" dialogues. In it, the two most different dialogues are placed at the ends of a scale, and the others distributed in between, in accordance with elaborate stylistic statistics—the particles used, the occurrence of the hiatus, and such matters. This scheme is accepted in general by the scholars—though there is still sharp disagreement over the place of particular dialogues on the scale, and the order within the first of the three groups is now not regarded as determined or perhaps determinable. Yet the whole device rests on assumptions so finespun as to be really convincing only to their makers.5

There is thus really no reason whatever to think that all the dialogues in the Platonic Corpus were written by the same man, or that there is exhibited in them any traceable development. Yet—it is a fascinating game. And there is here being presented a scheme of my own, with which the reader, I hope, will be misled.

5 This scheme was first worked out in detail by Wincenty Luto-slawski, *The Origin and Growth of Plato's Logic* (London, 1897; New York, 1905). It is well stated also in Constantin Ritter, *Platon: Sein Leben, Seine Schriften, Seine Lehre* (Munich, 1910, 1923).

IV

The Greek Heritage of Plato

PLATO is for us moderns the consummate expression of Greece. But what is Greece? For us, it is a group of literary monuments suspended in time, together with the archeological remains discovered during the last century. The documents are all we really know. They reveal a marvelous life, and must have been the product of a remarkable civilization and culture. Was the historical Greece really like that? Probably not; we can never know. Recent ancient historians have been doing their best to minimize the Greece of the documents, and to show that Greek society was actually a pretty poor thing, compared to the really prosperous civilizations of the ancient Near East. Our historians are probably right. But still, our Greece—the Greece of the documents—remains unique. There has never been anything like it in the world or in history. It comes out of a clear sky, with no real antecedents or beginnings: it springs up full-grown, like Athene from the brow of Zeus. The documents themselves reveal dim traditions of something that had come before, traditions hardly illuminated by archeology, which fails utterly to explain the Greece of the documents, the Greece that belongs to us, or its past. And our Greece was soon ended.

For us, Greece is Athens of the fifth and fourth centuries B.C., with a dim background of "early Greeks," and of course Homer and Hesiod. After that we find an Oriental and Mediterranean world, fascinating and enormously important for all subsequent cultural developments, a world we call "Hellenistic Civilization." This Hellenistic world molded all later thought; it gave us Christendom. But it is not Greece.

Before 500 B.C., Greece was unimportant: it consisted of a group of minor tribes of barbarians living on the fringes of the great Asiatic cultures. What happened in Greece—the wars, the intrigues, the politics—were of little importance in themselves. They have been tremendously important ever since, for they became universals, illustrations of human life. Yet Greece exhibits a unique intellectual life: the birth of science, of philosophy, of "reason." This life seems to us strikingly modern, more so than anything in Rome, or even in Alexandria, indeed, more modern than anything in the West until we get to the eighteenth century.

"Greece"

=

This life of Greece was fleeting. There is nothing before the battle of Marathon, in 490 B.C., save the Greek bible, Homer and Hesiod. Aristotle died in 323 B.C., and it was over: the Alexandrian period began, a culture living on past ideas, largely those worked out in Greece between 490 and 323. Everything that counts about Greece falls between those two dates. Sir Gilbert Murray calculated that we possess perhaps one-twentieth part of the fifth-century literature.

490 B.C. —

323 B.C.

These documents we can read and reread; from them we can work forwards and backwards, trying to understand them. We get some help from archeology, which tells us of a Greece, and a Near Orient, which the documents—

the Greeks themselves—knew nothing about. But the Greece of the archeologist appears no more significant than any other civilization of which we can dig up the potsherds, and a civilization unimportant in comparison with the Egyptian or the Babylonian. To the Greeks, this was all a dim background. We also get help from classical scholarship, which has produced our tantalizing "fragments" of earlier writings. We wish we had more. And the scholars have produced a host of neat little theories of how it all came about, theories that form admirable doctoral theses, but which may well be sheer fabrication.

Of classical, pre-Hellenistic Greek philosophy, we possess the writings of Plato and Aristotle—perhaps not even the latter. They make a tremendous impression today—though "Plato" is full of nonsense, inspired nonsense, to be sure, which we try to explain away as poetry, and "Aristotle" is full of sententious trivialities, which we try to see as profound. But we read these documents, and are led to exclaim, "Except the blind forces of nature, nothing moves in this world that is not Greek in its origin." That was said by Henry Sumner Maine,[1] and is of course not true: Maine had had a classical education. But we read the Greeks, and we find it inescapable.

We know actually very little about "Plato" and "Aristotle"—the traditional "Lives" that have come down to us are of little value. We know what some contemporaries were thinking. But our only real knowledge of the authors

---

[1] Sir Henry James Sumner Maine (1822–1888), Victorian comparative jurist and historian, author of *Ancient Law* (1861), which aimed "to indicate some of the earliest ideas of mankind, as they are reflected in ancient law, and to point out the relation of those ideas to modern thought."

of the Platonic and Aristotelian writings comes from internal criticism, from scholars like Lutoslawski, Ritter, and Werner Jaeger. "Plato" is probably a literary convention, and "Aristotle" a society of scientists, a research foundation. It is quite likely the author of neither Corpus as we have it was a single man. But the writings are there, to be studied and pored over.

These writings point to a past, what we call "Early Greek Philosophy." It is something dim and traditional, the backward look of Plato and Aristotle. Neither seems to have been especially interested in it. Many books have been written to show how Plato's views were the outgrowth of his opinions of this past. Moderns sometimes wonder at his inclusiveness, until they realize that the predecessors he failed to include are simply those he did not mention.

Plato had little we should call an historical interest at all. He quotes the statements that appear as fragments in our collections as opinions in men's minds, as facts in his living present. The dialogues are not historical: the *Protagoras* or the *Parmenides* appear to be something like G. B. Shaw's *Caesar and Cleopatra*. Socrates is a central figure in the dramatic Platonic dialogues. But was he actually like that? We do not know—probably not, since he had become a myth.

Aristotle is more interested in his predecessors, but not historically. They furnished him with scientific hypotheses; they were forerunners who were groping for truth. In Aristotle's account, in *Metaphysics,* Book A, their ideas appear as suggestions to be considered for their validity, not their genesis, or their original meaning. Both Plato and Aristotle exhibit, we say, little understanding of the earlier efforts. It takes a modern scholar really to understand the course of

Early Greek Philosophy; Plato and Aristotle were clearly not equal to it.[2]

But let us turn from the historical Greece to the Greece that was Plato's past, from the Greece of the modern historian to the Greece in Plato's own perspective, Greece as he understood it, how Greece and Greek culture looked to him. Now Greece is distinguished among human societies as one that managed to achieve a remarkable degree of self-knowledge; it produced a number of men capable of extraordinary critical reflection upon Greek civilization and Greek experience, who in the process worked out ideas capable of application to any civilization, any social experience—ideas of universal validity. These ideas were developed by thinkers working with particular elements of Greek culture, in the particular ways generated by Greek experience; and these distinctive ways of thinking the Greek writers, above all Plato himself, were keenly aware of. In the last analysis, this was the most profound meaning they gave to the antithesis between Greek and "barbarian."

These Greek tools of reflection formed the central core of Plato's thinking. They provided him with certain intellectual attitudes, certain controlling intellectual aims and values, that the Greeks sought to attain, and with certain basic concepts that grew out of these intellectual attitudes and aims.

There is first an openness of mind, an intellectual receptivity to the wealth of cultural materials the Greeks had at their disposal. These materials, they were keenly aware, exhibited an extreme diversity. Every element seemed to be there, from the most "primitive" to the most "modern,"

---

[2] See Richard McKeon, "Plato and Aristotle as Historians," *Ethics,* LI (1940), 66–101.

drawn from every great culture in that eastern Mediterranean world. There is no "Greek view of life" that can be statistically established—in Greece itself, though there have been many, and diverse, "Greek views of life" in different societies since. A civilized minority has left us the record; they are in great disagreement among themselves. Where can we find greater contrast than between Aeschylus, Sophocles, Euripides, and Aristophanes? There were social classes in Greek society; a landed gentry, a sturdy peasantry, keen business men, a rebellious proletariat. But they were of so recent formation, dating back merely to the social struggles marking the "industrial revolution" of the sixth century, that there was still no intellectual gulf between them. Sympathy and respect were still possible; thinkers were able to draw on and utilize a wide variety of experience, and were convinced of the necessity of doing so. Euripides, the most sophisticated dramatic poet, can yet display deep feeling for the most elemental sensibilities, as in his *Bacchae*. Hence the philosophies of Plato and Aristotle are able to possess a totality, a completeness of experience, that makes nothing thought or felt since, seem alien, a totality never approached in modern thinking.

There is, secondly, the sense of Greek life and culture as a human achievement. It had not seemed to the Greeks a growth, a natural evolution of social forces. Our own philosophies of social evolution and development are quite alien to the Greeks and their experience. Now this is a fundamental attitude shared by Plato, and given consummate expression in the dialogues. The Athenians felt themselves the masters of their social and cultural material, not constrained by it. They regarded their cultural materials, correctly according to our deepened knowledge, as richer but as no different from those of other peoples. The important difference lay in the *handling,* and the Greeks were keenly conscious of this fact, of their distinctive way of treating their cultural traditions.

This sense of human achievement was the basis of the Sophists' distinction between "nature" and "art," between *physis* and *texné.* To the Greeks, everything significant was the product of "art," of intelligence shaping natural materials: the city or *polis,* religion, the moral life, were all products of art. Hence "art" is a fundamental category in Plato and Aristotle. It led to a concern with the potentialities of things as intelligence discerns them, with the ends or perfectings of things, with what man can make of them, if not in practical activity, at least in imagination. Compare what the Greeks did to the Festival of Dionysus, the age-old ritual of fertility, the most primitive of materials. The Christians made out of that ritual Easter, the supreme hope of escaping from life. The Greeks made out of it tragedy, the supreme vision of the possibilities of human greatness.

This same attitude lies at the root of the Greek idea that all activity must aim at something definite and intelligible. The worst punishment is an activity that is not art, that continues without end or goal: the labors of Sisyphus, the vulture gnawing at the liver of Prometheus. The very idea of Infinity, endlessness, indeterminateness, was intolerable to the Greek mind. Only the finite, the limited, the determinate, was worthy or divine. Even the eternal circular motions of the heavens must have an eternal end or goal— the basic conviction of Aristotle's *Metaphysics.* The world to be intelligible must be a process of art, an intelligible striving toward an eternal perfection and completeness. Perfection, *to teleion,* is completeness, determinateness, finitude, being finished and limited. Thus the circle is complete, and in that sense perfect.

Modern religious thinking has been dominated by the notion that what can be grasped and understood is merely natural. Only the Unknowable, force, energy, the infinite, the unconditioned, only what eludes scientific and rational explanation, can possess religious value and be truly divine. To the Greeks, the Unknowable was mere chaos, mere formless material, a challenge to art and intelligence, but not the occasion for religious acquiescence. That which is clearest to intelligence, that which most fully reveals the intellectual shaping of materials, is most divine. Nature in its constitution is divine, not because the ways of God are mysterious, and His judgments past finding out; but because to a discerning mind nature can be understood, as an orderly process aiming at definite and intelligible ends, because nature can be understood as the supreme example of art.

In the fifth century, Greek life appeared to the Greeks as almost a literal conscious achievement. In the preceding sixth century, the time of the Greek industrial revolution, statesmen and poets had actually constructed the Greece we know. The *polis,* religion, art, literature, philosophy, all were very recent; they were still plastic and had not crystallized. Greece was poles removed from the societies of Egypt and Babylon. To the Greeks, the triumph of Hellenism over barbarism meant, the barbarians, the Egyptians, the Persians, the Mesopotamians, were slaves to their past, while the Greeks were masters of theirs.

This sense of the power of man the Greeks embodied in their myth of Prometheus, whose name means literally "forethought," intelligence. We have only to contrast the rebel Titan, Prometheus, with the tragedy, Greek in form but not in spirit, of Job. For the Greeks, "Forethought," Intelligence, could defy the power of the universe, and treat with it on equal terms. Job could only bear his afflictions with patience, and in the end bow to the Voice out of the whirlwind. The Greeks faced their world and understood it, they worked with it. The Hebrews found their world too much for them, they could not understand it. "Canst thou by searching find out God? Canst thou find out the Almighty unto perfection?" [3] The Hebrews could only endure, and purify their own souls.

This contrast between Greeks and Hebrews, as expressed in their respective consummate tragedies, can be phrased as the contrast between the temper of Humanism and the temper of Humility. Both are essential for any adequate religion. Both have been essential components in the Western religious tradition, in Judaism and in Christianity alike. The temper of Humility here attributed to the Greek tragedy of Job is a sense of unworthiness and impotence. It is familiar in Christian theologians like St. Paul, St. Augustine, and Calvin.[4] It is also expressed in philosophers like Spinoza and Pascal. Our psychiatrists have tended to oversimplify it as a neurotic guilt-complex, which certainly holds of that father of existentialist sensibility, Kierkegaard.

The temper of Humanism which characterizes the Greeks, and receives its highest expression in Plato, is more complex and harder to define. In the Western tradition it has always been supported by an appeal to the Greeks, by Clement of Alexandria, by Origen, by Athanasius, and by the supporters of the Humanistic values consecrated in the doctrine of the Trinity; by the more Aristotelian medieval

[3] Job XI:7.

[4] Karl Barth, who powerfully expressed this temper of Humility in our own day, is hardly a Christian, but rather an Arian in his earlier theology. Barth later drew closer to Humanism.

Schoolmen, like Abelard, St. Thomas, Duns Scotus, and William of Ockham; by German Idealists like Hegel, Heidegger, and Paul Tillich; and by Left-Wing Idealists like Whitehead or John Dewey. Humanism has meant since the Greeks man's awareness of a sense of human dignity and responsibility. This implies what has come to be called moral freedom: the conviction that man is a slave neither to something above him, to a God conceived as wholly "Other" and as inscrutable to man; nor is man a slave to anything below him, to any mechanistic order. The Greeks rejected both forms of heteronomy. Rather, they took moral freedom as such an obvious fact in human experience, that they very rarely discussed it—which is apt to puzzle us crypto-determinists today.

The tension between the aim and the obvious failure to achieve success is the root of the tragic sense of life, always associated with the Humanistic temper since the days of the Greeks and their tragic poets. Without the Humanistic sense of human dignity and human greatness, without both human freedom and human bondage in obligation to an ideal, there can be no genuine tragedy. Where human freedom is lacking, where a sense of unworthiness and impotence is very strong; and again where God's Providence is felt to be all-controlling, there can be little tragic sense of life, and very little tragic poetry. Only because the awareness of human greatness is rarely wholly lost is this tragic sense kept alive in periods of despair and cynicism, like our own Age of Anxiety; or in periods of great religious confidence, like those two Ages of Reason in our Western tradition, the thirteenth and the eighteenth centuries.

Greek intelligence could drive back Persia; but that was hardly its most important claim. It could achieve the Good Life: Athens had in fact managed to do it. Pericles' Funeral

Oration, as it appears in the pages of Thucydides,[5] is the supreme expression for the fifth century of the sense of the power of man—and also of the "hybris" or spiritual pride of such arrogance. Thucydides is of course perfectly aware of the hybris; and Plato gives a marvelous parody of the Funeral Oration in his *Menexenus*. For all his devotion to human dignity, Plato was able to *see*.

This power of man, for the Greeks, was not Baconian, not modern. It aimed, not at dominion over the forces of nature, but at controlling human nature—at the Good Life. It was directed, not toward man's environment—the Greeks were content to take that pretty much as they found it. It was directed toward man himself—toward self-control and self-discipline. It was early embodied in the sayings of the Seven Wise Men, who came bearing the first fruits of their wisdom as an offering to the gods at Delphi: "Know thyself," "Nothing in excess," "Self-control," "Excellence is knowledge." This was why the Peloponnesian War seemed so important, and so tragic: were the Greeks in the end to fail in their chosen aim? This social experience is the immediate background of Plato's dialogues. In them he is endeavoring to vindicate the faith of Humanism, the faith in the power of man to achieve the Good Life by human intelligence and art.

Sophocles is the most orthodox, the most pious, the most conservative of the great Greek tragic poets. Yet he—even he—could write the noble chorus from the *Antigone:*

> Many the forms of life,
> Fearful and strange to see,
> But man supreme stands out,
> For strangeness and for fear.
> He, with the wintry gales,

[5] In Book II, ch. 6, xxxv–xlvi.

O'er the foam-crested sea,
'Mid billows surging round,
Tracketh his way across.
Earth, of all Gods, from ancient days, the first
Mightiest and undecayed,
He, with his circling plough,
Wears ever year by year.

The thoughtless tribe of birds,
The beasts that roam the fields,
The finny brood of ocean's depths,
He takes them all in nets of knotted mesh,
    Man, wonderful in skill.

And speech, and thought as swift as wind,
And tempered mood for higher life of states,
These he has learned, and how to flee
The stormy sleet of frost unkind,
The tempest thunderbolts of Zeus.
So all-preparing, unprepared
He meeteth naught the coming days may bring;
Only from Hades, still
He fails to find a refuge at the last,
Though skill of art may teach him to escape
From depths of fell disease incurable.

So, gifted with a wondrous might,
Above all fancy's dreams, with skill to plan,
Now unto evil, now to good,
He wends his way. Now, holding fast the laws,
His country's sacred rights,
That rest upon the oath of Gods on high,
High in the state he stands.
An outlaw and an exile he who loves
The thing that is not good,
In wilful pride of soul.[6]

---

[6] *Antigone,* translated by E. H. Plumptre, lines 332–73.

Now, if life is essentially intelligence shaping natural materials, what was this intelligence? How was it conceived? What was it to aim at? This brings us to another attitude—the third being here emphasized—a certain conviction as to the ultimate intellectual ideal thought is to be directed toward. This is not a universal character shared by all Greek thinkers; but it is found in most of the greatest Greeks, and is a determining factor in Greek philosophizing. Certainly it is controlling in Plato, as perhaps the major intellectual drive he inherited from his culture.

To us—though perhaps not to the Greeks—this ultimate aim of thought seems to be in a certain disharmony with the conviction of man's power and achievement. This is probably because our own conception of human power is so different from the Greeks'. Its presence, though fundamental to any understanding of Greek philosophy, inevitably presents a problem to us moderns. It is indeed difficult to speak of this attitude without seeming to praise or to condemn it, the contrast with most of the spirit of modern culture is so profound. One's attitude toward it ultimately determines, consciously or unconsciously, the place one gives to Greek thought and philosophy today—whether, with a Santayana, we find it the highest wisdom, or with a John Dewey instinctively find something lacking in it.

I am speaking of the ultimate function and use of "mind," *nous*. The Greeks certainly had a sense of the enormous importance of what Americans have come to call "intelligence," or, in the vernacular, "know-how." They realized keenly the utility of thinking as a tool, the instrumental part it plays in human living. This certainly runs through the chorus from the *Antigone,* for example. Yet, in the last analysis, they were so fascinated by what thinking reveals to the discerning mind, that they disliked to use mind instrumentally: they felt mind was to be enjoyed rather than merely worked with. So for them the highest value of *nous* was to achieve insight, to see life as a dramatic spectacle, in all its shades and colors, with all its complexities and paradoxes; to see it as it *is,* to hold it up, to contemplate it, to see through it. Such "seeing" we enjoy in the theater at its best; and the Greeks called such an intellectual vision *theōria,* and praised the "life of *theōria."* "Theater" and *theōria* come from the same Greek word, and mean "spectacle" and "seeing," respectively.

So entranced were the Greeks by this achievement of mind, *nous,* that the power, even the desire, to control life gradually faded into the background; and they never really got around to doing anything about it. Hence they managed to achieve a supreme insight into the possibilities of human existence, a supreme vision of the Good Life; and proved at the same time miserably impotent to solve what seem to us the simplest problems of social organization. It is no accident that the teachings of Socrates seem to have produced an Alcibiades, and that the Periclean Age issued in the eternal visions of Plato, Aristotle, and Euripides, and in the complete and utter ruin of Greece itself.

This attitude made Greek science, when it was worked out, utterly different in spirit from our modern science. It had no desire to explain the world, in the sense of accounting for it, but rather to explain it, in the sense of "making plain" its main features, so that men might "see," gain *theōria,* intellectual and imaginative vision. The Greek scientists did not try to find the causes that produced its many processes, in the hope that by suitable manipulation men might make them produce something else. They sought instead to discriminate its characteristics, to see better what the world *is.* They asked, not "How did the world origi-

nate?" but "What is it *now?* What does it do, and how is
it acting?" This of course is the essence of the attitude of
Aristotle, and makes clear why the nineteenth-century
evolutionists disliked him and failed to realize his distinctive kind of wisdom. It is the source of the fundamental
tension in Plato between the drive to make human life
better, and the cool recognition of what men and human
nature are now. The Greeks, in a word, were seeking a
picture, not a blueprint. The spirit of picking apart and
analyzing to get a handle, a leverage for changing things, is
quite lacking in Greek science.

Hence the Greeks were able to see clearly certain fundamental characteristics of the world to which in the past our
modern science has been utterly blind; which it has often
denied, and to which it is only in our century awakening.
Yet they quite failed to see the simplest possibilities of control. Thus while they early discovered the basic idea of
physics, the idea of mechanism, they never saw in the
analytic concepts of atomism anything but a religious and
moral philosophy, a picture with a human relevance, not an
instrument for transforming the world. It is not till we get
to Hellenistic science, to the Alexandrians and the Syr-
acusans of the days of Hero and Archimedes, that we get
the modern, Yankee interest in machines and gadgets for
doing things making its appearance. In classic Greece, science remained a humanity, not the handmaiden of technology.

This is true even in the field in which the Greeks were
most interested in the problems of reshaping what they
encountered, in the field of human nature. For insight into
what human nature *is,* the Greeks, with Plato first of all,
are unsurpassed. They make our best modern psychologists
often look very crude. Yet even our own very adolescent

science of psychology gives us vastly more handle for reconstructing human personalities. Aristotle's *Ethics* is probably the wisest book ever written about the Good Life. Yet confront it with the crudest, most unintelligent Oriental prophet, and it proves impotent—it may be true, but it is powerless.

Because they recognize this quality in the "reason" of the Greeks, many contemporary prophets and existentialists, for whom knowledge must involve a commitment and an engagement, must be "participating" reason rather than mere "technical" reason, as Paul Tillich put it, are apt to scorn not only Greek rationalism but all intellectual methods. This is as though it were a simple alternative between this aesthetic *theōria* of the Greeks, and a gospel of irrational inspiration and revelation. It is as though the moderns had not developed, under the influence of our modern science, a conception and an instrument of intelligence as intellectual as *nous,* and both more powerful and more carefully directed than any brand of Romantic irrationalism and voluntarism.

How this method of intelligence has been elaborated, not through a rejection of, but through a criticism and extension of the Greek *nous,* intellectual vision, is the central strand in the development of modern philosophizing.[7] For intellectual method is the one strand in the philosophic enterprise that is most clearly cumulative and progressive. But it is well to remember, that intelligence is more than *nous,* not less: it must include *nous.* Scientific method without vision is not intelligence but disaster—just as vision without scientific methods is either disaster or impotence.

[7] It is made central in my *Career of Philosophy in Modern Times,* Vol. I (New York, 1962), Vol. II (New York, 1965); third volume in preparation.

This Greek *nous* made Greek religion a dramatic interpretation of human life, the subject matter for the poet and
artist, not for the moral reformer and the prophet. It made
politics likewise the material for the poet, and not the
statesman. And Plato is the poet in both religion and politics. Take Thucydides. His life was bound up with Athens
and the Athenian ideals. Yet he sees men so clearly, the
limitations and inadequacies of those ideals, their inevitable
fruits in the world of men and cities, that strive as he may
he cannot write a work of propaganda, but has to set down
a tragedy. He would like to see the great ideals of Pericles'
Funeral Speech prevail; yet he is quite aware of the hybris,
the tragic guilt, involved, and in the end their inevitable
doom proves more fascinating to him than those ideals
themselves.

Nous, the "reason" of the Greeks, is the reason, the intellectual vision and insight of the artist and poet and dramatist; it is not the intelligence of the engineer, not even of the
human engineer, the statesman. Inevitably it finds its highest expression in the poet and dramatist, Plato. And though
the greatest mind produced by the Greeks, Aristotle, found
supreme truth, it is the truth of him who has seen and
understood, not the truth of him who has *done* or will
do.

Nous, the ultimate achievement of the Greek mind and
culture, the instrument of the Greek philosophers, remains
the instrument for the imaginative artist, not for the scientist, or the statesman. Thinkers like Plato and Aristotle,
however much they may have wanted to be statesmen or
scientists, could never bend the Greek *nous* wholly to their
purposes. It always remained intractable; this was the
source of their major intellectual conflicts and tensions.

This is why the achievement of Greek philosophy is at

its best, in Aristotle as well as in Plato, an artistic achievement, a rendering of the world and of human life in terms of the artist's imaginative insight. And this has been the source of its undying power. Thus the Greeks invented the concepts in terms of which the religious life and religious problems have ever since been formulated and understood. But it took an impulse from a quite different and alien source and culture to give the Western world its religion. The Greeks likewise invented all the concepts and methods of science, which have determined the ways in which to this day the enterprise of science is understood. But it took a wholly different type of social experience to turn these concepts to the building of what we should recognize as science.

Both Aristotle and Plato are working with a *nous* that is essentially the *nous* of the artist. Aristotle could never quite decide between the Life of *Theōria* and the Life of Practice: his indecision has left insoluble tensions and contradictions in his *Ethics* and *Politics*. Should he advise practical men and rulers, or found a Research Institute of Advanced Studies? He remained torn between the Life of Intelligence and the Life of Vision; and like our modern Greek, Santayana, seems in the end to abandon intelligence, the Life of Reason, taken as the rational organization and perfecting of man's animal impulses, for what Santayana came to call the "spiritual life," the pure apprehension of essences, and what Aristotle himself called *nous,* in the sense of sheer intellectual vision of what is. In his metaphysical writings, Aristotle seems on the verge of developing conceptions to make intelligible the experience of the artist, the maker or *poiētēs,* of rendering the world as an artistic achievement, a creative or dynamic process; and then he seems to yield to the fascination of *nous,* of *theōria,* and reads it as a vision

of completed perfection. What started in him as the philosophy of the artist, the maker, of intelligence working with
materials, partly resistant and partly plastic, ends as the
philosophy of the aesthetic beholder, of a static Reason embodied in the universe. Beginning in the temper of John
Dewey at his best, he ends in that of Santayana at his
worst and most "spiritual."

And Plato, too, is torn by the same disharmony. Within
his soul there contended the prophet-statesman, aflame with
the moving vision of what the life of man might be, and
the artist-observer, with the cool perception of what it inescapably is. There follow naturally the recurrent quarrels
about the dialogues, from the *Republic* down. However
much Plato may have wanted to shadow forth the path
along which men might travel toward perfection, the poet
and the dramatist in the end got the better of him. The
dialogues emerge, not as programs of action, but as dramatic portrayals of the life of the mind—of the follies,
contradictions, enthusiasms, and greatness of human thinking, as beheld by a detached and ironic intelligence—by
Nous, Dramatic Reason.

V

Plato's Heritage from the Early
Greek Philosophers

WE have examined the intellectual instrument, the tools of reflection, with which the Greek philosophers, and above all Plato, worked—*nous, theōria,* intellectual and imaginative vision. On what cultural materials were these tools brought to bear? What were the traditional elements with which Greek thought began its examination and criticism? The Greeks did not set out with a firsthand observation of the world. It takes a great sophistication to look at the world and really see it. No real "observers" of the world appear among the Greeks before Aristotle and the Hellenistic astronomers—except in the medical tradition of Hippocrates—though observers of human life, discoverers of poetic insights into human nature, are present much earlier, from Homer down; and Plato was a consummate observer of men. But the Greeks in general set out from their cultural heritage. One strand of this was *religious,* which was used by art, science, and philosophy; this furnished especially the basic ideas with which the Early Greeks began, the basic notions underlying their religious heritage. Another was *political,* which strand formed the conscious starting-point of the Sophists, like Socrates. In a sense, Greek cultural experience can be summed up in the Gods and the City, the *Polis*. A third strand was the Greek *language* itself, discourse, *logos,* which was discovered by Parmenides and the Eleatics, who loomed as such large figures for Plato, and which was exploited by the Sophists. Its full implications as an intellectual instrument for the discovery of truth it remained for Aristotle to develop.

In the Greek religious tradition there were two major strands, the tradition of the Olympian deities, and the strand of the mystery cults. By the fifth century, both had come to furnish materials for poetry, art, and philosophy. The beliefs associated with them were no longer taken as literally true, they were not explanations. Explanation was to be sought elsewhere, though it was naturally colored by the religious traditions. The Olympians and their stories or myths had by then come to appeal to Greek intellectuals as symbolic truths, poetic visions: for them, the stories of the gods gave, not literal explanation of causes or origins, but an understanding of human life. It is in such fashion that the myths or stories are used in the Platonic dialogues: whatever be the philosophic function of Plato's myths, it is clearly not to furnish scientific knowledge. In the poets, the Olympian myths lent themselves to the expression of moral insight and vision, civic feeling, and common Hellenic sentiment—they gave the Greeks what Santayana calls another world of the imagination to live in.

The mysteries, or secret rites, and especially the esoteric teachings connected with them, are more important for Greek philosophy and especially for Plato, yet they remain puzzling. We get only tantalizing glimpses of their contribution to Greek sensibility. But they form the background of most Greek philosophy and science, and especially of the "Platonism" to be found as one ingredient in the Platonic dialogues. The philosophers were generally, like Plato, hostile to the Olympian official and political religion, or sharp critics like Euripides. The mysteries grew eventually to be less external, more spiritual, and with the Orphics came to express a deepened moral sense, as well as a concern with a personal way of life and salvation—what the philosophers like Plato naturally started with. They are usually overlooked in our generalizations about "the Greek view of life," and they triumphed in the later Hellenistic religions. But they were always there, not new after Aristotle; and they were being continually reinforced by religious currents from the Near Oriental cultures.

When sociological–psychological studies were first used to illuminate primitive Greek history, it was assumed that the Greeks developed their institutions and attitudes out of the sociological theories of the then reigning authority, Émile Durkheim (1858–1927). More recently, the Greeks have shown a tendency to originate them out of the views of Freud or Jung. The classical scholars Jane Harrison, Gilbert Murray, and Francis Macdonald Cornford,[1] who first introduced these perspectives into English studies of the Greeks, relying on the existing state of Greek archeology, held that the Olympian tradition was a relatively new layer of religious feeling and practice imposed by the barbarian Greek invaders from the north upon the deepest stratum of Greek religion, the religious rites of the underlying aboriginal Aegean or Helladic population conquered by the Greek invaders. This deepest Helladic layer, they main-

---

[1] Jane Harrison, *Ancient Art and Ritual* (London, 1906); Gilbert Murray, *Four Stages of Greek Religion* (New York, 1912); revised as *Five Stages of Greek Religion* (London, 1925); Francis Macdonald Cornford, *From Religion to Philosophy* (London, 1912); and *Principium Sapientiae* (Cambridge, 1952).

tained, was still preserved in the great Athenian festivals of the fifth century, the Diasia, the Thesmophoria, and the Anthesteria, which by that time were dedicated to Zeus, Demeter, and Dionysus respectively; but these gods they took to be late additions to a much more primitive ritual. Later historians find the gods much more ancient. Into this world the Greek barbarians brought the gods of invaders, who conquered the world, but did not create it. They were not omnipotent: they were subject to *moira,* Fate, which to the Durkheimian anthropologist like Cornford looks like the Great Tabu, read into nature, and setting bounds, limits, establishing a moral order in things, a "Justice" of things. This idea of *moira,* originally not a religious idea at all, but a poetic invention of Homer, is the basic idea the philosophers in Ionia, where critical reflection first arose, seized and built upon. And this idea of a moral order in the universe is central in Plato; he is so critical of the stories of the anthropomorphized gods of the poets, with all their goings-on, just because they seem to contradict this fundamental idea of a moral order in Nature. The conduct suitable in a nature principle of fertility seemed scarcely suitable in a personal Zeus, and the tales of his loves revolted Plato. Natural forces deserve respect; but if they are personified as "gods," as the poets had done, judged by human moral standards they deserve none.

The mysteries came to the fore in the sixth century, that time of social maladjustment and conflicts and unrest, demanding a more personal type of religion than the very political and official relations observed with the Olympian deities. Plato, we must never forget, writes in the time of disillusionment after the failure of Periclean self-confidence, when interest in the mysteries had been redoubled.

The mysteries continued much of the religious feeling and practice of the aboriginal Aegean or Helladic religion;

they seem to have been at times reinforced by currents from Egypt. Demeter, to whom the mysteries at Eleusis in Attica were dedicated, has many characteristics of the Egyptian goddess Isis. These Eleusinian mysteries, which were a state cult in Attica, attended by a great procession once a year over the mountain to the town on the Bay of Eleusis where Demeter had her shrine, in sharp contrast to the shadowy life after death of the official Olympian tradition, as portrayed in the Hades of Homer, promised their initiates a blessed immortality, to be gained by participation in the secret rites or mysteries. Something, we are told, was "done, shown, and said," after a prior ritual purification: the impressive hall, backed up against the hill, in which this took place, is still fairly well preserved. The goddess offered this gift to select and privileged initiates: she granted a personal salvation from Hades, and a prosperity on earth, such as the gods gave to the heroes and daimons of old. But the deep distinction between men and the gods, so marked in the official Olympian cult, still remained. In that cult, man's duties to the gods were purely formal and official: as a civic obligation, for the sake of the City, men must preserve the proper ritualistic and rather mechanical relations to the deities. In return for the favor of the gods, man owes them "piety," *eusebeia,* and above all, he must keep his own proper place, set bounds and limits to his presumption. Sin, *hamartia,* is exceeding these bounds, transgressing them. The whole relation is one of barter and contract. On the other hand, in the Olympian cult, morality is something social and human, not divine. The Greeks never forgot this distinction. The official charge brought by Anytus in the *Euthyphro* against Socrates is that of transgressing man's proper bounds, sinning against piety. There was still in the Eleusinian mysteries no "becoming divine" for man.

This gulf between man and the gods was broken down

in the worship of the god Dionysus, which promised, man can himself become "deathless and divine." Dionysus was the god of wild emotional cults, himself the fusion of several different Oriental religious traditions. These cults all aimed at achieving a rapturous frenzy or "ecstasy," *ekstasis*, a religious—and alcoholic—intoxication. They were known as the "orgies of Dionysus." They represented a coming together of first, the Phrygian worship of Dionysus as a wine-god, involving human sacrifice; secondly, the Thracian worship of Sabozios, the beer-god—Thrace produced grain—celebrated with the midnight dance of the women on the mountains; and thirdly, the Cretan worship of Zagreus, a wine-god. Zagreus parallels the Egyptian Osiris, and like much in Crete his cult shows strong Egyptian influence: aiming at "ecstasy" or "possession" by the god, involving prophecy, and reincarnation of the god in new members of the tribe.

Especially in its Cretan and ultimately Egyptian form, the original rite of fertility passed into a concern with immortality and salvation. There was a concern with the soul, and its sharp distinction from the body: a sharp dualism between Good and Evil, with the necessity for purification, at first purely formal and ritual, then moralized and spiritualized. The cult involved a revelation, an emotional vision, bringing a promise of deathlessness through "participation" in the god. This crystallized into the myth of the Savior of men who died, and then rose again: men can gain mystic union with him through the practice of asceticism and sacramental rites. The underlying notion was of a communion with all life, a becoming divine, *theios,* in marked contrast to the Olympian notion that it is *hybris* for man to emulate the gods. This cult represents a turning toward the Divine Force resident in the tribe, in social life, not to forces in nature, as with the Olympian cult. The mystery-god is human, the embodiment of the life of the group; the sacrament of union with him is a union with the Divine Power that pervades the group, and is the source of all its life and strength. The cult of Dionysus is thus closely allied with the Egyptian mysteries: its appeal is much like that of the Christian mystery of the Incarnation and the Resurrection. Both cults generated the same myth, which was widespread in the ancient Near East.

The cult of Dionysus, the Greeks believed, was introduced into Greece in the seventh century B.C., but the name has now been found as early as linear B. In that century, however, the cult was tamed, stripped of much of its orgiastic frenzy, and finally captured by the priests of Apollo at Delphi, the heads of the official Olympian cult. Dionysus had his grave at Delphi, at a place in back of the temple of Apollo. The cult of Dionysus was brought to Athens at the command of Apollo under Peisistratus, in the sixth century B.C.: Dionysus was thus a new arrival in Attica.

That form of the mystery tradition we know as "Orphism" is a reformation, or perhaps an institutionalization, of this religious cult and experience, in opposition to the official capture of Dionysus by the Olympian priests of Apollo—though it is still doubtful whether any sharp distinction can be made between the Dionysian and the Orphic forms of the mystery tradition. But like the Olympian version, Orphism is much more "Apollonian"— Nietzsche was fascinated by the contrast—more reflective and self-conscious. In Orphism is found an emphasis on individuality and personality, as contrasted with the pure cults of Dionysus. It is sacramental, ascetic, dualistic in an other-worldly sense: it promised a definite personal salvation in Heaven. The soul is of divine origin, but it has fallen, is now the prisoner of the body, and needs escape. But the soul is doomed to reincarnation, which is not a promise, as in the cult of Dionysus, but a punishment, unless it can be saved. Salvation is achieved not merely by initiation into the mysteries, but by living the Orphic way of life, a combination of physical and ritual purification with asceticism. The Orphics emphasized *beliefs:* the Fall, the Wheel of Birth and Death, the Cycle of Necessity. They had a Sacred Book, "The Holy Words." And they were strongly monotheistic as well as insistent on their way of living.

By the sixth century, the Orphic cults appear to have become strong in southern Italy, and in Attica, where they were allied with the traditional mysteries of Eleusis. Orphism is found in all the Early Greek philosophers coming from the Western part of the Greek world, from Magna Graecia, from southern Italy and Sicily. The Ionians—the succession of thinkers at Miletus, Thales, Anaximander, and Anaximenes—were relatively untouched, as was the medical school of Hippocrates at Cos, the immediate background of Aristotle.

Pythagoreanism, so influential in determining the attitudes of Plato, is a reformation of Orphism. In it the mystery tradition was still further moralized and intellectualized. The Way of Purification has for it become definitely the Way of Wisdom. The soul puts on divinity and deathlessness in the presence of Truth. What seem to have been Pythagorean beliefs appear as central in Plato, as the religious materials with which he was working: *Erōs* or love, reminiscence, purgation, the Last Judgment, the vision of the Ideas, the relation of "participation," *methexis,* are all originally Pythagorean notions. They are the source of most of Plato's illustrative stories or myths, which are all steeped in Orphic and Pythagorean imagery. They furnished Plato with his imaginative symbols: they are the source of the "Platonism" which is a central ingredient in the dialogues.

Plato refers to nearly all the figures we know as the Early Greek philosophers in the course of the dialogues. But three sets of ideas, those of two great figures, Heraclitus and Parmenides, and those of the Pythagoreans, play a central role in his own thinking. The Milesians, and the atomists, like Anaxagoras, Empedocles, and Democritus, appear but rarely, and then to be scorned, except for the *Nous* of Anaxagoras, which like Aristotle Plato vindicates. In contrast, it is precisely these natural scientists whom Aristotle takes most seriously: a knowledge of their ideas is central to an understanding of how he reconstructed their thought.

Of these three sets of ideas so influential on Plato, those of the Pythagoreans are by far the most important. The Pythagoreans stood for something dim, hazy, but powerful —certainly not very clear, something you feel rather than understand. Yet they stood also, especially for Plato, for the most abstract thought, mathematics, and were the founders of the Greek science of geometry. In Plato's day, the Pythagoreans were a group of secret societies, of men and women holding all things in common, especially a secret doctrine. The tradition had it that they had been founded by Pythagoras of Samos, who set up a religious society in Kroton, in southern Italy, on the ball of the Italian foot. His followers meddled in politics, they were driven out, and the society dispersed. We have references thereafter to a number of Pythagorean communities in Italy. Pythagoras himself is portrayed in the tradition as a kind of mixture of medicine man, prophet, and mathematician.

But most of our ancient accounts come from those we call the Neo-Pythagoreans, who lived eight hundred years after the legendary founding, and were an Oriental religious sect of the Hellenistic Age, who had to have a divine founder. They wrote "Lives" of Pythagoras, characteristic gospels, embellished with miracles. There is no conclusive evidence that "Pythagoras" is more than a typical myth, who dissolves before any kind of critical scholarship. Indeed, his name sounds suspiciously like the common Sanskrit term, "Pitta Goru," "Wise Teacher." The philological similarity is very suggestive as to the possible original source of the Pythagorean ideas. We can only say, the groups may have had a founder, about whom we know only myths. It is significant that Plato and Aristotle always refer to "some of the Pythagoreans," never to "Pythagoras." [2]

In any event, Plato was obviously fascinated by the Pythagoreans; and, if we may believe Aristotle, in the end they spoiled him. This interest is reflected in the "later" dialogues, the hard ones, and forms what is most characteristically the "Platonism" to be found in the dialogues— what moderns regard as least attractive, but what endured. Plato's stories or myths are made out of Pythagorean materials: remembering, the Last Judgment, purgatory, etc. The whole of the *Timaeus* is put into the mouth of a Pythagorean astronomer, Timaeus of Locris.

The Pythagorean cult was a variant of the Orphic religion, and retained many primitive elements. It had its tabus: never sit on a quart measure, always smooth out your impression in the bedclothes, never eat meat, above all,

[2] See W. K. C. Guthrie, *History of Greek Philosophy*, Vol. I (Cambridge, 1962), chapter 4; Erich Frank, *Platon und die sogenannten Pythagoreer* (Halle, 1923); M. T. Cardini, *Pitagorici: Testimonianze e Frammenti* (Florence, 1958).

never eat beans. Daring young Neo-Pythagorean heretics
rebelled, urging, "Eat beans." The Pythagoreans believed in
metempsychosis: Pythagoras one day heard a dog bark, and
said, "There's poor old so-and-so." They practiced rites of
purification and asceticism; but the best purification comes
from disinterested study—it does the soul good, frees it
from the body, and takes it to a realm of unchanging
Truth. There the soul can participate in the living *Nous* or
Reason, and become one with It—the Reason that was
Pythagoras, and is still Pythagoras, who still dwells among
the Pythagorean brotherhood, the one great body of
Pythagoras.

It is easy to see here the old ideas of the Dionysian and
Orphic religious tradition: the Group-Daimon or Soul, in-
carnate in the Hero, the One. This One goes out to the
Many and makes them divine; by appropriate rites, the
Many can lose themselves in the One, participate in it. And
yet—the important thing is that while all this mystic feeling, the ebb and flow of Divinity, is there, this soul has
become Mind, Reason, order, proportion; and it is by
assimilating our *minds* to it that we ourselves can become
Divine—by knowing.

Here is the mystic core of the "Platonism" of the dialogues, the Divine Ideas. In Plato, the whole relation between the soul of man and the Realm of Ideas is just this
mystic merging of the Many into the One; this is the emotional background of the logical relation of "participation,"
which is a technical Pythagorean term, *methexis*. The Way
of Life has become the pursuit of Wisdom: you must
purify your soul by study. The Pythagoreans were, the
Greeks thought, the first to call themselves "Philosophers,"
"Lovers of Wisdom"—they can thus be said to have invented "philosophy."

They had a doctrine of the Three Lives: at the games,

there are three classes of men, those who come to buy and
sell, those who come to compete, and the onlookers. These
lead the Apolaustic Life, the Practical Life, and the Theoretical Life, respectively. This threefold division lies deep in
Plato, in the *Republic*'s Lovers of Gain, of Honor, and of
Wisdom. Plato's threefold division of the soul is often
ascribed to the Pythagoreans.

We should study music—Orpheus was the god of music
—its harmony, and proportion of numbers; and the
harmony of music, numbers, and life is all somehow the
same. The Pythagoreans discovered proportion in music,
and it fascinated them. Burnet remarks, no one can hope
to understand Greek philosophy who does not possess an
elementary knowledge of the Greek lyre. All the musical
notes come from a mixture of numbers. The Pythagoreans
conceived numbers as things, both as elements and as relations. The great number was the *tetraktys,* ten dots ar-
ranged in a triangle. Everything is really contained in it;
the world came out of it, the movement of life and nature.

Yet—the Pythagoreans also discovered geometry and
mathematical science. We still speak of the "Pythagorean"
theorem. They were flabbergasted when they discovered the
fact of incommensurability, between the side and diagonal
of a square: this provoked a genuine crisis in Greek mathematics. All things are numbers: the world is made out of
triangles, pyramids, cubes, etc.[3] Is this a silly notion? It presided at the birth of our own exact physics: Archimedes,
Copernicus, Kepler, were all looking for simple mathematical relations in things, because they were touched by
"Pythagoreanism." The Pythagoreans used fantastic analogies: names are numbers, justice, *aretē,* are numbers. Justice

---

[3] This hypostatizing of numbers came from their notation, which
consisted of spatially related dots, as on our dominoes or dice.

is "4," square—and we still speak of a "square" man. First
was the One, then it split into the Odd and the Even, and
there ensued a process of cosmic generation, of *physis*. Yet
—harmony, balance, proportion, are all characteristically
Greek ideas—as is the "mean" of the unmathematically
minded Aristotle.

Indeed, the more you study numbers and mathematics,
the more hidden relationships are brought to light. Take
the magic squares of numbers, where all the columns and
rows and the two diagonals add up to the same sum. Why?
It must *mean* something. This sort of mathematical feeling
has an eternal appeal. It came down through the Middle
Ages, as the source of magic, and of thousands of mysterious theories. Mathematicians are always turning mystics,
and beginning to see things. We discover the fourth dimen-
sion, and are convinced we have at last found God. In the
"new infinite," the whole is equal to its part—clearly this is
the Trinity.

It is hard to make intelligible, if you do not feel it
yourself. It is very easy to say, there is nothing in it; it is
still easier to be it. It is impossible to explain rationally; it is
a kind of intellectual intoxication, like its source, the worship of Dionysus. It is a state of mind, a madness—perhaps
a Divine Madness. It is terribly dangerous, yet alluring and
seductive. It has probably ruined more good men than
strong drink. Yet it is almost impossible to resist, when we
feel it coming on. Something like this is what we mean by
Pythagoreanism. And it lies at the back of Plato's "later"
philosophy, especially his "unwritten philosophy," his mathematical cosmology, which the *Philebus* suggests and only
the *Timaeus* sets forth.

Two other major figures among the Early Greek philosophers meant a great deal to Plato, Heraclitus and

Parmenides: indeed, his philosophy was in the nineteenth century taken as a conscious attempt at a synthesis of their opposed ideas. Heraclitus is fully examined in the opening discussion of the *Theaetetus*. It is there said, the identification of knowledge with sensation, taken as the view of Protagoras, implies Heraclitus' conception of what is, of Being. Both Heraclitus and Parmenides were critics of the earliest conception of Greek philosophy, as found in the Ionian teachers of Miletus: the idea that the world is a process of birth, growth, maturity, decay, and death, a Coming-into-Being and a Passing Away, a living, physiological process, a Life, a Growth, a *"Physis"* or "Nature." Things are born, and live, and die; and the reason lies in some natural principle that for a time sustains them. The world, in a word, is a "Nature," a Career in time. This seems to have been the first philosophic idea the Greeks arrived at when they tried to get behind the surface of the ideas associated with their Olympian religious heritage. It is clear its background lay in the great Mesopotamian cosmogonies.4 Both Heraclitus and Parmenides agreed, the world is not like this: it is not a "Nature," not a career in time. And Plato accepted their criticism. Then Aristotle appeared to reinstate the idea of "nature," insisting that though his cosmos is not "a" Nature, it is full of "natures," processes in time.

Heraclitus among the Early Greeks at least offers us something tangible, a personality, vivid even in the frag-

---

4 See Guthrie, Vol. I, chs. 1 and 2. See also F. J. E. Woodbridge, "The Dominant Conception of Early Greek Philosophy," *Philosophic Review*, X (1901), 359 ff.; and W. Veazie, "The Meaning of *Physis* in Early Greek Philosophy," in *Studies in the History of Ideas*, Vol. I (New York, 1918). See also F. M. Cornford, *From Religion to Philosophy* (London, 1912); and *Principium Sapientiae* (Cambridge, 1952).

ments.5 His ideas have probably been distorted for us by being filtered through Stoic sources: the Stoics quoted him because they regarded him as their ancestor, taking his references to his *"logos"* in their own technical sense.

According to the tradition, Heraclitus enjoyed his *akmē* in 500 B.C.; he lived in Ephesus ten years before the war with the Persians. He was an aristocrat, a hereditary king or priest; but he gave it up, for he realized he had learned nothing, and then had found the Truth. He refused to make laws for his city, convinced that all men are bad. Instead, he went to play at dice with the children in the great Temple of Artemis. He wrote a book *Peri Physeōs,* "On Nature," and dedicated one copy to Artemis, for he cared not for the judgment of fools. He said, "The dry soul is best"; but, alas, he got his own soul wet, and died of dropsy. In the end he covered himself with dung, and was devoured by dogs. He was known to antiquity as the Obscure, the Weeping, the Dark Philosopher, in contrast to Democritus, who is always called the Laughing Philosopher. He looms as a large figure for Plato, and was later canonized by the Stoics as their first Sage.

When we read his fragments, diligently collected, what impresses us most? "It is wise to hearken, not to me, but to my Word (*Logos*), and to confess that all things are one." (1)

5 See Guthrie, Vol. I, ch. 7. See also R. Mondolfo, *Eraclito* (Florence, 1961), Vol. IV, Part 1, of *La Filosofia dei Greci nel suo Sviluppo Storico;* Philip Wheelwright, *Heraclitus* (New York, 1964). The quotations from Heraclitus are taken from John Burnet, *Early Greek Philosophy* (2d ed.; London, 1908), ch. 3, "Herakleitos of Ephesos," and follow Burnet's numbering. See also G. S. Kirk and J. E. Raven, *The Presocratic Philosophers* (Cambridge, 1957), ch. 6; and Hermann Diels, *Die Fragmente der Vorsokratiker,* ed. Walther Kranz (7th ed.; Berlin, 1954), Vol. I, ch. 22, "Herakleitos."

"Though this Word is true evermore, yet men are as unable to understand it when they hear it for the first time as before they have heard it at all. For, though all things come to pass in accordance with this Word, men seem as if they had no experience of them, when they make ulal of words and deeds such as I set forth, dividing each thing according to its nature and showing how it truly is. But other men know not what they are doing when they are awake, even as they forget what they do in sleep." (2)

"The learning of many things teacheth not undertanding, else would it have taught Hesiod and Pythagoras, and again Xenophanes and Hekataios." (16)

"Hesiod is most men's teacher. Men think he knew very many things, a man who did not know day or night. They are one!" (35)

"For what thought or wisdom have they? They follow the poets and take the crowd as their teacher, knowing not that there are many bad and few good. For even the best of them choose one thing above all others, immortal glory among mortals, while most of them are glutted like beasts." (111)

"In Priene lived Bias, son of Teutamas, who is of more account that the rest. (He said, 'Most men are bad.')" (112)

Thus many of the quotations are negative: everybody is wrong, they are all fools, even those esteemed most learned. *I* alone have found the Truth. Heraclitus is combating common beliefs, and also earlier teachings of poets and wise men. What *is* this Truth?

"Of all whose discourses I have heard, there is not one who attains to understanding that wisdom is apart from all." (18) Wisdom is apart from all, it is the one thing needful. And it is not common knowledge, not anything apparent at first glance, but:

"Wisdom is one thing. It is to know the thought (*gnōmē*) by which all things are steered through all things." (19) There is one thought:

"The one is made up of all things, and all things issue from the one." (59) All things are one—that is the one thing needful.

All things pass through all things, and a thought, a *gnōmē,* steers them. Everything is in flux: there is nothing permanent, no element is permanent, there is no "source" of things, on which they all depend. There is no *archē,* no "principle":

"Fire lives the death of air, and air lives the death of fire; water lives the death of earth, earth that of water." (25)

"You cannot step twice into the same rivers; for fresh waters are ever flowing in upon you." (41, 42)

"The way up and the way down is one and the same." (69)

see T. S. Eliot Four Quartets

"We step and do not step into the same rivers; we are and are not." (81)

Only one thing is permanent: Heraclitus gives it different names: Strife, God, Zeus, Wisdom, Fire. It is an intelligible principle:

"This cosmos, which is the same for all, no one of gods or men has made; but it was ever, is now, and ever shall be, an ever-living fire, with measures kindling and measures going out." (20)

"Homer was wrong in saying: 'Would that strife might perish from among Gods and men!' He did not see that he was praying for the destruction of the universe; for, if his prayer were heard, all things would pass away." (43)

"War is the father of all and the king of all; and some he has made Gods and some men, some bond and some free." (44)

"We must know that war is common to all and strife is justice, and that all things come into being and pass away through strife." (62)

But not only do all things pass into each other; all *are* each other. Opposites are the same. Day and night, wet and dry, war and peace, surfeit and hunger, even Good and Evil, are one. What does Heraclitus mean?

"Men do not know how what is at variance agrees with itself. It is an attunement of opposite tensions, like that of the bow and the lyre." (45)

There is a harmony of tension and balance between opposites:

"It is not good for men to get all they wish to get. It is sickness that makes health pleasant; evil, good; hunger, plenty; weariness, rest." (104)

All things are thus really parts of a process. The world and human life appears a confused flux; in reality, it is the soul of harmony and order:

"To God all things are good and fair and right, but men hold some things wrong and some right." (61)

There is really a cosmic harmony, a balance in everything. Justice really holds the world together.

Is all this the scientific explanation of anything? No, it is a spiritual attitude; it does not increase our knowledge, but it does our soul good—it is the One Thing Needful, the vision of harmony and justice in the midst of confusion and strife. Heraclitus has caught dimly something of the vision so clear and precise in Spinoza.

Is Heraclitus, then, the first Idealist? Is he stating the notion of natural law? Is he an anticipation of modern physics? Does he hold the doctrine of the relativity of all things? Yes —and no. Many have found one or another of these ideas there. Hegel found the Hegelian Dialectic clearly stated, and Ferdinand Lassalle wrote a large two-volume work on Heraclitus—the biggest book on the partisan of flux.[6]

Let us ask, what is Heraclitus opposing? A view affirming some permanent element on which the processes of the world depend, some element the senses can grasp—affirming a process of birth, growth, and death that is real. Heraclitus insists, there is no beginning, and no end, and therefore no process, and no permanent element, only ceaseless change—together with a harmony, a measure, a thought, a justice, that keeps it within bounds.

Is Heraclitus then a mystic opposing naturalism? He is pointing to one continuous life, the one way or path. Everything is a part of it, and caught up in it. There is no mixing, but a continuous stream. Heraclitus seems to be reflecting the ideas and feeling of the Dionysian religious tradition. He is not Orphic: there is no emphasis on individual personality.

Yet Heraclitus' vision is akin to that of science, of reason, and order—to George Meredith's "Army of unalterable law," or Spinoza's "God or Nature." There is an enduring intelligible structure in the midst of ceaseless change.

Heraclitus is a recurrent figure, and he has beheld a vision that is universal. Like all the Early Greeks, he became a symbol—a symbol that has entered into the heritage of every educated man in the West. Thus when Ralph Barton Perry wrote a review of Dewey's *Experience and Nature,* he could entitle his comment, "A Modern Heraclitus"; and every educated reader knew what he was trying to point out.

---

[6] Ferdinand Lassalle, *Die Philosophie Herakleitos des Dunklen von Ephesos,* 2 vols. (Berlin, 1858).

For Plato, Heraclitus was a most important figure: his ceaseless flux became Plato's world of Becoming; while his "thought" that "steers all things through all things," his "measures kindling and measures going out," became the factor of the Ideas and Forms accessible to *nous*.

Parmenides was assigned his *akmē* at the same time as Heraclitus: the two clearly form a related if opposed pair. Parmenides, tradition has it, was a citizen of Elea in southern Italy. He gave his city a constitution. He was himself the disciple of Xenophanes, the poet-prophet, the reformer of men's religious ideas, who for sixty years wandered up and down Greece, bearing his burden, and who appears as a kind of Voltaire, who delighted in playing men's superstitions off against each other and offering rational explanations. And, as Aristotle put it, "He looked at the whole sky and declared One is, namely, God."

At first Parmenides had been a Pythagorean; 7 then he saw the Truth, and repudiated his earlier beliefs. He came, the Platonic legend has it, to Athens as an old man. Socrates met him as a young fellow: Plato has written his most puzzling dialogue about this encounter. The *Parmenides* dialogue is not easy to understand; there is still no agreement among scholars as to just what Plato is trying to do in it. One suspects that this is just what Plato intended to be the effect of the writing—it is the whole point about Parmenides. The old philosopher makes even Socrates

---

7 On Parmenides, see Guthrie, Vol. II (Cambridge, 1965), ch. 1; Kirk and Raven, ch. 10, pp. 263–86; Leonardo Tarán, *Parmenides: A Text with Translation, Commentary, and Critical Essays* (Princeton, 1965); Mario Untersteiner, *Parmenide: Testimonianze e Frammenti* (Florence, 1958). The quotations from Parmenides are taken from John Burnet, ch. 4, "Parmenides of Elea," and follow Burnet's numbering. See also Diels, Vol. I, ch. 28, "Parmenides."

dizzy with his brilliant dialectic. Yet we are also left with the conviction that Parmenides was a great philosopher, profound and impressive. He had a large following and many disciples: such a thinker would have, and always does. There was also an ancient proverb: "Lead a life like Parmenides."

Parmenides wrote a poem; so far as we know, it was, after Xenophanes, the first philosophic poem of the Greeks. It is not a very good poem, but very earnest. It is setting forth a new Truth, like Heraclitus. It opens with the picture of an eager youth, seeking a Way of Life, the Truth about Life—not a theory of the Universe. He journeys to the abode of a distant and far-off goddess, who reveals to him the Way of Truth, and the Way of Error: She welcomes him: "Welcome, O youth, that comest to my abode on the car that bears thee tended by immortal charioteers! It is no ill chance, but right and justice that has sent thee forth to travel on this way. Far, indeed, does it lie from the beaten track of men! Meet it is that thou shouldst learn all things, as well the unshaken heart of well-rounded truth, as the opinions of mortals in which is no true belief at all. Yet none the less shalt thou learn these things also—how they should have judged that the things that seem to them are—as thou goest through all things in thy journey." (1)

The Way of Error is, that there is a big black thing like Night, and a bright thing like Fire. The two are married by Eros, and proceed to a physical generation—a process of birth, growth, decay, and death, a process with absolute beginnings and endings. But this Way of Error is all wrong. Could Parmenides here be setting forth the Pythagorean doctrines he has repudiated?

The Way of Truth is very different.

"Come now, I will tell thee—and do thou hearken to my

saying and carry it away—the only two ways of search that can be thought of. The first, namely, that *It is,* and that it is impossible for it not to be, is the way of belief, for truth is its companion. The other, namely, that *It is not,* and that it must needs not be—that, I tell thee, is a path that none can learn of at all. For thou canst not know what is not—that is impossible—nor utter it; for it is the same thing that can be thought and that can be." (4, 5)

"The thing that is to be thought and that for the sake of which the thought exists is the same; for you cannot find thought without something that is, as to which it is uttered. And there is not, and never shall be, anything besides what is, since fate has chained it so as to be whole and immovable. Wherefore all these things are but names which mortals have given, believing them to be true—coming into being and passing away, being and not being, change of place and alteration of bright color." (8:34–42)

It is! But what does it all mean? What Parmenides is against is clear; he is absolutely opposing all births and deaths, all beginnings and endings, all comings into being and passings away. But why?

"It needs must be that what can be thought and spoken of is; for it is possible for it to be, and it is not possible for what is nothing to be." (6)

"For this shall never be proved, that the things that are not are; and do thou restrain thy thought from this way of inquiry." (7)

"One path only is left for us to speak of, namely, that *It is.* In it are very many tokens that what is, is uncreated and indestructible; for it is complete, immovable, and without end. Nor was it ever, nor will it be; for now *It is,* all at once, a continuous one. For what kind of origin for it wilt thou look for? In what way and from what source could it

have drawn its increase? I shall not let thee say nor think
that it came from what is not; for it can neither be thought
nor uttered that anything is not. And, if it came from
nothing, what need could have made it arise later rather
than sooner? Therefore must it either be altogether or be
not at all. Nor will the force of truth suffer aught to arise
besides itself from that which is not. Wherefore, Justice
doth not loose her fetters and let anything come into being
or pass away, but holds it fast. Our judgment thereon depends on this: '*Is it* or *is it not?*' Surely it is adjudged, as it
needs must be, that we are to set aside the one way as
unthinkable and nameless (for it is no true way), and that
the other path is real and true. How, then, can what *is,* be
going to be in the future? Or how could it come into
being? If it came into being, it is not; nor is it if it is going
to be in the future. Thus is becoming extinguished and
passing away not to be heard of. . . .

"Since, then, it has a furthest limit, it is complete on
every side, like the mass of a rounded sphere, equally poised
from the center in every direction; for it cannot be greater
or smaller in one place than in another. For there is nothing
that could keep it from reaching out equally, nor can aught
that is be more here and less there than what is, since it is
all inviolable. For the point from which it is equal in every
direction tends equally to the limits." (8:1–23, 43–50)

What is it that *is,* anyway? Something unchanging. Is
Parmenides teaching the sphericity of the earth? Is he the
first materialist? Perhaps—though materialists do not talk
that way usually. But that is unimportant. He is trying to
say, there is something Real, and everything else just
"seems" to be. He is, we must remember, talking about a
Way of Life. The things that really count, the great, divine,
stable things, are all one. God is! That, at least, is what

Parmenides meant to Plato: "Seen things are temporal, but unseen things are eternal."

How are we to *find* "what is"? Parmenides' *method* is the most important thing of all about his message. We must find them by "Mind," by *Nous*, Reason—the senses give no help.

"For it is the same thing to be thought and to be." "To think and that for the sake of which we think, are the same." In other words, whatever is, is accessible only to thought—the criterion of "what is" is that it be thinkable. Whatever may seem to be, if it prove not to be thinkable, cannot really be—that is only the way of Opinion, not the Way of Truth.

Parmenides is the father of that long line of thinkers, willing to subject the best-attested facts of experience to the test of thinkability, of Intelligibility; and finding them by that test unthinkable, willing resolutely to proclaim them "unreal," and mere "seeming." These are the men who have proclaimed a standard of intelligibility, by which apparent facts must be judged, and, if needs be, condemned. He is the father not only of the long line of rationalistic philosophers, down to F. H. Bradley, who insist that Reality must be intelligible, and find all ordinary beliefs and experience self-contradictory, and unintelligible, and therefore mere Appearance. He is also the father of the long line of scientists, including Copernicus and the great seventeenth-century figures, down to our own physicists, who reject the most obvious facts of experience beecause they can prove by thought—by mathematics—something else to be true. And he is the father of their critics as well, who can prove their scientific theories unintelligible.

Parmenides sent forth in his day a band of eager young followers we call the Eleatics, who proved, in terms of his very simple conception of "what can be thought," that no other theories could be thought consistently: time, change, motion, divisibility, plurality—all such notions are unintelligible and self-contradictory. Naturally this provoked a further scrutiny of "what can be thought"—of the nature of the test of intelligibility—of the nature of what came to be called "logic."

Parmenides offered a challenge to thinkers to determine "what can be thought," and how to think the facts of experience. How to think "what is not" remained a perplexing problem, which was not solved till Plato's *Sophist* dialogue. And how to think what is experienced and seems to be, was not solved till Aristotle undertook the careful analysis of change, motion, and time—of *kinesis* or "process."

We can say, if we take the argument of Parmenides seriously, that the attempt to understand process in terms of structure alone breaks down. Any change or activity approached in such structural terms remains unintelligible, and has to be accepted as a brute fact.

But was Parmenides saying, "Reality and Thought are One?" So Hegel held, and he just devoured it. We can only say, "Yes—and no." Was he a mystic? If so, it is the kind of mysticism that is reached by passing through logic and coming out on the other side—as in Bertrand Russell's famous essay on "Mysticism and Logic." [8] He is clearly the enemy of "Naturalism"—no wisdom lies in a knowledge of natural processes. In ancient times he was called the *Aphysikos,* the "Opponent of Nature, of *Physis.*" His great message remained for Plato: *It is!* And one suspects he springs from an Orphic background with its one Divine Life—as does his teacher Xenophanes.

[8] In Russell, *Mysticism and Logic and Other Essays* (New York, 1918), pp. 1–32.

ꞋVIꞌ

Plato's Immediate Background:
The Sophists

THE figures and the interests of the Early Greek philosophers were not the immediate setting for Plato and Aristotle. Their thought, especially that of Plato, deals with an entirely different set of concerns, and was not the outcome of Early Greek philosophy. Plato and Aristotle drew on these thinkers for ideas, Aristotle on a different group than Plato, notably Anaxagoras and Empedocles rather than Heraclitus and Parmenides and the Pythagoreans. We know the Early Greeks largely because Plato and Aristotle were interested in them, quoted them and talked about their ideas. But the problems of Plato owe little to the Early Greeks. Plato employed their distinctions, but in a quite different context, to illuminate different problems, Athenian problems. The only clear development we can discern in Early Greek philosophy tended toward the working-out of atomism, which was completely irrelevant to the concerns of Socrates and Plato. Democritus was a contemporary of Socrates; yet, so far as the dialogues reveal, neither Socrates nor Plato had ever heard of him. Only in the *Sophist,* that "late" dialogue, do the partisans of "body" as

Being make their appearance, and then only in the most general of terms.

Some misguided Sophists, to be sure, came to Athens to lecture on the latest ideas about "nature" and natural science, like Hippias in the *Protagoras*. But they soon learned better—it did not pay, it did not interest the Athenian youths. In Greece science, in our sense, developed outside Athens: Aristotle was no Athenian. Socrates is typical of Athenian interests: he was concerned, he tells us, not with trees and fields but with men, as found in the agora, the market place, and he has only scorn for the Anaxagoras and Empedocles who attracted Aristotle's scientific interest in nature.

Athens was a different world. It enjoyed a political life, a life belonging to the *polis,* the city, a life of intense but narrow concerns, which engaged the practical-minded. Athenian interests were broadened and deepened, to be sure, after the failure of the Periclean commercial prosperity; and it is essential to remember that Plato wrote after the Peloponnesian War. He then viewed, and has made his readers view, the problems and the chief figures of the period of Athenian prosperity and uncritical self-confidence with something of the cold and fishy eye with which, say, Englishmen have come to regard the booming times of the Age of Kipling and Empire. Under Pericles, even the religious interest, in the mystery as well as the Olympian tradition, faded into the background; it revived only when depression and failure demanded consolation. Its place was taken by patriotism, by civic feeling directed toward the *polis,* the pride of wealth and power and empire.

Fifth-century Athenian life was born of the city, of the market place, the gymnasium or exercising field, the theater, and the common table. English classical scholars naturally speak of it as the kind of life led in the clubs of gentlemen. One gets the impression that the Athenians never went home. They lived in the open, as men still do in Mediterranean countries, and engaged in talk, talk, talk. What did they talk about? About human problems, in the professional sense, problems of moral and political conflict. We get the impression of something like the eager discussion in the towns in the American colonies before the Revolution, as Burke depicts it; or, better, of something like the English governing class in the Victorian Age, in that age of great liberals, who believed that talk, free discussion, would be able to settle all human problems—the world of the Oxford Union, of Parliament, of the political novels of Trollope or Mrs. Humphry Ward.

The Athenians talked, that is, about the surface of human conflicts and relations, as intelligent governing classes do, in a time of assurance, of expanding social life, of untroubled confidence in fundamentals. It was a time of rapid commercial growth; the old hold of the clannish landlords had been broken. Cleisthenes had given Athens a democratic constitution, which seems to have meant what democracy usually means in a prosperous, commercially minded society. The older traditions, the stable mores of an agricultural society, based on an economy of scarcity, were going by the board. Men now had freedom—the freedom to talk.

Then came the Persian Wars, and the great victory. There was a new outburst of the feeling of pride and patriotism, a new enthusiasm for wealth, power, and empire. There ensued the rapid building of a richly varied life. It took all men's energies; and it was new. The picture is clear in Thucydides. In his dialogue, the *Menexenus,* Plato has written a brilliant parody of Pericles' Funeral Speech, which extolled this new confidence. It is clear that with the wisdom of hindsight Plato saw, and saw through, this complacency.[1]

In this new and rapidly changing social situation, the old traditional Greek education broke down. There arose the demand for more instruction, in the practical and professional sense. How were the young aristocrats to hold their own, how were the new rich to succeed, with the arena now open to all comers? It was something like the interval between the two world wars in England. A comparison with pre-Labour England is inevitable: for Athens exhibited much the same combination of political democracy with a strong aristocratic governing-class intellectual tradition, the same plutocracy in combination with older feudal landlords and with empire. A young fellow, it was clear, now needed to have training. It paid.

To meet this demand, the Sophists appeared as professional trainers.[2] These wandering teachers taught "How to

---

[1] For a brilliant picture of the Age of the Sophists, see George Grote, *History of Greece* (rev. ed.; London, 1925), ch. 67; and A. W. Benn, *The Greek Philosophers* (2d ed.; London, 1914), ch. 3.

[2] Ryle emphasizes that what the Sophists taught was the "Socratic method," or "eristic," satirized in Plato's dialogue of the *Euthydemus*. He judges it was Protagoras who introduced it into Athens.

"Protagoras taught the art of elenctic disputation to young men and did so for a fee; the teaching of this art subsequently became widespread. Often, if not usually, it was taught to students who were also studying rhetoric. Eloquence and clarity of presentation were reinforced by cogency in destructive argumentation. Probably Protagoras thought of this new exercise only as a good training for future politicians and 'lawyers'; and, to start with, young men paid to be coached in the exercise partly because it was an amusing and exciting contest but chiefly because of its career value." Ryle, "Plato," *Encyclopedia of Philosophy,* ed. Paul Edwards (New York, 1967), VI, 317.

succeed in life." Now to moderns this still means, we may suppose, how to secure a good income and an established position. To the Athenian governing class, it meant, how to get ahead in politics—what Hippocrates in the *Protagoras* calls, "How to win power over men and affairs." Yet the means were not so different: how to talk well, how to persuade your audience. Today we call it "salesmanship," or "advertising." The technical term is, "the science of public relations." The Greeks called the skill "eristic" and "rhetoric." And they had a word for the aim of success. They called it *aretē,* translated, ironically enough, by the Victorian Benjamin Jowett with the Sunday School term, "virtue." The method of politics in Athens was still oral discussion, talking; and what most young Greeks wanted when they wanted to acquire *aretē* was "success"—the kind of success that comes from talking plausibly, from having the right know-how.

The Sophists were a kind of popular lecturers, half professors, half journalists. Like many modern teachers, they were slightly bewildered. What should they teach? The traditional content of Greek education, the classics and the poets? The new science of nature? What their students wanted was the political skill to win "success." So accordingly the Sophists like Protagoras came to offer courses in "Success in twelve lessons, or your money back." We can imagine what they thought of Socrates, who persisted in asking, "What is success anyway?"

The first Sophists, the original teachers, had high ideals: they were trying to raise professional standards and improve social conditions, like our better law schools. But go into the lounge of any law school, and ask the students there, what is justice? The students have little enough interest in justice; they want to win cases. The Sophists grew commercialized; they came to give their public what it wanted. By Socrates' day the Athenian parents complained, the Sophists were corrupting their sons. But it is clear what was really happening: the sons were corrupting the Sophists. In a generation, the Sophists had come to stand for practical, professional training in eristic and rhetoric as opposed to the liberal education Plato and then Aristotle had now begun to offer. The latter were schoolmasters also, and it has been suggested that their dislike for their fellow teachers sprang from the fact that they did not like the competition. Their scorn, in any event, is directed against the last representatives of the Sophistic movement, their contemporaries. They always show a genuine respect for the ealier, less-corrupted teachers of the Periclean Age —so long, at least, as they did not try to teach "success."

But the Sophists always remained suspect. To the conservatives, they stood for a novel kind of education, which seemed a subversive and clearly un-Athenian activity. Then, too, they were professionals, not amateurs and gentlemen. To the people, the Sophists were clever foreigners who taught the rich young anti-democratic conspirators. To them, *arete* in practice seemed to mean, how to get off in the law courts when you were caught—that knowledge so useful to politicians. To both, they were unsettling, and corrupting the youth, like the worst of them, Socrates himself. They went around raising questions and starting issues. Why could they not let well enough alone?

The Sophists were originally conservative enough, preachers of a conventional morality, like Prodicus, or defenders of the established order, like Protagoras. But something happened. Political inquiry is a dangerous thing. You go around discussing issues; you have no sure knowledge, and can reach no certain conclusions. The outcome is bound to be skeptical. The Sophists made a great distinction, in both knowledge and conduct, between Law or Convention, and Nature, between *nomos* and *physis*. They suggested that laws, being conventions, are malleable, and can be changed; they are to be judged by the standard of "nature." This distinction came from the problems facing lawgivers, in the founding of new colonies, and as the outcome of the social struggles of that turbulent time. It also grew out of the Sophists' own experience as, traveling from city to city to lecture, they observed the multiplicity of different laws and customs—the equivalent of the experience of our anthropologists for the last century. Now this is a very dangerous idea to set afoot. It suggests that the laws of any city are not sacred, but human and purposive. Inevitably, men arrive at the question, are they doing all they might?

Among the Sophists, two main parties emerged. There were first the liberal reformers, who had learned that laws are human instruments, and should be revised and adapted to new social needs. Then there were those we may call the radicals. They held that all laws are bad; they are the weapons of the ruling class, and should be broken and destroyed. Both programs were unsettling and clearly subversive.

Thus the Sophistic movement exhibited two parallel developments. There was the degeneration from a broad liberal education to a narrow, professional, rhetorical training. At the same time took place the shift from respect for law and order and convention to a "realistic" position. This means, to seeing man, as "realists" put it, "as he is," by nature: ambitious, unscrupulous, grasping, and dominated by class interests. And both groups grew more and more scornful of scientific education, of the philosophers interested in nature, and of their critics, the Eleatics.

Actually the different teachers included in the Sophistic movement had many different interests and are reported to have taught many different doctrines. There is the large figure of Gorgias, about whom Plato wrote an important dialogue, and whose teachings he comments upon in another through the device of examining what he has taught his pupil Meno. Gorgias claimed to be a rhetorician, and there are several parodies of his style in Plato, in the *Symposium* and the *Phaedrus*. Gorgias wrote a book *On Non-Being or on Nature,* in which he turns Zeno's dialectic against Being itself. Is it or is it not? he asked, aping Parmenides. Such talk is nonsense. It is nothing; and if it were something, we could never find it out or know it. And even if we could know it, we could never teach it to others, nor could they learn it. For if they did not already know it, how could they look for it? And if they did know it, how could they then be taught it? Anyway, it is nothing to me. But I can teach rhetoric, how to use fine words. And that is just what Gorgias has taught Meno.

Gorgias was therefore an artist in words, with a distinctive euphuistic style that lent itself to parody. He was also an honest teacher, who made no pretense of teaching "success." He had a fine scorn for the humbug of philosophy.

Prodicus, who appears in the *Protagoras,* lectured on science, especially on definitions and on precise distinctions between words. He had apparently learned linguistic analysis, and was for Plato a semanticist. He had been, we are told, one of the teachers of Socrates. He also taught a safe morality; he was a pessimist, who held that the only salvation is work—do not expect to be happy.

The greatest of these teachers was clearly Protagoras. He stood for a classical, humanistic education in the poets. And he had a great faith in the power of education, and in society as a human achievement, in Law, *nomos.* There is no guidance to be found in Nature. He was skeptical of science, and of any certainty in theology. He opened his book *Concerning the Gods* by saying, "As to the gods, I have no means of knowing either that they exist or that they do no exist. For many are the obstacles that impede knowledge, both the obscurity of the question and the shortness of human life." [3] All our good comes from social institutions, so we should study them. Protagoras is clearly no individualist, and is possessed of a strong institutional sense, of what you can do with laws and courts and punishment. They determine what men will be, and furnish our real education. But institutions are not immutable, they are the product of human art, and men can improve them and make them serve better the Good Life. For this task, men need further training, they need an education in political skill and intelligence, in *aretē* in the best sense.

Protagoras understood Pericles and his aims: we have only to compare the Funeral Oration with the myth put into his mouth by Plato in the *Protagoras* dialogue. He was one of the lawgivers for the last Greek colony to be sent out, Thurioi, in 444 B.C. He wrote a *Republic,* like Plato, and we are told the arrangements of the perfect city in Plato's *Republic* are borrowed, in many details, from that of Protagoras: there was the same emphasis on institutions.

Protagoras, we are told, had no faith in the fantastic and radical conclusions of dialectic; he disliked mere arguing, debating, he hated everything the word "sophistical" has come to connote to us. On every issue, he held, there are two theses, two *logoi,* directly opposed to each other, and each can be supported equally well by argument and dialectic. But one of the two opposites is "better," "stronger,"

[3] Diogenes Laertius, *Lives and Opinions of the Philosophers,* IX.51.

more normal, than the other. In this famous position of his, Protagoras was appealing to common sense and common experience against the Eleatics, and against Sophists like the Socrates of the *Protagoras* dialogue. His philosophy of common sense fitted in well with his democratic and conservative temper.

The other famous saying of his runs, "Man is the measure of all things, of things that are, that they are, and of things that are not, that they are not." 4 What precisely did he mean? We do not know; this was the beginning of his book *On Truth.* Did he mean that the individual man is the measure? Was he stating a theory of sense-perception as knowledge, as is suggested in the *Theaetetus,* and as Sextus Empiricus takes it in quoting the statement—though Sextus takes it as applying to opinions as well as to sensations? But it is also there insisted that the views being discussed under the name of Protagoras were not those actually held by the historical Protagoras. That this was the identification of knowledge with the individual's sensations is very difficult to believe. From everything else we are told about Protagoras, by Plato himself, he was not that kind of individualistic thinker. Was it a vindication of common sense against Parmenides' follower Zeno? Were the arguments directed against Zeno's dialectic? It is hard not to suspect that this aphorism of Protagoras is not an obscure theory of knowledge, but rather an affirmation of the consciousness of human power, that human interests and concerns must be determining.

Is Protagoras, then, a figure like that of A. J. Balfour? 5 Is he bidding us, amidst all our theoretical uncertainty, to

---

4 Sextus Empiricus, *Against the Logicians,* Book I, par. 60.

5 Balfour, the Tory Prime Minister of Great Britain, wrote *A Defence of Philosophic Doubt* (1879), the manual of Victorian skepticism.

join the Established Church because we can be sure at least that it is established? The analogy is hardly complete, for in Protagoras there is the strong sense of the power of Intelligence to improve man's life, individual and social— the power of education.

There were other Sophists who inclined not to Law, *nomos*, but rather to Nature, *physis,* as the standard. There is the Hippias who appears in the *Protagoras* lecturing on Nature. In the Platonic Corpus are two dialogues, known as the *Hippias Major* and *Minor,* in which he appears as an evangelist of the "Back to Nature" gospel, foreshadowing the eighteenth-century physiocrats. Proclaiming that society is not important, that a man should do everything for himself and be self-sufficient, he stands for the Robinson Crusoe ideal. He appears at the Olympic games, announcing he can lecture on any subject; he is a universal genius, he has made all his own clothes and ornaments himself. In philosophy, he held that human laws conflict; men need something more, a higher law, a divine and natural law, a universal and fixed standard.

There is Antiphon, a fragment of whose writings was found on papyrus. For him, all laws are bad: evade them if you can. Follow only the natural law of self-preservation. Antiphon is subversive and iconoclastic: he maintains the natural right of the strongest.

Such cynics appear also in Plato's pages. There is Glaucon in the *Republic,* who holds that men desire power, and in the struggle for it naturally get hurt. So they band together, and set up laws only to avoid something worse; law is thus a second best. John Stuart Mill called him the first protagonist of the social contract theory.

Then there is the Callicles who disputes with Socrates in the *Gorgias.* He maintains the natural right to whatever a man can get away with. Law is a kind of slave morality; the strong man deserves his success. Power and might are the source of right. Naturally, for almost a century Callicles has appeared as a Nietzschean, proclaiming a new morality based on natural superiority. In Plato's portrayal he is revolutionary and idealistic, the superior individual and personality fighting the mob. In the *Gorgias* he stands for what we call the Romantic ideal of life: live at high pressure, seek to enjoy all experience, try everything. To this ideal, Plato makes Socrates oppose wisdom and self-control. It is well to recognize that the typical Athenian—if there was such an animal—was probably a good deal of such a Romanticist—like Alcibiades. Callicles has no use for the wisdom of moderation, and regards Socrates as an old moralizer. Our generation, reading the *Gorgias,* is apt to sympathize with the Romantic ideal of Callicles. There is much in the modern temper that wants to live life to the full, to get a thrill out of it, rather than to live with Socratic wisdom. In the face of the breakdown in Athens of the traditional mores, Plato presents the contrast, and leaves it to the reader to decide. Christians have usually decided against Callicles for Socrates' ideal; the *Gorgias* is hence traditionally taken as one of Plato's more "Christian" dialogues.

Finally, there is the position maintained by Thrasymachus in the *Republic;* here the whole long discussion is presented as the attempt of Socrates to answer him. "Right" is all nonsense. Men will, and that is all. What is called "Right" is what power, any power that can get away with it, decrees. "Justice is the interest of the stronger," Jowett puts it. Whatever is, is right—till something stronger appears. The position is cynical and brutal—and very modern.

Why was this the outcome of the educational movement

of the Sophists? In the light of twentieth-century experience, we say, it was the effect of Athenian imperialism,
based on sheer power. The well-known Melian dialogue in
Thucydides, where the Athenian delegates take just such a
position in arguing their right to destroy the city of Melos
for strategic reasons, well illustrates the effect of war on
men's idealism. That is the way the State acts; why should
not individuals act that way too, if they can? It has been a
recurrent argument in defense of the strong man, the
demagogue, the tyrant; in modern times it has been familiar in Machiavelli. It expresses the disintegrating effects, not
of the Sophists' teaching, but of empire and war. Naturally,
among many Athenians there was a reaction to law, and an
admiration for Sparta and its close regulation, its socialism,
organization, and specialization. The reverberations of this
cultural conflict dominate the *Republic* of Plato.

⸝ VII ⸝

The Historical and the Platonic Socrates

WE actually know less about Socrates than about any other great figure of history—except Jesus of Nazareth—and for the same reason: he has meant so much to later ages, he has stood for so much, and has become a symbol. The living Socrates is still among us; the man who walked the streets of Athens has been forgotten. Socrates was the great inspiration of Plato. So legend affirms; and even if it did not, the dramatic dialogues make him so central a character that we should in any event be forced to affirm Plato's debt to Socrates. But for surviving as the living Socrates, the son of Sophroniskos also owes a great debt to Plato.

What was Socrates like? We possess two gospels, the gospel according to Xenophon, and the gospel according to Plato. As so often happens, the two gospels conflict. Socrates had many disciples, who were in violent philosophical disagreement with each other. Are the gospels true accounts of the historical Socrates? If so, which? And how much? We do not know how to answer these questions: we merely argue.

In the nineteenth century, the higher criticism naturally got busy on Socrates. Theories were worked out galore.

Every possible view, one is tempted to say, has been maintained, together with many views clearly impossible. Is Plato's gospel to be trusted? We should certainly like to believe so—but how far can we go? Was the Platonic Socrates the real man? What would it involve to take this position? Did Socrates teach all of Platonism, including the political theories of the *Republic,* and even the famous theory of Ideas? Were Plato's own views entirely different, and not to be found in the dialogues at all? This position was seriously maintained early in this century by John Burnet and A. E. Taylor. But it seems to be one of the impossible theories—we cannot give up Plato, and the dialogues are all we possess that is tangible.

Is Xenophon's gospel rather to be trusted? Was Socrates after all only a respectable Benthamite, spouting tedious, dogmatic platitudes? It is clear Xenophon's Socrates is a spokesman also; but certainly not the philosophical inspiration the historical Socrates was and has remained. Were he the true Socrates, the Athenians would never have put him to death.

No, it is clear that like all gospels, both Plato's and Xenophon's are a mixture of *Dichtung* and *Wahrheit.* To continue the figure, Plato's is like that of the Beloved Disciple, St. John the Evangelist, giving a philosophic interpretation of the master's significance; Xenophon's is more like the synoptic gospels.

Where, then, lies the truth? Shall we go to the Apostle to the Gentiles, who spread his gospel but never actually saw Socrates? Shall we go to Aristotle? He tells us that Socrates was the first to seek for general definitions, and that he was the first to practice systematic induction. This is doubtless so; Aristotle ought to know. But it is Aristotle the logician speaking, and he seems to be emphasizing the least important point as he so often does, except when he is touching on his own great passion for sheer knowing.

If we turn to the summary of *"Das Sokratesproblem"* in Ueberweg-Praechter, the problem which has so exercised scholarship, we find that of the four or five leading interpretations, one, that of Karl Joël, concludes: Go to Aristotle. Xenophon did not know what he was talking about, and Plato knew only too well; another, that of August Döring, says: Go to Xenophon. Aristotle was ignorant, and Plato was a liar; a third, A. E. Taylor's, holds: Everything Plato puts into Socrates' mouth was taught by Socrates, as the head of an organized school of Pythagoreans; a fourth maintains: Only the Platonic *Apology* and the "Early" dialogues tell us anything about Socrates; a fifth concludes: "Socrates" is a pure myth; there never was any such man; and one, the wisest of all, reaches the truly Socratic conclusion: We only know that we know nothing. This view has recently received new support from O. Gigon.[1]

This is not quite true. We do know one thing about Socrates: Socrates died a martyr to the Truth. Why did he? We do not know that, nor even the meaning of the charge against him, or the real reason why he was put to death. Modern historians, however, have produced some lively accounts of "Socrates with his halo off."

After Socrates' death, many "apologies" were written, setting forth how he ought to have defended himself. It became a stock literary theme—like setting down the sayings of Jesus among the early Christians. Is Plato's to be trusted? Socrates seems too self-conscious, too clear in his life's aim, like Bernard Shaw's St. Joan. Men do not usually know what they are going to stand for to future ages; and

[1] O. Gigon, *Sokrates* (Bern, 1947).

if they do, they usually do not tell. It seems clear, Plato's *Apology* is hardly a literal account of what Socrates actually said at his trial; it is rather the expression of what he meant to Plato. But the Platonic *Apology* is what Socrates has meant, and continues to mean to us. It is after all the only thing we really possess to go upon—it is our Socrates. It is the figure to whom Erasmus exclaimed, "St. Socrates! Pray for me."

The personality of Socrates, as revealed in the *Apology,* is probably correct enough; it would at least explain why he had so many different disciples founding so many different philosophical sects. He appears as a self-confident, independent, egotistical figure, a man of strong passions and even stronger self-control. He is a glorified common Athenian, prosaic, unimaginative, homely—yet obviously inspired. He loved questioning and discussion better than anything else in the world. He was very politically minded; he fitted into the Age of the Sophists, and till he died he was clearly Athens' prize Sophist. And he asked no fee—you could not hire him to stop performing.

He was passionately eager to find knowledge, real knowledge, though he scorned natural science. He was impatient of pretense, something of a skeptic, more of a mystic. He was convinced he was the wisest of men, for he knew his own ignorance. But everybody else was worse off—they did not even know that. So he went about, playing the part of the gadfly, or the torpedo fish, showing up the pretensions of others. This profession of ignorance is what we call the Socratic "irony." He was looking for some truth; if he could only find it, then he would possess the secret of a satisfying life. He was an interesting personality, but terribly annoying.

Socrates was always surrounded by a band of clever,

brilliant, bad young men. They applauded his attacks on the respectable citizens, the Babbitts of Athens. Socrates shook their adolescent faith, punctured the moral pretensions of the older generation, and held their beliefs up to ridicule, to the immense delight of the clever young fellows. They, of course, did not share his own faith in the Good Life—they knew too much. We can say, Socrates was trying to substitute self-discipline for the rigid discipline of tradition. Tradition is easy enough to topple over, when changed conditions conflict with it; but it is none too easy a task to offer a viable substitute. So Socrates was undoubtedly a subversive moral influence; but at the same time he was intellectually a magnificent teacher.

Finally, the Athenians could stand it no longer. They brought him to trial: he made the worst sort of defense, for he had no more tact than the average radical. He was put to death. It does not really matter why; it was probably a frame-up, for the Athenians were out to get him.[2] He died a sacrifice to the resentment and fear inspired by the reformers and intellectuals, by the talkers—by the whole Sophistic movement. Socrates was apparently an easy victim, since he was backed by no party—he had alienated them all by his outspoken criticism.

Socrates died to find everlasting fame. He became a great memory, a tradition. Would we ever have heard of Socrates if he had not been made a martyr by Athenian stupidity? His death changed everything: he became the

---

[2] See Ryle's argument about Socrates' trial, which leads him to the conclusion: "Plato's Apology must, in bulk, be totally unhistorical. . . . There is much more fiction than is sometimes supposed in the dialogues' picture of Socrates." Gilbert Ryle, "Plato," *Encyclopedia of Philosophy,* ed. Paul Edwards (New York, 1967), VI, 316.

symbol of Philosophy. When alive, he was an amusing old fellow, rather monotonous and boring, to be sure, but good fun for a time, when taken in small doses. He was a "character"; but hardly to be taken seriously, of course: a fit theme for those "Follies of 423 B.C." Aristophanes put on in *The Clouds.*

Then came the incredible death, which transformed him into the Inquisitor of Athens, the finger of conscience pointed at her soul. Socrates became a myth—like Abraham Lincoln. He was always an appealing character, essentially comic, but certainly not so tremendous or overshadowing until he was dead and sainted. Then every philosophic school, including so unlikely a candidate as the hedonistic Cyrenaics, tried to use him—as the Republicans have used Lincoln—to cover their sins. The actual man, whatever he may have been, was forgotten: a myth is the best way to forget. He became an idealized, impersonal convention; and, as it was put by Hegel, who was nothing if not unsentimental and realistic, "the patron saint of moral twaddle."

The personality of Socrates has probably come down to us clearly enough, at Plato's hands. But what about his teaching, his method and doctrine? We do not know. It became the fashion to write Socratic dialogues; many, we are told, were written, for it had become a conventional literary form. Those of Xenophon have been preserved, in addition to Plato's. Plato was a great artist and a creative thinker, so he could make the most of the literary form.

The Socrates who figures as a dramatic character in the Platonic dialogues does, of course, have a very precise method and a definite teaching, for which Plato is clearly responsible. The method of the Platonic Socrates is to discuss and argue and browbeat his victims interminably, till they are willing to agree to anything to get rid of him. He says much about a so-called dialectical method, so much that classical scholars have been apt to take him at his word, and argue solemnly about "the logical structure of the Socratic dialectic." But, as Plato actually—and maliciously, and perhaps ironically—portrays him, the only method he is really made to use is dialectic in the very literal sense of talking everybody and every subject to death —*to dialegesthai.*

Plato makes his character employ every trick of logic and rhetoric: "Flattery, cajolery, insinuation, innuendo, sarcasm, feigned humility, personal idiosyncrasies, browbeating, insolence, anger, changing the subject when in difficulty, distracting attention, faulty analogies, the torturing of words, making adjectives do the work of nouns and nouns of adjectives, tacking on verbs to qualities which could never use them, glad of an interruption or a previous engagement, telling stories which make one forget what the subject of discussion was, hinting that he could say much more and would if his hearers were up to it, promising more tomorrow if they are really interested and want to go on—an accomplished sophist if there ever was one.

"[In a word] Plato has made him the incarnation of all the subleties men use in argument to confirm or destroy opinions." 3

The teaching of this dramatic character of Plato, as revealed in the dialogues, is very simple: "Know thyself." Socrates uses all the tricks of the trade developed by a community of talkers, not to defend opinions, but to bring to light what they are. He claims, he can himself teach nothing. The dialogues convince us he is right. He upsets

³ F. J. E. Woodbridge, *The Son of Apollo* (Boston, 1929), pp. 269–70.

the confident opinions of others without putting another confident opinion—least of all his own—in their place. The constant outcome of the discussions in the Socratic dialogues is inconclusiveness. This is obviously deliberate on the part of the skillful author, Plato, who knew just what he was doing. The effect is to reveal men to themselves, to make them see just what their opinions really amount to. To make such self-knowledge emerge is far more important than any determination of the question discussed, than any certified conclusion about the theme chosen for discussion, could possibly be. Since this is the effect the dialogues produce, it is clearly intended by the author.

It is necessary, therefore, for such a dramatic character as the Platonic Socrates to possess no knowledge of his own, no personal bias, so that he can reveal the bias of the other characters. He must show to what human opinions actually lead. If he himself held opinions of his own, they would be like the others. Plato uses Socrates as a mirror in which to reflect man thinking. Such a mirror must reflect without distortion. The story runs that his friends consulted the oracle at Delphi about him, and received the truly Delphic answer, "He is wisest who knows he knows nothing." Plato makes us believe this is true of his Socrates: its truth is the very essence of the dramatic character of Socrates—it is illustrated in every Socratic dialogue. Thus in the *Protagoras,* Socrates reflects the opinions and methods of Protagoras. In the *Meno,* he is made to reflect those of Gorgias; and so on. Plato uses his Socrates as the instrument for conducting his dramatic commentary on the opinions of those men whose ideas he judges are worth thus revealing though the mirror of Socrates.

Is this what the Socrates of Athens was really trying to do? Is this the method and teaching of the historical Socra-

tes? Or is this a dramatic—and therefore a philosophical—
device of Plato's, a dramatic character created by Plato for
his own philosophic purposes?

For us, the method and teaching of the historical Socrates, who finally went home to meet defeat at the sharp
tongue of Xanthippe, and the method and teaching of the
Socrates who is a character of Plato the dramatic poet, the
writer of intellectual comedies, have become one and insep-
arable. Are the dialogues all stenographic transcriptions of
what the historical Socrates actually said? Or are they
imaginative and poetic renditions of what he might have
said, or ought to have said, to be what he actually was—in
this respect, like the speeches in Thucydides? Was Plato
himself the second- or third-rate thinker the Aristotelean
commentators tell us of, much given to Pythagorean
mumbo-jumbo? Or are the Socratic dialogues all dramatic
expressions of Plato's own philosophic insights, in which he
uses, for his own philosophic purposes, the dramatic character, Socrates, his poetic gifts enabled him to create, borrow-
ing certain traits—we do not know just which—from an
historical figure named Socrates, about whom we know
literally nothing? Was the historical Socrates just the ques-
tioner, the gadfly?

We do not actually know enough about the historical
Socrates to give any sure answer. But it really does not
matter. We possess Socrates, the leading character in Plato's
comic dramas. The question, what was the real Socrates
like, before Plato's genius got busy working on him, is
suspiciously like asking seriously, "What was the real
Amlet, Prince of Denmark, like, whose name Shakespeare
used, perhaps in vain, in a well-known play?" That is,
God—and Sophroniskos—may have created the historical
Socrates. But it was Plato, with but little help from God,

who created the Socrates of the dialogues, and the philosophical tradition—though perhaps Plato was "participating in the Divine" when he did it.

What this means is that Plato was far greater than Socrates. He could see all around Socrates, and view him, as we say, objectively. It is the hardest thing in the world to understand a great man, to feel his greatness, and still not transform him into a plaster saint. If you can really do it—as Plato could do it with Socrates—you are greater than he. In a word, Socrates was no poet, while Plato was.

✽ VIII ✽

Plato's Circle and Audience

THE dialogues of Plato were not written for a classroom audience. They were not composed to contribute to the professional training of philosophers and teachers of philosophy. They presuppose an entirely different kind of audience, an audience of intellectuals, as we have called them, in a quite nonprofessional sense. They were written for the kind of people who attend the latest plays and read the latest books, the kind that read the more sophisticated weeklies. They were the audience that paid to hear the newest Sophist arrived in Athens, that lingered while Socrates belabored a companion in the agora.

What was this audience in Athens like? Certain of the Socratic dialogues seem to have as their primary dramatic intention to portray this audience busily arguing with the Sophist or playing him off against Socrates. They offer a dramatic picture of Plato's circle. Three in particular seem far more interested in portraying such a picture than in arguing for any conclusion, or even in suggesting one dramatically. They have traditionally been called "inconclusive." Their philosophical concern lies in a dramatic commentary on the ideas of the central figure or protagonist, a commentary that brings out his position and appraises its

strength and its limitations. These three are the *Protagoras,
the Meno,* and the *Gorgias.* The first is a full-scale portrait
of the Sophists at work: besides Protagoras himself, we are
shown two other famous Sophists, Hippias and Prodicus,
the latter of whom is supposed to have been one of Socrates' teachers. Protagoras is very sympathetically presented:
he is a great teacher, with certain distinctive ideas which,
rightly understood, are provocative and stimulating. He is
made to tell a "story" which is one of the wisest in all Plato,
a story which expresses the faith in the educational power
of social institutions Plato shared with him. We can well
believe the report that Protagoras' *Republic* formed the
basis for the Perfect City in Plato's *Republic.* The *Meno*
and the *Gorgias* are about another Sophist, Gorgias. The
Meno examines his ideas in terms of what he has taught his
pupil, Meno—a cruel procedure. The *Gorgias* brings him
on stage personally, together with one of his followers, Callicles. Again we have a searching commentary: how far
Gorgias is right, and wherein lie his limitations. Gorgias
was a famous rhetorician, and some of the speeches in Plato
are said to be parodies of his style—notably Agathon's
speech in the *Symposium.* Plato took him very seriously, as
he did most of the great teachers of the Periclean Age.

The *Protagoras* is an account, narrated by Socrates to a
friend, of his meeting with the great teacher; this affords
the chance for many shrewd comments of Socrates upon
the whole procedure. Socrates tells how he was awakened
early one morning by the young fellow Hippocrates rush-
ing in eagerly. The Sophist Protagoras has arrived in town,
and they must both hurry not to miss anything of his per-
formance. The youth is so eager because he hopes to learn
about *aretē* from the teacher, which clearly means for him,
how to achieve "political eminence," "how to speak and act

in the affairs of state." "Excellence" is for him political skill
and know-how, the power to achieve "success" in politics.
Socrates cautions him: to whom is he proposing to entrust
his soul? for the Sophist cannot possibly know how to
teach what he professes to impart. Hippocrates replies that
he certainly is a "master of making one a clever speaker."
They hurry out quickly, despite the dangers; and when
they come to the house of Callias, where Protagoras is
speaking, they find Hippias of Elis, another Sophist, seated
in the doorway and answering questions about nature and
the heavenly bodies. Hippias is a partisan of nature
throughout the discussion, interested in astronomy and the
cosmological theories of the Early Greeks. Prodicus of Ceos
is still in bed in a store-room, talking to an eager band
which includes the Pausanias and Agathon of the *Symposium*. Prodicus is a linguistic analyst, at the slightest
chance making nice distinctions between words. These
teachers are not Athenians, they are foreigners; and not
gentlemen, they are professionals who take money. Hippocrates is as scandalized as Anytus in the *Meno* at the suggestion that he himself might want to become a Sophist.

Protagoras claims to be a Sophist, and to educate men:
he tells Hippocrates, "You will go home a better man." He
scorns Hippias' teaching of arithmetic and astronomy and
geometry and music. His own teaching consists in "good
judgment in one's own affairs, showing how best to order
one's home; and in the affairs of one's city, showing how
one may have most influence on public affairs both in
speech and in action." Socrates puts it: "You appear to be
speaking of the political art (*hē politikē technē*) and
undertaking to make men good citizens." "That is exactly
the purport of what I profess," runs the Sophist's reply.

The talk, then, is to be about politics and political

affairs: actually it is about everything else. Socrates starts by asking, "Can this political art, this *aretē,* be taught?" Is "excellence" teachable? The theme is chosen, it is clear, to have something to talk about: and this is what such a group would be likely to discuss, as Americans in the 1960s might discuss civil rights. There is no point in finding an answer: Protagoras will go on teaching it in any event. Protagoras starts by telling a fable or myth, which raises doubt whether it can be taught, and he proceeds to argue against his own thesis. Socrates denies excellence can be taught, then argues for a conception of it which by making it knowledge would seem to make it teachable. A major point of Plato's is plainly, this is the way men discuss and argue.

In the discussion, the character most clearly "sophistical" in common parlance is Socrates. Socrates also, after voicing his distrust of men who tell stories instead of arguing, tells the longest and most improbable story. The wisest speaker is clearly Protagoras himself, though he distrusts argument and cannot do it very well. And actually, of course, there is no real disagreement between him and Socrates. As he says, "My view, Socrates, . . . is precisely that which you express, and what is more, it would be a disgrace for me above all men to assert that wisdom and knowledge (*sophia kai epistēmē*) were aught but the highest of all human things." [1]

What is Plato doing with Protagoras? Is he trying to disprove his contentions, what he stood for? Not at all! He is having fun with him. What he is doing is to use all the characteristic devices associated with Protagoras against him. One of Protagoras' most famous dicta was that on

[1] *Protagoras* 352 C, D.

every issue there were two antithetical positions, two *logoi;* both these *logoi* could be defended equally well by argument, and equally well demolished. Hence the recurrent arguments by opposites, as showing that folly is the opposite of every excellence. The argument about the Simonides poem is introduced as an interlude or kind of chorus, like Agathon's speech in the *Symposium.* It too yields two opposite interpretations that can be supported equally well. It is introduced because Protagoras stood for a classical education, the traditional Greek education in the poets: even Protagoras' favorite subject matter betrays him at Socrates' hands.

Socrates' myth is presented as a parody of Protagoras' democratic myth. The latter tells how Prometheus and Epimetheus, Forethought and Afterthought, bestowed gifts and talents on all mortal creatures at their creation. But Epimetheus, Afterthought, "being not so wise as he might be, heedlessly squandered his stock of properties on the brutes; he still had left unequipped the race of men, and was at a loss what to do with it." [2] So Prometheus stole for man the fire of Hephaestus and the wisdom in the arts of Athene. "Now although man acquired in this way the wisdom of daily life, political wisdom (*hē sophia politikē*) he had not, since this was in the possession of Zeus." [3] Prometheus could not easily enter the citadel of Zeus, and the guards of Zeus were terrible. So men invented sounds and words, but lived alone, without cities, the prey of beasts, as they had no political skill to join together. And when they tried to, they found themselves in a Hobbesian war of each against all. "So Zeus, fearing that our race was

[2] *Protagoras* 321 B, C.
[3] *Protagoras* 321 D.

in danger of utter destruction, sent Hermes to bring respect and right (*aidō ḳai diḳē*) among men, to the end that there should be regulation of cities and friendly ties to draw them together." But Zeus bade him not distribute these as special gifts, like medical skill: "Let all," said Zeus, "have their share; for cities cannot be formed if only a few have a share of these as of other arts. And make thereto a law of my ordaining, that he who cannot partake of respect and right shall die the death as a public pest." 4 Hence while only a few share artistic excellence or good craftsmanship, "when they meet for consultation on political excellence (*politiḳē aretē*), where they should be guided throughout by justice and good sense, they naturally allow advice from everybody, since it is held that everyone should partake of this excellence, or else that cities cannot be." Yet we are also told that this political excellence is not "natural or spontaneous, but is something taught and acquired after careful preparation by those who acquire it." There are, to be sure, no special teachers set apart. We might as well ask who is a teacher of Greek: men learn political excellence and justice as they learn their language, from the whole round of their living, from what we call their "social heritage." The citizens admonish their sons from earliest childhood to the last day of their lives. They charge the schoolmasters to continue this moral training; what the schools teach inculcates the same lessons. Everyone is a teacher of excellence to the extent of his powers; and the worst of men possess more of it than the barbarians. Excellence is teachable and is so deemed by the Athenians. "If there is somebody who excels us ever so little in showing the way to excellence, we must be thankful. Such an one I take myself to be, excelling all

---

4 *Protagoras* 322 C.

other men in the gift of assisting people to become good and true." 5

Ah!, says Socrates, if you think everybody can teach excellence, I can give you a better example. You know, the Spartans, whom we Athenians think to be narrow and stupid and unintellectual, are really and in secret philosophers, who far surpass us feeble Athenians at divine philosophy. And so Socrates is launched on his parody.

That the positions of the two disputants are completely reversed is noted at the end: it is a cardinal illustration and proof of Protagoras' doctrine of the two *logoi,* turned against his own profession.

Our discussion, in its present result, seems to me as though it accused and mocked us like some human person; if it were given a voice it would say: "What strange creatures you are, Socrates and Protagoras! You on the one hand, after having said at first that excellence cannot be taught, are now hot in opposition to yourself, endeavoring to prove that all things are knowledge—justice, temperance, and courage—which is the best way to make excellence appear teachable: for if excellence were anything else than knowledge, as Protagoras tried to make out, obviously it would not be teachable; but if as a matter of fact it turns out be entirely knowledge, as you urge, Socrates, I shall be surprised if it is not teachable. Protagoras, on the other hand, though at first he claimed that it was teachable, now seems as eager for the opposite, declaring that it has been found to be almost anything but knowledge, which would make it quite unteachable!" 6

The concluding discussion of the art of measuring pleasures, which John Stuart Mill called the first statement of Utilitarianism, is an illustration of another central idea

---

5 *Protagoras* 328 A, B.
6 *Protagoras* 361 A, B, C.

associated with Protagoras' name: Man is the measure of all things. Plato seems to be saying, this is what it could mean if it is to make sense.

The impression left of Protagoras is: he cannot argue, and distrusts dialectic, but his views on public education are sound. His myth stating the philosophy of democracy, with its faith in nonprofessional education, and concern with improving human affairs through popular intelligence, is far from radical and dangerous: it is eminently respectable. It is just the respectability of Protagoras' views that permits Plato to let Socrates and his companions have fun with the supporter of the Athenian Establishment.

The other portraits are also sharply and ironically lined. Hippias the partisan of natural science and nature, not of law and society, is always bumptiously offering to explain any difficulty: he can explain anything, as he claims in the two *Hippias* dialogues. "We are all friends by nature!" he repeatedly interjects. "I shall explain it for you." Prodicus is forever introducing his fine distinctions, between "fear" and "terror," etc. Socrates, his pupil, uses his method, with his distinctions in the Simonides poem between "be" and "become," between "bad" and "evil," and the rest.

What is the final attitude Plato leaves with the beholder and the onlooker at this gorgeous canvas? These Sophists are all good teachers—of everything but "excellence," *aretē*. This is clearly Plato's artistic and philosophic intention, in presenting us with this picture of his circle and audience.

The *Meno* is a dramatic commentary, in a very similar ironic spirit, upon the ideas of another great Sophist, Gorgias, Meno's teacher. Since the theme is what can be taught and what cannot, it is appropriate to examine the teacher by inquiring what he has been able to teach his pupil. Gorgias has succeeded in teaching Meno nothing but persuasive definitions. Socrates, inquiring of Meno what excellence is, is told that excellences are relative and specific: each man and each situation has its own specific excellence, which Meno tries to state; he cannot generalize. When pushed, he calls excellence "the power of governing mankind." There are also courage, and self-control and wisdom, and loftiness of mind. Socrates tries to make Meno see he wants a general definition, like that of geometrical figure as "the limit of solid." He proposes Empedocles' physical definition of color: "Color is an effluence of figures, commensurate with sight and sensible," which meets with Meno's approval, since it is in "the high poetic style" he is familiar with in his teacher Gorgias. So Meno tries again. "Excellence is to desire what is honorable and to be able to procure it." It is "ability to procure goods." But that is not enough, so Meno adds: "Excellence is the ability to procure goods things with justice." When Socrates has got through with this, Meno compares him to the stinging and benumbing torpedo fish. Socrates explains: "It is not from any sureness in myself that I cause others to doubt; it is from being in more doubt than anyone else that I cause doubt in others."

Is Socrates really in doubt? Meno recalls his master's teaching:

Why, on what lines will you look, Socrates, for a thing of whose nature you know nothing at all? Pray, what sort of thing, amongst those that you know not, will you treat us to as the object of your search? Or even supposing, at the best, that you hit upon it, how will you know it is the thing you did not know?

Soc. Do you see what a captious argument you are introducing—that, forsooth, a man cannot inquire about what he knows, or about what he does not know? For he cannot inquire about what he knows, because he knows it, and in that case is in no need of inquiry; nor again can he inquire about what he does not know, since he does not know about what he is to inquire.7

This is the argument stated in the beginning of Gorgias' famous book, *On Nature and Nothing,* repeated by his pupil. Socrates proceeds to attack it. He tells how the soul is really immortal, and learned all things before being born; hence all knowledge is actually recollection. The reminiscence myth and doctrine is introduced to refute Gorgias. If all inquiry is really remembering, "We must not hearken to that captious argument: it would make us idle, and is pleasing only to the indolent ear, whereas the other makes us energetic and inquiring."

So they call in a slave boy, and "remember" him a proposition in Euclid. Socrates is a good teacher—or rather, "rememberer"—of geometry.

Soc. You should take heart, and whatever you do not happen to know at present—that is, what you do not remember—you must endeavor to search out and recollect. Most of the points I have made in search of my argument are not such as I can confidently assert; but that the belief in the duty of inquiring after what we do not know will make us better and braver and less helpless than the notion that there is not even a possibility of discovering what we do not know, nor any duty of inquiring after it—this is a point for which I am determined to do battle, so far as I am able, both in word and deed.8

Gorgias has been refuted.

Anytus enters, and bursts into a tirade against the

7 *Meno* 80 D, E.
8 *Meno* 86 B, C.

Sophists, about whom he knows nothing but against whom he has strong prejudices—even against Protagoras, who, Socrates mildly objects, "retains to this day the high reputation he has enjoyed all that time." No! explodes Anytus, "Any Athenian gentleman he comes across, without exception, will do Meno more good, if he will do as he is bid, than the Sophists."

But have these admirable gentlemen, Socrates asks, proved good teachers of their own excellence? "Did the good men of our own and of former times know how to transmit to another man the excellence in respect of which they were good, or is it something not to be transmitted or taken over from one human being to another?"⁹ Can excellence be taught? Even Pericles was not able to teach it to his own sons.

Here Meno recalls his own teacher once more:

Soc. What of the Sophists? Do you consider these, its only professors, to be teachers of excellence?

Men. That is a point, Socrates, for which I admire Gorgias: you will never hear him promising this, and he ridicules the others when he hears them promise it. Skill in speaking is what he takes it to be their business to produce.¹⁰

Since it appears no one is able to teach excellence, "The result of our reasoning, Meno, is found to be that excellence comes to us by a divine dispensation, when it does come."

Gorgias claims, in his book, that strictly speaking we can teach nothing, and inquire into nothing. Plato's dramatic commentary on this doctrine runs: Gorgias is right —he has been able to teach Meno nothing but fine words, persuasive definitions. He has taught him nothing about

---

⁹ *Meno* 93 A, B.
¹⁰ *Meno* 95 C.

excellence, which he professes not to teach. Yet—some things can be taught—geometry, *ta mathēmatika,* the teachable things. Gorgias forgot mathematics. Yet on the broader question, Can excellence be taught? Gorgias is right—he has not taught Meno, nobody has taught it, even Pericles could not teach it to his own sons. The professed teachers, the Sophists, have been good teachers, but not of excellence, not even Protagoras, whom Socrates defends against the prejudices of Anytus.[11] "Now are we to take it, according to you, that the Sophists wittingly deceived and corrupted the youth, or that they were themselves unconscious of it? Are we to conclude those who are frequently termed the wisest of mankind to have been so demented as that? . . . . Tell me, Anytus, has any of the Sophists wronged you? What makes you so hard on them?" [12] The Athenian statesmen and gentlemen have no true "knowledge" (*epistēmē*) of excellence, they possess only "right opinion" (*orthē doxa*). So excellence must be after all a divine gift. On this ironic note the dialogue ends. Yet it has already been made clear, that men are not good "by nature."

Soc. Since it is not by nature that the good become good, is it by education?

Men. We must now conclude, I think, that it is; and plainly, Socrates, on our hypothesis that excellence is knowledge, it must be taught.[13]

The upshot is, Gorgias is right; and Socrates makes a vigorous defense of all the Sophists. Plato has presented one

[11] Anytus is the man who brought the suit against Socrates himself, as portrayed in the *Euthyphro.*
[12] *Meno* 92 A, B.
[13] *Meno* 89 B, C.

Sophist in terms of his product. In so doing, he has given a dramatic commentary on the teacher, Gorgias, and pointed out the sense in which he is right, and the sense in which he is too sweeping, in forgetting the teachable things, that mathematics can be taught. In his educational program, as presented in the *Republic*, Plato bids us begin at least with what can be taught, mathematics.

In the *Gorgias* dialogue, the famous Sophist and rhetorician Gorgias of Leontini appears in person, on a visit to Athens, where he is staying in the house of Callicles, a young man with many of the traits of Alcibiades. Here too he has an enthusiastic young disciple and admirer, Polus of Agrigentum, from Sicily. Socrates is asking about the art of rhetoric, which Gorgias professes: rhetoric is the ostensible theme under discussion. But the talk soon develops into a concern with the Good Life; Socrates relentlessly pushes his questions about the good with Polus, until Callicles bursts forth with an Alcibiadean—or Nietzschean, the modern reader will inevitably add—defense of the Romantic ideal of living life to the fullest, squeezing the utmost possible out of experience. Thereafter Plato is interested in presenting and contrasting the two ideals between which the Greek intellectual class were torn, now that customary morality had broken down—the Romantic will to power of Alcibiades, and the self-discipline of Socrates. Which is it the part of wisdom to follow? The young Plato leaves it to the reader to decide. The dialogue bears many marks of youth; it belongs with the earliest Socratic dialogues, in its immaturity of style—it uses direct dialogue, it divides the discussion into talks with three successive debaters with Socrates, etc. Still, it has many moving and eloquent passages. These have been used normally in the Christian tradition to sanctify the Socratic ideals; and it has always been a prime favorite with the lovers of great ethical literature. Most of all, perhaps, the *Gorgias* makes it clear that for its audience the question of life and the way it should be lived was deeply entangled with rhetoric and language.[14] The *Gorgias,* in displaying far more ethical fervor than the *Protagoras,* gives us an insight into how the problem of the Good Life appeared a real issue for that generation alienated from the moral tradition, and how it could win the enthusiasm of the young Plato before his sense of the irony of life and his detachment had matured.

"What is the power of the art of rhetoric which Gorgias teaches?" Socrates asks. Gorgias has just given a long and tiring speech, so his student Polus acts as his stand-in. The art of manipulating words is "the finest art of all." But Gorgias favors long speeches; Socrates, as he had done with Protagoras, asks for the brevity of dialectic. Gorgias complies: rhetoric deals with words. Does it also deal with understanding the things about which they speak? Gorgias is forced to admit, yes—his fatal admission. He sticks out his neck, and answers, "Rhetoric deals with the greatest and best of human affairs." It persuades the minds of its hearers, in the courts or in the assembly, about the just and the unjust (*dikaia kai adika*). But, Socrates points out, it

---

[14] A. E. Taylor well characterizes the *Gorgias:* "The true object of the whole work thus emerges: it is to pit a typical life of devotion to the supra-personal good against the typical theory and practice of the 'will to power' at its best. We are to see how the theory of the 'will to power,' expounded by a thoroughly capable, intelligent, and far from merely ignoble champion, like Callicles, and the 'practice' of it as embodied in Periclean Imperialism, look from the point of view of a Socrates; and also how the convictions and career of a Socrates look to the intelligent worshipper of 'strength'; and when we have looked at each party with the eyes of the other, we are to be the judges between them." *Plato: The Man and His Work* (New York, 1926), p. 106.

merely persuades men that certain beliefs are so; it teaches no true knowledge of right and wrong. Hence rhetoric must be used fairly (*dikaiōs*). The user of words must know what is just; hence, "He who has learnt what is just is just himself," and he must wish to do what is just. Polus accuses Socrates of unfairly forcing the answer on Gorgias: the rhetorician must teach others what justice is.

Socrates regards rhetoric, not as an art, but as a form of flattery, what he calls a mere "cookery" of the soul. Polus holds the rhetoricians powerful, like tyrants: they can get men to do what they wish. No, they are weak, says Socrates, for they do not really will evil—their bad effects are not intended. But to do wrong is the greatest of evils. To do injustice is worse than suffering it: no unjust man can be happy. Consider Archelaus, King of Macedon; he cannot possibly be happy, for he is unjust. A good and honorable man or woman is happy, and an unjust and wicked one is wretched. Yes, says Polus, if he is punished and made miserable. No, runs the reply:

In my opinion, Polus, the wrongdoer or the unjust is wretched anyhow; more wretched, however, if he does not pay the penalty and gets no punishment for his wrongdoing, but less wretched if he pays the penalty and meets with requital from gods and men.[15]

"He becomes better in soul if he is justly punished, and he who pays the penalty is relieved of badness of soul." It is pleasant to be medically treated, and although those who undergo such treatment do not enjoy it, it is beneficial, because one is relieved of a great evil, and hence it is worth while to endure the pain and be well. A man, says Socrates, developing his ideal of self-discipline, "must keep a close

[15] *Gorgias* 472 E.

watch over himself so as to avoid wrongdoing, since it would bring a great deal of evil upon him."

So far, Socrates has had it all his own way. He has got Polus to admit that doing evil is the greater "disgrace," an admission fatal to his whole contention. But now Callicles jumps into the argument, disgusted with Socrates' sophistry. "Is Socrates in earnest, or only joking?" Callicles is a lover of Demos, the Athenian people; Socrates is a lover of Alcibiades—the ambivalent relation between Socrates and the Alcibiadean ideal of Callicles is clearly suggested. Polus' fatal admission was just like Gorgias': that doing evil is "fouler" and a greater "disgrace." Callicles is a partisan of Nature, not of convention (*physis,* not *nomos*); the two are sharply opposed. By Nature, suffering injustice is worse; by convention, performing it.

Indeed the endurance of wrong done is not a man's part at all, but a poor slave's, for whom it is better to be dead than alive, as it is for anybody who, when wronged or insulted, is unable to protect himself or anyone else for whom he cares. But I suppose the makers of the laws are the weaker sort of men, and the more numerous. So it is with a view to themselves and their own interest that they make their laws and distribute their praises and censures; and to terrorize the stronger sort of folk who are able to get an advantage, and to prevent them from getting an advantage over *them,* they tell them that such aggrandizement is foul and unjust, and that wrongdoing is just this endeavor to get the advantage over one's neighbors: for I expect they are well content to see themselves on an equality, when they are so inferior. . . . Nature, in my opinion, herself proclaims the fact that it is right for the better to have advantage of the worse, and the abler of the feebler.[16]

[16] *Gorgias* 483 B, C, D.

"The right has been decided to consist in the sway and advantage of the stronger over the weaker." What other right did Xerxes have to invade Greece? Callicles defends the "law of Nature" (*ho nomos tēs physeōs*).

But when some man arises with a nature of sufficient force, he shakes off all that we have taught him, bursts his bonds, and breaks free; he tramples under foot our codes and juggleries, our charms and "laws," which are all against Nature; our slave rises in revolt and shows himself our master, and there dawns the full light of natural justice.[17]

"So put aside philosophy," Callicles concludes; "that is all right for callow youths. Get into political life."

After this Nietzschean tirade, Socrates can only ask, Are those "superior" in power really "better"? Is it possible to be better and yet inferior and weaker, to be stronger and yet more wicked? The many are the stronger, so their ordinances are by nature "fair." But, snorts Callicles, by "superior" I do not mean numerically stronger, I mean wiser, "men of wisdom and manliness in public affairs, the rulers." "Do you mean those who can rule themselves, and possess self-control, temperance?" "The temperate are fools!"

He who would live rightly should let his desires be as strong as possible and not chasten them, and should be able to minister to them when they are at their height by reason of his manliness and intelligence, and satisfy each appetite in turn with what it desires.[18]

But desire is a sieve, interposes Socrates; the intemperate is never satisfied. And some desires, like the desire to scratch an itch, are bad. I say pleasure is the good, objects

[17] *Gorgias* 484 A.
[18] *Gorgias* 491 E–492 A.

Callicles. But wants and desires, rejoins Socrates, are bad; the satisfaction of pleasure thus implies previous pains, so pleasure cannot be the good. Callicles then makes *his* fatal admission: some pleasures are bad. Hence not pleasure but the Good is the standard, and that depends on knowledge. Socrates had brought even the Romanticist around at last. He tells a typical Orphic myth about the Last Judgment, with something of the otherworldliness of the *Phaedo* about it. Indeed, much of the temper of the *Gorgias* is so close to that of the *Phaedo* that one suspects it was written shortly after Socrates' death, when Plato could not contemplate without emotion his teacher's departure.

Man has one resource: if he had stood up for himself by avoiding any unjust word or deed in regard either to men or to gods. For this has been repeatedly admitted by us to be the most valuable kind of self-protection. Now if I were convicted of inability to extend this kind of protection, to either myself or another, I should be ashamed, whether my conviction took place before many or few, or as between man and man; and if that inability should bring about my death, I should be sorely vexed: but if I came to my end through a lack of flattering rhetoric, I am quite sure you would see me take my death easily. For no man fears the mere act of dying, except he be utterly irrational and unmanly; doing wrong is what one fears: for to arrive in the nether world having one's soul full fraught with a heap of misdeeds is the uttermost of all evils.[19]

The *Gorgias* gives an inimitable picture of the atmosphere in which Socrates carried on his ethical discussion. There was a crying need for a new rationale for the moral life, and for Socrates' attempt to substitute self-discipline and conscious ethical reflection—"Know Thyself, an exam-

[19] *Gorgias* 522 C, D, E.

ined life"—for the older stable customary morality of an agricultural society now rapidly giving way to a new commercial existence. This new life afforded opportunities to the strong individual like Alcibiades to free himself from convention in order to develop his own personality, and to run the full gamut of experience. What was needed was a new standard for judging man's individual opportunities— a standard for what was worth knowing and incorporating into one's own life of Reason. The Socratic dialogues of Plato take up this problem, and were written for an intellectual class confronting it as no mere theory, but as a practical choice.

IX

Plato the Artist–Philosopher *

To exhibit what Plato is—the artist-philosopher—it is well to start by disposing of certain things he is not—certain things that are not to be found in the dialogues. And here I am yielding to the temptation to be rather dogmatic. If these things are found in the dialogues—as much of the tradition has found them—it does not accord with a present-day reading.

In the first place, there is to be found in the dialogues no system of doctrine. The search for such a system finds the dialogues themselves very elusive and even slippery. Plato, we may say, knew too much about life to put it into a system. Systems can afford great illumination; but the light is always shed from a single source and center. Like a searchlight directed into the dark, they reveal much, but they leave far more in outer darkness.

All the systems the wits of man have ever devised, one comes to believe, are there in the dialogues, waiting only to be discovered, from Christian theology to Freudianism. Again and again the reader is convinced Plato must have

* This chapter and Chapter X appeared in unrevised form in *The American Scholar*, XXXVII (Summer, 1968), 502–11.

agreed with him, so clearly are his own ideas developed by
one of the characters. Then he finds their very antithesis in
the mouth of another. The dream of Plato himself—that he
was transformed into a swan who flew from tree to tree,
while the bird-catchers tried in vain to snare him; just
when they crept up and thought they had captured him he
flew to another tree—was a true dream. And Simmias' interpretation of it: that all men would desire to catch the
spirit of Plato, but none would succeed, for each would
interpret him in his own fashion, is clearly the best interpretation of Plato.

There is in the dialogues no system of doctrine. But
there is a tremendous incentive to system-building. Plato
has been the inspiration of the architects of all the great
edifices of ideas down through the ages.

(2) Then again, Plato is not a wonderful metaphysician—if
by "metaphysics" we mean with Aristotle the science of
what is. The metaphysical doctrine traditionally attributed
to Plato cannot be said to hold true of the world we encounter. "Platonism," taken literally—as the Neo-Platonists
did, or the Christian Platonists, or the German Idealists—is
a beautiful, inspiring, but in the end tragic illusion. It is not
supported by any evidence that would hold water. It is not
descriptive of what is, but rather a cosmic metaphor—
seductive and misleading.

Plato, then, is not a wonderful metaphysician. But he
has been the inspirer of every great metaphysical vision in
the Western tradition, from Aristotle down to the present.
(3) Then, Plato has no passion for truth, literal truth, if by
"truth" we mean the actual facts about the world. He has
only scorn for the plain, downright, honest scientist like
Anaxagoras, with whom Socrates is made to exhibit so
much dissatisfaction in the *Phaedo*. Plato is completely in-

different to Democritus and his atomic theory. The atomists appear in his pages only once, in the *Sophist,* and then only to be swiftly refuted. But if by a passion for truth we mean a passion for what really is, for the real things in life, not those miserable, disconcerting little facts, through ferreting out which we get steam-engines and autos and planes—and H-bombs—then Plato has a passion not for truths but for Truth, for what is really worthwhile, for what ought to be true, whether it happens to be so or not. He has a passion for the Good, for the Perfect—and literal truth, at the hands of mortals at least, and in their eyes, is often bad. But perhaps what Plato is devoted to is the only Truth. If we believe that, then we are Platonists.

No, Plato has no passion for literal, scientific truth. Yet every great advance in natural science, in Hellenistic times, in the Middle Ages, in the early modern period, in this century in geniuses like Einstein, seems to have come from thinkers who were in some sense followers of Plato.

Again, Plato is not a great logician. There are, we are told, three kinds of logic: deductive logic, the kind Aristotle perpetrated; inductive logic, the kind John Stuart Mill made up out of whole cloth; and the kind Plato's characters and the rest of us actually use, seductive logic.

A French writer of the turn of the century, Émile Faguet, has well illustrated the kind of logic that often appears in the dialogues:

> Is not the whole, Callicles, greater than the part?
> Without doubt.
> And the part is smaller than the whole?
> Assuredly.
> But if the part is smaller than the whole, then the whole is greater than the part?
> So I believe.

And if the whole is greater than the part, then the part is smaller than the whole?

Certainly.

Is it as certain as that? Could you conceive a part which would contain the whole?

Never.

But you do conceive a whole which contains a part?

Surely.

And the whole, containing the part, is greater than it?

Yes.

It follows that philosophers should be the rulers of the State.

How does that follow?

There can be no doubt. Let us begin again. The whole is greater than the part. . . .[1]

This is the logic of Plato's characters much of the time. It is human logic, the kind of logic and reasoning we mortals use.

Plato is not a great logician. Yet he can still drive a hardboiled modern young thinker into a passion for dialectic.

And Plato is not an epistemologist. He is not even a poor one. The same author, Faguet, tells us that Plato can even be defined as the thinker with the least possible resemblance to Immanuel Kant. In this sense, one cannot discover in the dialogues any "theory of knowledge." What we do find is a *theōria,* a vision, of what is worth knowing. Now perhaps the scholarch of the Academy had a theory of knowledge. If he did—when he wrote the *Theaetetus*—it was in essence the same as Aristotle's, only not so precisely expressed. But it is doubtful whether the writer of the So-

---

[1] Émile Faguet, *Pour qu'on lise Platon* (Paris, 1900), pp. 3-4. See also Rosamond K. Sprague, *Plato's Use of Fallacy* (New York, 1962).

cratic, the dramatic, dialogues had any theory of knowledge.

Plato is not what moderns call an epistemologist. Yet he has lured generations, from Aristotle down, into regarding a theory of knowledge as of transcendent importance.

And Plato is not a social reformer, a utopian. He obviously liked social reformers, and had a generous sympathy for them. But he knew too much himself about human nature, he had too keen a vision of man, to join them in commitment. Perhaps he had been one in his youth; but when he wrote the *Republic* he had learned better. One has a dreadful suspicion: perhaps the flesh was weak, and Plato did succumb to the call of Dion—if Dion really called. And could the author of the *Republic,* which so clearly depicts both the value and the limitations of social idealism, of what today is called "perfectionism," have so far forgotten his insight as to write the *Laws?* It seems most improbable that the same man could write works of so different a temper. But it remains possible, human nature being what it is. Aristotle assures us the *Laws* was Plato's last work.

Plato was not a social reformer. Yet he has remained the patron saint of all social idealists down through the ages. And he has been the greatest revolutionary force in the Western tradition, with the exception of the Prophets and the Gospels.

These negatives can all be summed up by saying, Plato was not a "Platonist"—any more than Jesus Christ was a "Christian." "Platonism" is a disease you are likely to catch if you read Plato without much imagination. And Plato himself was immune. It is a kind of madness, such as the *Ion* tells us of—a divine madness, perhaps. But Plato himself was not mad. He knew most other men were, that men could in fact hardly live without a touch of it. But he himself was one of the sanest men who ever lived. At least such is the conviction the dialogues bring.

Is all this the Truth about Plato? Probably not, in any literal sense. To be strictly accurate, it would demand a host of dull academic and scholarly qualifications and reservations. And judged by such standards, it is probably an overstatement. It can be considered what the *Republic* calls "royal lies." But it is a pity if the reader of Plato does not believe them.

If these things are what Plato is not, what then is Plato? Plato is an artist and a poet, with a truth of perception that strikes us as approaching finality. If we like to classify the dialogues, we can see the *Protagoras* as a comedy, the *Euthydemus* and the *Cratylus* as farces. The *Phaedo* is a tragedy, as moving a tragedy as any Greek poet ever wrote. The *Republic* is more like our philosophical novels—like Thomas Mann's *The Magic Mountain*. It is not so closely knit as a play. Or it is like *Faust* in its two parts. Like Goethe, Plato seems to have put his whole life—at least his pre-schoolmaster life—into it.

Let us take the *Symposium*, though that is hardly fair: the *Symposium* is clearly Plato's dramatic masterpiece. It has a unity lacking in the *Republic*—though there is much more unity there than is usually suspected. The *Symposium* follows all the dramatic conventions of the Greek stage: it has a chorus, a rising and descending action, a climax, a peripety, and all the rest. It exhibits not so much philosophy, as the fruits of philosophy; not so much reasoned discussion, as ardor and enthusiasm. It is the supreme example of what philosophy can do. It takes a very unpromising material, and proceeds to show its imaginative possibilities. Then it confronts those possibilities, that imaginative vision, with the bare facts, and makes us "see"—it generates *theōria.*

The theme is, What is love? And the answer, dramatically displayed, shows us what love really is, "Love itself," Absolute Love, the very Idea of love. Is love a thing perched in the firmament? No, it is a perfecting in imagination of what is in fact not perfect, it is an intense human experience, and a theme for inspiring discourse—for those "words which surpass realities." At bottom, love is a physical relation between two mortals, the delight of perfect intimacy. In reality, it is the love of mankind, the love of the saints, the hunger and thirst after righteousness, the aspiration after the divine perfection. Is any human love all that? Of course not, literally. Human love is primarily rooted in a biological urge. But it might be, and it ought to be, much more, and if you do not see love as a biological urge that might be and ought to be a love of all truth and all beauty and all good, all perfection, then you do not see love as it really is, you have no true knowledge of love—you are only a Freudian.

In fact, the human love from which the Platonic love of the *Symposium* sets out is something rather more disreputable than the notion usually associated with Platonic love since the Renaissance. It starts as the love of a man for a youth, in what used to be called in pre-Kinsey days "sexual perversion." That is the bald fact. Yet from that—even from that—love can grow into the love of philosophy: such are the ideal possibilities of even the crudest physical love. Plato might have taken any other existent love as his starting-point and natural basis. One suspects, indeed, that Plato chose the least promising material to make his point all the stronger. He has won his reward today: as recent criticism puts it, an example of our own fashionable Freudian theories of art, "Plato's style has all the characteristics of homosexuality." At least, the *Symposium* is a supreme example of "sublimation."

The *Symposium* is a closely knit drama: every word has its function and purpose. There is in it as great an artistic economy as anything to be found in Sophocles, or among moderns, in Ibsen. Nothing could be pruned away. The climax of the discussion in words is approached in the discourse of Diotima; everything before has been a skillful preparation. But we cannot stay with the Divine Love. We must come back to the earth and humanity; in the figure of the *Republic*, we must return to the cave. In comes Alcibiades, roaring drunk, and turns the whole discussion into a praise of Socrates, the human embodiment of the object of love. Look on the Divine Love with the priestess of Mantinaea, and you will then appreciate Socrates; you will love him, and properly, and not some beardless youth. Such are the genuine fruits of idealism.

It is the entrance of Alcibiades, not the tale of Diotima, that is the real climax of the *Symposium*.[2] And this fact suggests that love is not to be explained or understood in terms of the fine words it inspires alone. Love is something to be felt and "seen," by the spectator of life's drama. Plato lets Socrates transform a passion of the body into a vision of the soul; and then he abruptly confronts love as an imaginative experience with love as an animal fact. The effect is to convince us that love is not to be seen as a vision of perfection alone, nor yet merely as Alcibiades creeping under the cloak of Socrates. Love is to be seen truly only when you can behold both, in the dramatic and irrational juxtaposition of life itself.

Consider the setting of the *Symposium*. Agathon, "the

[2] Herbert W. Schneider holds that the entrance of Alcibiades is the *denouement* rather than the climax of the *Symposium*. The climax he takes to be the revelation that Love is not a god at all, but the offspring of Poverty and Plenty.

Good," has won the first prize for his tragedy, and a cele-
bration is in order. Socrates goes, uninvited, attended by his
little barefooted admirer, his "Boswell," Aristodemus. After
dinner, the question is raised, what shall they do next? Last
night they had all got drunk on wine; the scene is laid the
day after that first exuberance. Eryximachus, the physician,
advises them to get drunk this time on talk, about love.
The whole dialogue is presented as a rational form of
intoxication, a kind of temperance debauch. Pausanias and
Agathon are "Greek lovers"; this is the fact coloring the
whole discussion.

Phaedrus speaks first, and praises the fruits of love. Love
is noble because it is not self-centered, but self-sacrificing,
and the inspiration to noble deeds. Phaedrus is clearly an
instrumentalist. Then Pausanias speaks, Agathon's lover.
He makes a distinction: there are really two Aphrodites,
the Earthly and the Heavenly. The point is not merely to
love, but to love well and worthily. Pausanias raises the
level of the discussion: we must love that which is worthy
of love, the mind as well as the body (his own beloved has
just won the prize for tragedy). Love means companion-
ship, friendship, *philia*. Love is lasting and enduring only
if it is of spiritual beauty.

It is now the turn of Aristophanes. But he has drunk too
much, and has the hiccoughs. So while he is recovering on
the physician's advice, the chance goes to Eryximachus,
who is evidently eager to expound his own pet ideas: he has
suggested the theme on purpose. He is a physician, and has
read Empedocles: he makes love a cosmic force. The distinction between the earthly and the heavenly love is a
cosmic distinction: there are in the world forces of disintegration and integration.

Aristophanes, by this time recovered from his hiccoughs,

proceeds to explain love in terms of its origins; though, since we do not know the origin of love, this has to take mythical form, as in our own psychologies. In modern terms, Aristophanes outdoes Freud. He offers the only attempt at what we might call a scientific, genetic explanation of love; and he is exhibited as drunk. The point is, this is not the final truth about love. He tells the myth of love's origins: once human beings were united together, two in one body, with four arms and four legs. For their misdeeds Zeus clove them asunder. But ever since the two halves have yearned to be joined together once more—to be back in the mother's womb again, a modern might put it.

The theme has now been set forth, and distinctions made, and made first cosmic, then comic. It is now the turn of <u>Agathon</u> himself. He makes no contribution to the discussion, but furnishes rather an interlude, performing the function of a chorus. He praises the beauty of love, not its fruits: love is the supreme experience. Agathon is clearly no instrumentalist. His speech is a parody on the speeches of Gorgias the rhetorician, and was much admired in antiquity as such. It expresses how it feels to be in love. Socrates complains that Agathon's speech is too rhetorical and then proceeds to deliver his own speech!

<u>Socrates</u> announces, it is now the time to define love—he *would* try. He will tell what love really is. Diotima 3 is made to unfold the science of love, what love is, and what it is good for. It is a vision, and an experience, an inspiration to perfecting, a human experience bearing fruits in achievement, the attainment of deathlessness itself. And it

---

3 Whether there was a Diotima before the *Symposium* was written is doubtful. But there is no question there was one thereafter. She is depicted on one of the best fourth-century steles in the National Museum at Athens.

is reached, not by forsaking the human, earthly love, but by perfecting it in imagination. Starting as the child of poverty and plenty, love can arrive at the vision of perfection. Things are good, they possess value, in the measure that they lead us to what is supremely good and valuable. The worth of life lies in its stimulating the love for a more god-like life. Such is the deathless quality in the soul of man. True deathlessness is the creation of heaven, in man's soul, out of the materials of earth.

These are the words of philosophy. But life bursts in at the door. There is turmoil and confusion, and we are left with the picture of the fruits of philosophizing: Socrates remains discussing, while everybody else is under the table, dead drunk. Socrates goes off soberly, to bathe and attend to his day's work. If, having known the intoxication of love, you can go soberly about your business, confessing yourself both a tragic and a comic figure—Socrates in the end holds that tragedy and comedy are one—you have found what love really is. You have grasped the fact that love is at once tragic and comic.

X

The Philosophy of the Artist and the Artistic Experience

WHY have I been at so much pains to point out that Plato is a poet and an artist? It seems an obvious fact, obvious at least to anyone but a professional philosopher, to whom nothing is, on principle. Why not accept the fact gracefully that Plato could give consummate literary expression to his ideas, and then turn from his technique of expression to his ideas themselves? Just so we thank God that Santayana has a style, and is not like Dewey, or the Logical Positivists; and proceed to search out his metaphysics.

The answer is, because if you think Plato developed a philosophy, and then put it into dialogue form in order to popularize it because he happened to possess literary ability also—you will never arrive at the slightest understanding of the philosophy actually present in and expressed through the dialogues. You may be a "Platonist"; but Plato will remain a closed book to you—just as Santayana will, if you do not make his style central.

The most important and basic fact about the philosophy of the Platonic dialogues is that it is the philosophy of a man who *had* to write imaginative dialogues, a philosophy such as only a writer of dialogues could have worked out, and a philosophy capable of expression only in dialogue— that is, in *dramatic* form. You can no more understand Plato without starting from that fact, than you can understand Spinoza without starting from the fact that he wrote of the means of attaining supreme, continuous, and never-ending blessedness, in a series of geometrical propositions modeled after Euclid.

It is quite possible, of course, to be impressed by Plato the artist, by the dialogues as dramatic portrayals of human thought, and to stop there; to consider them as fitting materials for the study of Greek literature and poetry, but rather irrelevant to the achievements of Greek philosophy; to see in them a dramatic treatment of the perennial human themes of politics, education, love, and death; to find in them a "theory" in the sense of a *theōria,* a vision of the world and human life, but not a "theory" in the sense of an explanation of them; to find a program for the guidance of the spectator of the drama of life, but not a program for the actors in that spectacle; to find "seeing" exalted above both doing and explaining; to find *nous* contemplating all life, itself included, with detached objectivity, as in a theater, the proper home of *theōria,* but not intelligence participating in it and perfecting it, in fact and in imagination. Woodbridge, in *The Son of Apollo,* did something of that sort. He chose to do it, partly because he was so provoked by the refusal of other scholars to recognize such a *theōria* in the dialogues, that he wanted to emphasize it, even at the cost of minimizing everything else. He did it partly because he himself was not a Platonist, but an incorrigible Aristotelian.

Now, such a realistic vision is certainly there; and in the last analysis *theōria is* exalted above *technē,* practice, *nous* above intelligence. But—to stop there is to overlook the fact that the hard and fast distinction between theory and practice, between insight and intelligence, is to be found in the facile and polemical interpretations of Greek thought by moderns, like John Dewey, but is to be found only dubiously in the Greeks themselves. The Greeks viewed theory and practice, insight and intelligence, as very intimately connected. They remained puzzled by their precise relation, and never really satisfactorily solved the problem, never even made up their own minds, Aristotle is far more devoted to pure theory than Plato. Yet every student of his thought knows that the relation between the two presents in his writings insoluble contradictions.

To stop with dramatic insight overlooks the fact that if Plato offers realistic vision, he also provides imaginative inspiration. If the dialogues have shown men what they are, and given them self-knowledge, they have also revealed to men what they might become, and given them the compelling urge to perfect their human life.

Such stopping overlooks the fact that Plato is not only an artist, but also an artist-philosopher, an artist who not only saw life, but loved wisdom, loved wisdom as only an artist can, and loved the kind of wisdom only an artist can see. Plato, in a word, is not merely an artist, but the philosopher of the artistic attitude, starting from the artist's experience, and developing the philosophic implications of the artist's outlook on life, employing the artist's method and technique to do it.

If we take Plato the artist-philosopher seriously, we shall find in the dialogues not merely a dramatic picture of life, but a dramatic development of the implications of the artistic attitude and experience, a dramatic presentation of the artist's philosophy—almost the only one in our Western

tradition.¹ So, at the risk of offering merely one more interpretation of Plato, I want to suggest what Plato portrays as
the philosophic implications of the artistic attitude.²

Plato is an artist, and his philosophy is the philosophy of
the artist, his aim is the aim of the artist in vision and in
creation. And his followers, significantly enough, have uni-
formly been artists, men of imagination. When they have
been men of religion, like the great Christian theologians,
St. John the Evangelist, St. Augustine, the long line of
Augustinian Platonists, culminating in Malebranche, they
have been essentially poets in religion, making the most of
the artistic and imaginative materials in the Christian tradition. And appropriately, the greatest Christian Platonist is a
supreme poet, Dante.

When the followers of Plato have been humanists, like
the poet-philosophers of the Renaissance, they have been
artists of human life. Inevitably, it seems, the great out-
bursts of creative artistic energy in the Western cultural
tradition, like the Renaissance, and the Romantic movement, have turned for their philosophic expression to some
form of Platonism. Even when they have been great scien-

---

¹ With Plato may be placed Schelling, in his *Identitätsphilosophie,*
probably Whitehead, and John Dewey, in the manipulative sense of
"art." There are, of course, plenty of philosophies of the aesthetic
attitude and experience, but that is quite another thing.

² This interpretation has one advantage over all others that have
been advanced. They have been only what different men have found
in Plato. while this one points out what is actually there. This one
is true.

Curiously enough, in preparing this statement I had a dream
myself the night before. I dreamed I saw a swan, eluding his pur-
suers and pouring forth his voice in song. I exclaimed, "O Swan,
I can understand your song." Whereupon that swan flew down
and perched on my shoulder. This dream was obviously sent by
Apollo himself.

tists, like Kepler, Galileo, Descartes, Newton, or Einstein, they have been great scientists because they have possessed the artist's insight and imagination. Like Bertrand Russell in his Platonic periods, they have sought in science chiefly the beauty of the harmonious order of natural law, not the sweat and dirt of the multitude of facts.

Take the two great objects of Plato's interest, the Good Life, and Knowledge, which ultimately merge into one. In the dialogues they are seen through the eyes of the artist, and treated by the hand of the artist. The Good Life, both individual and social, there is treated as what the artist can discern of human possibilities, what he can create from the given human materials—an affair of imaginative vision, and of blending, reworking, remolding in the continued light of that vision. Knowledge is taken to be what the artist's imagination perceives, the possibilities resident in his materials. Conceived as a human experience, the experience of knowing is the emotional experience the artist feels in the presence of the objects discerned by his imagination.

We moderns are apt to feel that Plato must have shared our own interest in knowledge, that he must have been a scientist concerned with the causes of things, with the relations they display, with the permanent uniformities in events; that he must have been a mathematical logician interested in the logical structure at times exemplified in the world, though handicapped by the lack of the precise vocabulary we have developed. We write books like Paul Natorp,[3] trying to show that Plato's Ideas are really scientific laws, that he was working at our enterprise of unifying all the permanences and uniformities of experience into one perfect, all-embracing postulate system. We are convinced

---

[3] Paul Natorp, *Platons Ideenlehre* (Leipzig, 1903).

that if he had only heard of Whitehead and Russell's *Principia Mathematica,* he would have fallen on their necks. A. E. Taylor puts it: "We may say that what the *Republic* calls 'dialectic' is in principle simply the rigorous and unremitting task of steady scrutiny of the indefinables and indemonstrable of the sciences, and that in particular his ideal is just that reduction of mathematics to rigorous deduction from expressly formulated logical premises by exactly specified logical methods, of which the work of Peano, Frege, Whitehead, and Russell has given us a magnificent example." 4

Now it is true, Plato can inspire us moderns to such an enterprise—as to so much else—but nothing was actually farther from his own mind and intent. Plato is not a scientist; and the whole realm of modern natural science he relegates to "opinion," *doxa,* even "mere opinion." There is in the dialogues no conception of uniformity or "law of nature" whatever. And Plato is not a modern logician. He is concerned not with mathematical structure in itself or in things,5 but with ends and functions—with discovering "all that which is best in existence," unified in the vision of the Idea of the Good. Even Taylor has to admit, Plato is seeking a "teleological algebra"; but it is difficult to conceive what this has to do with mathematics or with logic, or indeed what it could mean.

No, Plato's interest is the artist's interest in knowing, in what is worth knowing, from the artist's viewpoint: the possibilities of things, their uses, their opportunities—what

---

4 A. E. Taylor, *Plato: The Man and His Work* (New York, 1926), p. 293.

5 Not at least in the dramatic dialogues. There is such a concern in the *Timaeus* and the *Philebus;* the former has been an ever-renewed inspiration driving men to construct a mathematical physics.

you can do with them, what you can make out of them, if you possess the artist's imaginative and constructive power. In Plato, the realm of *nous,* of "mind," is not the realm of science, but what since the Romantic revolution we have called the realm of the "imagination"—that realm in which we can see life perfected and clarified, made whole and complete, a perfected work of art. As an artist, Plato is convinced, we do not see things as they are, really, until we see them thus perfected in imagination. True knowledge, *epistēmē,* is to see the world imaginatively, in the light of the totality of its possibilities, of the "Idea of the Good."

We moderns are also puzzled by the way Plato is moved by the experience of knowing it is for him something profoundly emotional, and he tries hard to convey something of its savor to the reader. We exclaim, he must have been a mystic! And we then confront the problem, how could he have been both the scientist and the mystic? Our interpretations of the two poles of knowing, as Plato presents them, thus generates an antinomy. But Plato is not a mystic, in any specialized sense; at least there is in him nothing of religious *Schwärmerei*—though Platonists often exhibit such emotion.[6] Rather, Plato is an artist feeling the creative experience, in which one is led on and on, yet ever conscious of the vision of something that lies beyond. Hence Platonic dialectic is not, as Taylor supposes, symbolic logic, nor yet the religious quest for the Divine, as Plotinus saw it. It is rather the imaginative experience of the artist, his flight of soul as his vision enlarges to embrace all truth and all beauty.

[6] It is more accurate to say that in the dramatic dialogues Plato is primarily concerned with what today is called "existential knowledge"—what Paul Tillich calls "participating knowledge." For him the object of knowing is at the same time, and in the measure it is truly known, an object of passionate commitment, of what the *Symposium* calls *erōs,* love.

At this point a caveat is in order, lest the position be misunderstood. It is contended, Plato is the philosopher of the *artistic* attitude, not of the *aesthetic* attitude: the two are quite different. The *aesthetic* attitude emphasizes the delight attending seeing and hearing, of body and mind. It is an attitude of enjoyment, of receptive appreciation, a passive openness and receptivity, to sense-impressions, like Walter Pater, or to essences, pure forms, like Santayana. In it perception goes out to tendencies already completed and brought to a happy fruition. There are plenty of such aesthetic philosophies in our time, that bid us engage in the contemplative enjoyment of past achievements, of the finished forms and structure of the world.

When brought to knowledge, the aesthetic attitude emphasizes the fixed structure of the world, an intelligible Logos; or even, at its purest, a realm of detached essences, irrelevant to existence and its problems. When forced to take change seriously, it finds an immutable structure of change, a single unified dialectic of history.

When brought to conduct, the aesthetic attitude emphasizes passive enjoyment and pure hedonism, the enjoyment of the beauties and refinements of existence, with no incentive to creative activity, to embodiment. It is content to appreciate existing goods, but has little desire to extend that enjoyment to other men, or to bring further goods to pass. When logically consistent, as in Santayana, it refuses to make any distinctions of value. To make such distinctions, to feel the pull of certain goods above others, to strive for them, is a sign of "animal arrogance and moral fanaticism." 7

---

7 George Santayana, *Platonism and the Spiritual Life* (New York, 1927), p. 31.

At its best, the aesthetic attitude can achieve insight and understanding, but not love and devotion. "Love," says Santayana, "is something material, based on craving and a sense of want; it is a sense of urgency in values"; while "wisdom," what Santayana came to call the "spiritual life," is "a disintoxication from the influence of values."[8] In another language, it is release from existential commitment.

Now, Plato is clearly not the philosopher of the aesthetic attitude. Love and devotion toward what the imagination discerns is central for him; knowledge is fundamentally "existential," involving passionate commitment. To be sure, plenty of Platonists, seizing on "Platonism" as a finished, static system, rather than a spirit and a life, have been aesthetic philosophers. This is an excellent shibboleth for distinguishing Plato himself from "Platonism." At its clearest, we can see what the aesthetic attitude makes out of Plato in Santayana, the later Santayana. The earlier Santayana was far closer to Plato, when he defined: "The Life of Reason is that part of experience which perceives and pursues ideals."[9]

For Plato the artist, both knowledge and conduct seize on what does not already exist as a completed perfection, on what is discerned by *nous,* by mind. For Plato, the basic distinction between what is and what ought to be, between the actual and the ideal, is not a metaphysical dualism; it is not fixed and absolute. It is a fluid distinction made in experience, made by men dealing with their world. Plato himself—in the dramatic dialogues—is not a dualist, but, like Aristotle, a naturalist—though his followers have usu-

---

[8] *Ibid.,* pp. 29, 30.
[9] George Santayana, *Reason in Common Sense* (New York, 1905), p. 3.

ally converted the artist's distinction made in experience into a gulf dividing the universe into two different "realms."

In Plato himself, in the dialogues, the "Ideal" does not appear as a realm apart, an isolated abode of detached essences, as the conventional tradition has it. Plato presents it dramatically rather as the sum of possible perfectings of existent natural and human materials. The Ideal, we can say, is treated as a "process," not as another realm at all. It is a process to be found operating in the imaginative experience of men—of men loving and talking, aspiring and thinking. Knowledge is not a glimpse into some impossible heaven, but an illumination cast upon actual human life by the discernment of its possibilities. Philosophy, Plato tells us, is the pursuit of what is "eternal" and "perfect." But "eternity" is a quality of human vision, not a description of authentic Being; and "perfection" is no attribute of any existence, but experience clarified and made whole by the spirit of man—of man the artist.

This is the conviction the dialogues leave with us: this is the *theōria* of the Ideal that if we are perceptive and endowed with imagination we are inescapably made to see. The very elusiveness of the Platonic Ideas—the difficulty of fixing precisely their status—is an indication that they are not what they have been taken to be by a literal-minded tradition: a fixed and static structure of a separate "intelligible realm," remote from the passions of living, but rather a process of human idealizing, a living direction of natural events and tendencies to a perfected form—they are a process of human art. "Ideas" are that vision that haunts the artist as he works with his materials—in Plato's case, an entire civilization—something living, growing, organic, the

object of intellectual vision, of knowledge, of *nous,* and of
aspiration, of love, of *erōs.*

Take the relation of "participation," with all its problems
and paradoxes. How do things participate in an Idea, and
how does the mind of man share in it? This is solved in
the experience of artistic creation: in that experience, in
writing the *Antigone,* in building the Parthenon, the many
beautiful do embody the one Beauty. The whole multifari-
ous Greek life does participate in the plays of Euripides—
and so does the soul of the poet, and thereby achieves not
only deathlessness, but generation, creation in deathlessness.
Schopenhauer was, it seems, right. He was wise enough to
know that the realm of Ideas is the realm of art; though,
because he was fleeing to the enduring art of the past as a
refuge from the pains of living, fleeing to a realm of peace
and certainty, Schopenhauer is primarily a philosopher of
the aesthetic and not the artistic attitude, a "Platonist," and
not one who has caught and exemplifies the spirit of Plato.
For Plato was no refugee.

This insistence is meant seriously. It is here being urged
that the great system of philosophy, of metaphysics, built
up around Plato, with all its logical and metaphysical problems that have proved over the centuries insoluble, is in the
last analysis irrelevant to the philosophy set forth in the dialogues, to the philosophy of Plato himself. It is suggested
that there *is* a perfectly definite and coherent philosophy set
forth in the dialogues. It is proposed that the many problems, insoluble in the long Platonic tradition, and in all the
books about Plato, from Aristotle down, can be solved
clearly and satisfactorily by asking the dialogues, if we approach them and read them as is here being suggested.

This philosophy is to be discovered, and the problems

solved, by observing with care what is the *method* of Plato, and by taking that method seriously.

The method of Socrates, the talker, is the method of dialectic, of discussion and talk. But the method of Plato, the poet, the dramatist, the artist, is the *dramatic* method. And this is not a mere technique of exposition, but an art of discovering and discerning Truth. Truth, Plato is convinced, is many-sided and complex. It is to be found, not by investigation—by scientific inquiry—and not by mere talk, discussion, dialectic. Truth is to be found by the dramatic balancing of human minds and personalities and opinions against each other, and by setting what men say and feel over against that about which they are talking and feeling, and by thus making us *see* both.

For Aristotle, truth is the expression in logical form of what can be *said* about a subject matter, what can be said rightly in words. But that subject matter is there all the time, underlying all discourse, and controlling it. And one can never say all that might be said about it.

In Plato, we are not only allowed to hear in endless talk much that may be said; Plato dramatically presents to us that underlying and controlling subject matter itself, and makes us *see* what the talk is about—lest we forget, like many moderns, and imagine the talk is about talk itself, about words. The Truth we are made to see is not a fixed body of doctrine, but itself something dramatic—a never-ending process, a life. The dialogues themselves present to us the very Idea of Truth; they go on and on, they are ever creative. In the *Lysis,* for instance, two beautiful boys, and two ugly old men, meet and proceed to talk about friendship. Though they are friends, they cannot manage to say just what friendship is. But we are made to *see.* "Friendship" emerges, the Idea of Friendship, from the living dialogue.

Mē philosophia, says Plato, *alla philosophein,* "Not Philosophy, but philosophizing." For philosophy is itself an Art.[10]

---

[10] It should be pointed out that Plato rarely uses the term *technē,* "art," generically, as Aristotle so frequently does. The various "arts" usually mean for Plato the different "sciences," as Aristotle was to call them. On the other hand, Plato uses the term *epistemē,* "science" or "true knowledge," generically: all "science" is ultimately *one* for him, and for the Platonic tradition.

Again, Plato *never* employs *technē* or "art" to mean what moderns distinguish as the *beaux arts,* the "fine arts." For Greeks this distinction simply did not exist. Consequently, there is in Plato *no* "theory of Art" in the sense of a theory of the Fine Arts. What has been taken by moderns to be Plato's "theory of Art" is actually his theory of poetry, *poiēsis.* Incidentally, that theory of poetry is *not* to be found in the *Republic,* Book X, in the discussion of *mimēsis,* imitation. This discussion is *not* about poetry, but about what happens to poetry in the efficiently organized state, where it becomes mere "imitation"—in modern terms, where it is limited to "socialist realism"—or its stereotyped perversions.

See Paul O. Kristeller, "The Modern System of the Arts," in *Renaissance Thought II* (New York, 1965), pp. 163 227.

∮ XI ∮

The Theme of the Good Life *

PLATO could go as far as he did in developing the implications of the artist's outlook on life, because what we have been calling the "artistic attitude" was very conspicuous in Greek civilization. The greatest achievement of Greek life was an artistic achievement, and not only in architecture, sculpture, and poetry, but also in religion, politics, ethics, and science. The ultimate intellectual interest of the Greeks, *nous,* "Reason" in the sense of *Vernunft,* not *Verstand,* as leading to *theōria,* intellectual vision, was to see the world and human life as the artist sees them, to enjoy them as the artist enjoys them, and to remold them in imagination as the artist remolds them.

Plato was fortunate in being able to take over this attitude, elaborate it, and bring it to its highest expression. The whole relation of Plato to his environment is not that of the prophet opposing what he encounters, and proclaiming the one thing needful; it is not that of the scientist observing and describing what he sees and finds, picking it apart and manipulating it. It is that of the artist discerning its possi-

* This chapter and Chapter XII appeared in the *Journal of the History of Ideas,* XXVIII (July–Sept., 1967), 307–24.

bilities, and perfecting them in imagination. Plato was able to create an immortal vision of Greece—not of the Greece that actually was, but of what the artist could make out of it.

Hence it is a mistake to look for originality in the themes Plato selects to discuss and elaborate, or in the general notions and attitudes with which he starts his discussions, in the artistic materials he takes over from his culture and works with intellectually. It is easy to discover certain positions, certain assumptions underlying the discussions of the dialogues, and shared by all the characters:

1. Knowledge is essentially functional in character; it is directed toward knowing the uses, the possibilities, the ends of things.

2. The aim of politics is to organize and adjust different classes, by the scientifically trained expert, in the light of the best knowledge, and in the interest of bringing out the particular excellence of each class.

3. The Good Life is an achievement, an artistic master piece, to be attained by human intelligence and skill.

Now it is natural for most readers to assume that these ideas are distinctively Platonic conceptions, that this is Platonic doctrine, that these are the ideas Plato is trying to teach, because we learn about them from his pages. In reality, these are the commonly accepted notions of the Greek, and especially of the Athenian, intellectual class. They differ widely from the notions on the same themes met with among the Hebrews, or the Romans, or the Christians, or modern Americans; but they are encountered again and again in Greek thought—in the Greek thought of the documents that have come down to us from the classic age.

Plato's originality—the distinctively "Platonic" note,

"Platonic doctrine," if we will, consists not in these ideas themselves, but in what Plato *did* with this familiar material, in what he made out of it, in how he developed and elaborated its implications. These conceptions, in a word, are not Plato's philosophical *conclusions,* but rather the *starting-point* of Plato's philosophizing.

For example, we often imagine that Plato invented the idea that philosophers should be kings, that experts should rule the city, that education is the way out of our social problems. This is really like thinking that Abraham Lincoln invented democracy or that Dante invented Christianity. We imagine that Plato was concerned to work out the details of what a perfect city would be like, or even that he was the first to sketch out a utopia. And so we are apt to be shocked, when we are told that the scheme of the perfect city in the *Republic,* down to almost the last detail, was merely taken over bodily by Plato from the familiar *Republic* of Protagoras, whose social philosophy Plato presents so sympathetically in the *Protagoras* dialogue.

Though we cannot check on these reports—Protagoras' utopia is lost—they are quite credible. For it is clear the scheme of the perfect city, and the details of its organization, are quite irrelevant to Plato's political philosophy. It is clear that Plato's fundamental interest lies, not in the details of the utopia of Protagoras, or of any other—least of all in one of his own devising—but in where men get when they try to elaborate a social ideal. It lies, formally speaking, in the nature and function of political discussion, in the nature and function of social idealism and social reform, in what a social ideal is, its values and its limitations. Naturally he had to take one particular social ideal for his illustration, to work with; and naturally he chose an ideal familiar to his audience: Protagoras' utopia—or, if you prefer, the ideal of the Spartan state—as his philosophical material. But Plato might have chosen any other social ideal, and made the same points, developed the same political philosophy. He might, if he could, have taken the ideal of the Roman Empire, or of the Christian Church, or of Russian Communism, or of American Liberal Capitalism, or of the Welfare State—and carried out the same philosophical intent.

Now we may not be particularly attracted or seduced by Plato's own illustration—by the idealized Spartan state, clarified and elaborated, purified and perfected through discussion—though at least one modern state, Prussia, took this ideal as expounded by Socrates very seriously, in the nineteenth century, and tried to model its *Beamtenstaat* upon it—which, incidentally, is why Karl Popper during World War II came out so strongly against Plato. And we must at least respect the power and the appeal of its closest analogue in our world today, the ideal of the totalitarian state—besides being in an excellent position to appreciate what Plato points out as the more unpleasant features involved in that ideal—in the ideal of the perfectly just city. But we have ideals of our own, and we find Plato's dramatic comment on political ideals, his philosophy of politics, as pertinent to our social ideals as to his Greek illustration.

Plato's philosophy of politics, pulled out of its dramatic setting, and stated crassly, would run something like this: political discussion has many values. The highest is to provoke vision, to discern imaginatively what would be really best, to have an ideal, to formulate it clearly, to see all it really involves. But—to *have* an ideal is not to *be* an ideal, it is to *use* it. Man cannot live without ideals, but equally man cannot live by ideals alone. That is not the Good Life, but fanaticism or lunacy. To take the *Republic* literally, as a suggested practical program of political reform, is to make Plato a fanatic, and yourself an insensitive and imperceptive reader.

We say, Follow the pole star. But does that mean, get a ballistic rocket and embark for the stratosphere? Do not *fly* to it, chart your course *by* it. To employ Plato's own figure: the sun is the only source of all light, of the possibility of any discrimination of objects. But does that mean, Look only at the sun? That would be folly indeed.

Life must be lived by the proper use of natural human materials. Order it as wisely as you can, so that you may gain a vision of heaven, and in the light of that vision, go out and order it better. The ultimate end is vision: Plato is after all a Greek, not an American; he is devoted to *theōria,* not to endless progress.

There is the constant temptation to live *in* the vision, rather than *by* vision: to want to go to Heaven, like the Christians, or to bring Heaven here to America, like the moderns, instead of living well a human life, *with* vision. There is the temptation to demand perfection, and to condemn all existence because it falls short of what it might be, as it naturally must, instead of using the vision of perfection to discriminate between what is better and what is worse in our relatively, and inevitably, imperfect world. This is just the difference between Plato and "Platonism," between Plato's "realism" and what it is the fashion to call today "perfectionism." This, it may be, is the truth that lies behind Plato's ironical warning that the effect of poets is often bad: because men are apt to be too stupid to realize that they *are* poets, and to take them literally, instead of seriously.

Something like this is what the artist-philosopher made

out of the particular political discussion, the elaboration of the particular ideal of the Good Life furnished by Greek culture. And what he made out of Greek attitudes and sensibility is obviously a universal philosophy, applicable to any of man's ideals. Because he was an artist-philosopher, he was able to find the particular ideal of Greek culture very congenial: that the Good Life is not a theory to be expounded, nor a law to be proclaimed and followed, but an art to be practiced, a technique for the better ordering of human life, an artistic achievement.

What was this conception of the Good Life that had emerged in fourth-century Athens, and that was accepted, elaborated, and clarified by Plato? It was:

1. The Good Life is not righteousness, obedience to commands and law, either divine or natural. Its converse is not sin, taken as disobedience, transgression, breaking the law. This is the conception expressed in a central strain in Hebrew thought: that morality is a matter of taboos, of commandments, and obedience to the Law. This we call the ethics of Legalism.

2. The Good Life is not purity, holiness, it is not the ascetic flight from anything, involving so much repression of man's natural impulses that it is inevitably supernatural, and can come only through the miracle of grace and redemption. This is the conception expressed in a central strain of Christian thought; this we call the ethics of Asceticism.

3. The Good Life is not pleasure, the mere enjoyment of the goods proffered by existence. Pleasure, the Greeks thought, is not something bad; it will be a natural part, an accompaniment, of the Good Life. But to aim at pleasure alone means missing so many possibilities of human living; and "pleasure" affords no means of discrimination: for any-

thing can give one pleasure, especially if it is familiar and accustomed. This is the conception we call the ethics of Hedonism.

4. The Good Life is not "being natural," following impulse, "expressing oneself." This often seems to be our modern superstition. We used to say, "Be good, sweet maid, and let who will be clever." But more recently we have taken to saying, "Be yourself, kid, and let who will be careful." Did Sophocles write the *Oedipus* by just "being natural"? Did Ictinus and Pheidias build and adorn the Parthenon to "express" themselves? Some poems and plays are written for that purpose. In our modern world even some buildings seem to have been erected from that motive. But this hardly happened in Greece. Such a view was impossible in Plato's world. This is the conception we call Romanticism.

No, for the Greeks the Good Life is a conscious human achievement: it is an art, guided by vision and skill, a masterpiece to be created. Socrates is constantly appealing to the experience of the craftsman, the shoemaker, the weaver, the carpenter, the wagon-driver, the navigator. How can we find a *technē,* a skilled craft for achieving a good man, like their skills? *Aretē* in Plato means "skill," "craftsmanship," and its converse, *hamartia,* means "missing the mark," failing to achieve, clumsiness. Man is neither naturally full of original sin, nor is he naturally good. The good man is not developed by putting the child in a flower-pot, watering him, and just watching him grow in goodness.[1] The good man is a work of human art, not of nature.

Aretē, "excellence" (probably the most useful transla-

---

[1] This is a figure used by Graham Wallas to characterize permissive education.

tion of this central Greek term into our vernacular), is "the health of the soul," say Plato and the Greeks. But does this mean that it is something spontaneous, natural, and effortless? Not to a Greek. For him health, bodily excellence, was a matter of constant exercise and intelligent concern.

The Good Life is what man can be made into, his possibilities, his Idea, as Plato would put it—what our present-day existentialists call "man's essential being." To see man as suggesting it to the artist's imagination is to see man as he really is. There follows naturally the importance of *knowledge* of the Good: it is the knowledge of man's possibilities. A good man is like a good horse, a good ax, a good ship: to know what is a good specimen of any of these things, you must know what that kind of thing is good for. To know what is a good ax, you must know what an ax is good for. To know what is a good horse, you must know what a horse is good for. To know what is a good man, you must equally know what a man is good for. This is the kind of knowledge of the Good Socrates and Plato are looking for.

Now to know what a man is good for is not an easy question to answer. For a man is obviously good for so many different and incompatible kinds of thing. To make the question a little easier, we can follow the Socrates of the *Republic* and turn to "man writ large," to society, to the city. We can ask, what is a good industrial system? To answer that question, we have to ask in turn, what is an industrial system good for? We have to explore the possibilities of our technology, to find its Idea, the ends it might bring about. What could our machine and electronic technology give us? Clearly it could give us many things, some of which we should find fitting, and should like to secure, like freedom from want; and some not so fitting, like H-bombs and ICBM's. This unfortunate but inevitable fact, that an industrial and technological system is good for so many different and incompatible things, raises the fundamental problem of selecting and harmonizing, and it demands clearly the search for a principle of adjustment and adaptation. Just so it stands with the question, what is a man good for? That question raises the same problem of selecting and harmonizing; and it likewise demands the search for a principle of adjusting and adapting to each other the many different things a man is good for.

And since the highest object of knowledge is what a man is good for, man's possibilities, what a man can become, we cannot help "loving" this highest object of knowledge and aspiring to it. For it is the Ideas, or as we should say, the ideals arrived at by a realistic analysis of human nature—of what a man is good for. Hence "knowledge *is aretē*," excellence. For to "know" what we might become is to want to become it—it is to "love the Good." [2]

This is the theme of the earlier, the Socratic or dramatic dialogues. The several *aretai* discussed in the *Charmides,* the *Lysis,* the *Laches,* the *Euthyphro,* and the *Protagoras* are different human excellences; they are all particular kinds of skill, appropriate to the occasions to which they are suited. To find the fitting excellence in any particular case implies an intelligent direction and ordering: it is a matter of measuring, of correct proportion, of adjustment and adaptation to the occasion. It is thus a matter of what Aristotle was to call finding "the mean."

The Greek *aretai,* excellences, that appear in Plato: *sophia* or wisdom, *andreia* or courage, *sōphrosynē* or self-

[2] This is the "existential" conception of knowledge that runs through the Socratic and dramatic dialogues.

control, and *dikaiosynē* or justice, are all human arts and techniques for dealing appropriately and fittingly with different situations. Thus courage, in the *Laches* and the *Protagoras*, is knowing what is worth doing, when it is worthwhile to take the risk, and when it is not, and having the power of character to do it. This last, *thymos*, is "spirit-edness," "honor," something like what we call colloquially "will power," strength of character: it is the nonrational factor in conduct, one of the noble steeds in the chariot figure of the *Phaedrus* myth. The whole of each excellence is thus knowledge adapting impulse to appropriate ends.

Knowledge thus enters into every excellence or *aretē*, without being identical with it. This knowledge is four-fold:

1. Of what the possibility is, of its end.

2. Of its worth, the sense of feeling of it from within, in that sense of knowing in which to know self control is to practice it.

3. Of skill in attaining it.

4. Of the occasions on which it is appropriate.

To know a good ax, we must know what an ax can do, the worth of doing it, how to do it, and when to do it. It is the same with these human excellences. But knowledge is only one factor in the Good Life; there must be impulses and enjoyments also. Knowledge is so important because we need both the vision of perfection, the imaginative insight into the possibilities, and also intelligence, the skill, the ability to harmonize the impulses and get the right admixture, fitting to every occasion.

The fundamental problem of the Good Life, of ethics, thus becomes, to adjust all these excellences, through a principle of organization in the soul, which Plato calls *dikaiosynē*, "Justice," in the light of the totality of human excellences, which he calls "the Idea of the Good." The moral or point of the myth of Er at the end of the *Republic* is that the fruit of human experience is to have learned how to mix and harmonize them properly. The "mixed life" taken as the ideal in the *Philebus* seems to be an explicit statement of what is dramatically implied in the "earlier" or Socratic dialogues. In the *Philebus* it is said, the Good Life is an intelligent and artistic blending of many materials, an affair like weaving, mixing, harmonizing and adjusting, involving *nous* both as insight, vision, and also as intelligence, ordering the ingredients in the right measure and proportion.

This whole conception demands all the materials available, all the natural and social goods. A good leaf must grow on a good tree, in a good soil, in a good climate. If you have not got the necessary elements—if you have no money, or live in a bad city—the good life will be impossible for you, you cannot be a good man. This may well be regrettable, but it remains a fact. Of course, if God has laid the injunction on man, to follow the law of righteousness— Be ye perfect, even as your Father in Heaven is perfect—it is then manifestly unfair to demand what is not possible for every man, however adverse his circumstances. The Good Life must then be pared down to an irreducible minimum —to righteousness or purity of heart. The great moral faiths of the East—Buddhism, Judaism, Christianity—express an ethic of despair, of renunciation. Such an ideal is natural enough in societies where the opportunities were very meager, in the poverty-stricken and class-ridden Oriental lands. They offer the promise that even the penniless beggar, the lame, the halt, and the blind, even they can attain the highest. It is clear why Nietzsche, saturated in this very

different Greek ethic, called them forms of "slave morality."

But—if the Good Life is to be rather the best life con-
ceivable in imagination, the kind of life men might lead in
paradise, the creation of a perfect masterpiece out of natural
human materials—how can you hope to make a good pair
of shoes, if your leather is poor and you have no thread?
How can you hope to make a good man, if the essential
materials are lacking? This Greek conception is an ethic of
achievement, for a situation in which the materials are all
available. It is an ethic of prosperity, of abundance. In practice, given the actual paucity of materials available in classical Greece, it is the ethic of a privileged class, of an élite.

But, the modern objects, this is not democratic! Of
course it is not. No art can be in that sense democratic. It
refuses to sacrifice its vision of the Good Life, just because
the great mass of men has to put up with something second
best. There must be, Plato holds, no compromise with me-
diocrity. Plato shows he has no illusions about the actual
privileged class in Athens: he portrays them as a pretty sad
lot. But he is no democrat. He has no cheer for the op-
pressed. If that is what you are looking for, go follow An-
tithenes, the proletarian philosopher, be a Cynic! But at the
same time, Plato offers no "opiate of the people," no "pie in
the sky." Plato could sympathize with democratic moral
ideals: they have never been more powerfully set forth than
in the *Gorgias* and the *Phaedo*. Generations have read these
dialogues, and exclaimed, "How Christian!" But Plato refused to give up his vision of the life that is really best.

No, the task of ethics and politics is alike: they face the
same problem. It is not to find a type of goodness available
to any man at any time, but to discern the possibilities of

human life at its richest, fullest, and best, and to adjust these possibilities to each other, and to their natural basis and conditions.

We may here say a word on Plato's philosophy of education:

For such a conception of the Good Life as an artistic achievement, education is naturally of primary importance; just as for the legalistic morality, the important thing is moral training and the discipline of habits, and for the ascetic morality, the emotional shock of conversion. For Plato, the end of education will be to provoke a desire and love for the great things of life, to give a sense of what is worthwhile, a sense of relative values. Plato himself states it as "a discernment of all that is best in existence, and how they are related to each other."

Since for Plato the ultimate goal is *theōria,* vision, the means will be to remove the soul for a time from practice, so that it may get a disinterested outlook, and see what is, beyond all opinion and all debate. Plato thought that the only real science the Greeks had so far developed—except for the medical science of the school of Hippocrates, from which Aristotle was to set out—geometry, which takes the mind out of the welter of conflicting opinion, into a realm of fixed and certain knowledge, and confronts it with the compelling inevitability of what is, is the best preparation for seeing oneself and one's fellows with detached objectivity—for seeing impartially what you and they are, and what you and they might become.

For you can teach even an ignorant slave-boy the truths of geometry, because it is not debatable, while the wisest of men cannot teach their own sons moral excellence, *aretē.* Only when we have escaped the relativities of opinion in that realm in which there can be no differences of opinion, in which what is true can be taught—the realm of *ta mathē-matika,* the "teachable things," mathematics—can we hope to escape from mere opinion in that realm where there is no school and no teacher, where we must teach ourselves before we can expect to be taught, and where in the end it seems we have to fall back on the grace of God. Only when we have learned what is, in that world we never made, where our private preferences do not count, where we are not asked, "What do you think? What is your reaction?" but only, "How much have you found out?" can we hope to discern what is best, and to discriminate what we love. Plato is convinced, the best way of gaining imaginative insight into the problems and opinions of men, which is the goal of the philosophic life, and without which the intelligent direction of human life and of the cities of men is quite impossible, is the disinterested study of what is not man's to alter.

And this is Plato's philosophy of education: the art of the statesman must be founded on scientific knowledge; and the best way of preparing ourselves to find out what we must learn in order to guide human affairs wisely, is to study what the scientists—and we must remember, for Plato this meant the geometers—have already discovered about the world, and to learn scientific method from them. Only thus can we escape the unending and inconclusive discussions of the Sophists and the professors of education.

Putting Plato's philosophy of education into modern terms, he definitely rejects a humanistic education in the classics, the traditional Greek education in the poets, and also our own traditional education since the Renaissance—though few modern men can still remember it. This was the philosophy of education of Protagoras, who was a clas-

On education

sical humanist. In the dialogue that bears his name, Plato makes fun of Protagoras' literary humanism.

Plato rejects also any education in the social studies; that is all "mere opinion." There is no evidence that good citizenship, which is what *aretē* means in this context, can possibly be taught.

Plato comes out strongly for an education in the sciences. They can be taught, above all, the "teachable things," *ta mathēmatika,* geometry. This conviction forms a large part of the attraction the Pythagoreans had for Plato.

It is significant that Plato does not stand for teaching the social sciences: he was convinced there is no such thing. And though he talked much about a science of the Good, according to the commentators it turned out to be nothing but mathematics. It seems clear that were Plato teaching today in a modern university, he would be teaching in the Faculty of Pure Science, and not in the "non-being" and "mere opinion" of the college of education.

XII

The Efficiently Organized City: The Republic

ALL this philosophy of the Good Life is to be found in the *Republic*. It is brought out, partly in the words the characters are made to speak, partly in the author's dramatic commentary on those words. And we can neglect the latter only at the peril of wholly misconstruing Plato's philosophy.

The *Republic* has as its central theme *dikaiosynē*, or "Justice"—the principle of organization, of coordinating the separate excellences in men and in cities—the fundamental problem of Plato's conception of the Good Life as a harmonizing of possibilities. This principle of organization is clearly dependent on knowledge: it must be an ordering by wisdom and intelligence. And so the treatment of the theme of knowledge is inextricably interwoven with the treatment of the theme of the organization of the Good Life —of Justice.

How far can you carry the ideal of organization, of Justice, if, because it is so obvious and essential a good, you take it as the supreme and only good, if you let the mind play with it, as men do in discussion, and push it as far as you possibly can? What would an "absolutely just man," that is, in modern terms, a "perfectly adjusted man," or what would an "absolutely just state," that is, a "state organized with perfect efficiency," be like?

It is clear, you can carry the ideal out to the bitter end, in imagination; and Plato shows the end is bitter! So Plato has Socrates, maliciously and ironically, elaborate, shall we say, Protagoras' scheme for a perfectly organized state—a perfectly planned society, we moderns put it—till in the end we have a picture of *auto to dikaion,* of "Justice Itself," Pure Justice—the Perfect City, from which every other consideration has dropped away, which exists for the sake of efficient organization, and efficient organization alone.

But Plato warns us, we must know what we are about, just what we have been doing. We have arrived at a vision of Justice, of what he calls the Idea of Justice. It is surely a marvelous guide and inspiration—in imagination. But could we ever hope to make the city of Athens—or the city of New York—like that? This question, Socrates is made to point out, is completely irrelevant to what we have been doing. When pressed by his eager young hearers, anxious to proceed forthwith, he replies, "Yes, we could if we only turned philosophers into kings—or perhaps kings into philosophers—and then established a perfect system of education; if we drove all the citizens over ten years of age out of the city, as hopelessly miseducated; and then proceeded to transform the human nature of the children under ten left. Yes, we could then establish the perfectly organized city on earth—if we only did a few more little things like that." Here is obvious irony.

Would we *want* to bring the Perfect City down from the sky—which is clearly for Plato its only possible abode— and set it up among the human cities of men? In order to achieve perfectly efficient organization, would we really want to sacrifice everything else? And Plato makes it abundantly clear, it would in the end involve just that—the sacrifice of any individual happiness, of any genuine moral education, of all poetry, art, wisdom, and philosophy—all would have to go by the board. Or, in individual terms, would you want to be, in Plato's unforgettable picture, a "perfectly just"—that is, a "perfectly adjusted man," and be at the same time perfectly miserable?

The answer, for anyone in his senses, and certainly for any perceptive and imaginative reader of the *Republic*, is clear. Justice, organization, efficiency, is only one element in the Good Life, or in the Good Society. Would you want any one excellence, at the expense of giving up all the rest? Would you want to be courageous, and nothing else? Or to be self-controlled, and nothing else? That way lies only madness.

No, Plato tells us, above Justice, organization, is the Idea of the Good, a harmony of all values, a principle of more inclusive adjustment, not merely of efficiency, organization, Justice. The more we contemplate the vision of the perfectly organized city, of the perfectly planned society, the more we realize, without losing sight in the slightest of the very real importance of efficient organization, the need of adjusting the values of organization to all the other values, in the light of the totality of values—of the Idea of the Good.

Plato tells the myth of Er to point the moral of his long discussion or organization or "Justice." The souls gather at the river of Lethe to choose the lots that will determine what their next reincarnation will bring them: Plato is once more drawing on Orphic and Pythagorean mythology. The choice is made on the basis of what they have learned through their earthly experience in this life. The first soul to select makes a stupid choice: he elects to be a tyrant, though he does not see he is fated to devour his own children, and suffer other horrors. Plato continues:

When he inspected his lot at leisure, he beat his breast, and bewailed his choice, not abiding by the forewarning of the prophet. For he did not blame himself for his woes, but fortune and the gods and anything except himself. He was one of those who had come down from heaven, a man who had lived in a *well-organized city* (*en tetagmenē politeia*) [emphasis mine] in his former existence, participating in excellence by habit and not by philosophy (*ethei aneu philosophias aretēs meteilēphota*); and one may perhaps say that a majority of those who were thus caught were of the company that had come from heaven, inasmuch as they were unexercized in suffering. But the most of those who came up from the earth, since they had themselves suffered and seen the sufferings of others, did not make their choice precipitately. For which reason there was also an interchange of good and evil for most of the souls, as well as because of the chances of the lot.[1]

Along came the soul of Odysseus, who had spent his life in anything but a well-organized and just city, but had knocked about the world more than most men.

And it fell out that the soul of Odysseus drew the last lot of all and came to make its choice, and, from memory of its former toils having flung away ambition, went about for a long time in quest of the life of an ordinary citizen who minded his own business (*bios andros idiōtou apragmonos*), and with difficulty found it lying in some corner disregarded by the others, and upon seeing it said that it would have done the same had it drawn the first lot, and chose it gladly.[2]

[1] *Republic* 619 C, D.; tr. Paul Shorey.
[2] *Republic* 620 C, D.

Could Plato be saying more clearly that the moral of his whole discussion is to defend the Athenian ideal he states explicitly in the *Laws,* to be good "not by external compulsion but by inner disposition"? ³ The life lived in a "well-organized and just city without philosophy" brings no education in moral excellence. We must not forget, in Socrates' perfect city only the ruling class "participates in philosophy."

Yet men have read the *Republic,* and imagined that Plato is urging a practical political program—they have been insensitive enough to Plato's irony to think, Socrates is taking the stump for the Perfect City Party in Athens! They have judged that Plato was himself eager to catch a king, and to train him into becoming a philosopher. It is really hard to understand that over the ages readers of the *Republic,* with its layer upon layer of dramatic irony, have assumed, from the literal-minded Aristotle on, that Plato himself wanted or that any sane man in his senses could want, to *live* under such institutions as Socrates is made to elaborate—institutions so fascinating to talk about, but so intolerable to have to endure.

No, Plato is not offering a new constitution for Athens —or for Syracuse—or for any human, earthly city. He is trying, dramatically, to make us "see" where men get when they allow their imagination to carry them away as they talk about a perfect constitution. Plato is offering, not any political program, but a picture—the Idea of Justice. "Idea" is a sight word, and means "something seen"—the picture of perfect organization, taken as an end-in-itself. Plato is offering an imaginative vision, with all the imagination's

³ *Laws* 642 D.

ruthless disregard of any other value than that on which it is for the moment focused.

What is the value of talking about perfect organization, of contemplating it in discourse and in imagination, as Socrates and his companions are made to do in the *Republic?* What is the value of elaborating and clarifying an ideal of a perfect social order? It makes you see more clearly, surely, the very real value of efficient social organization—and of its implications—and it makes you realize also the importance of other values we want to possess. This, Plato shows us, is the value of clarifying any ideal. We at once find a particular perfection inextricably involved in other ideals; and we are led on to the problems of harmonizing and adjusting them all to each other. This unification of values is the essence of what Plato calls the approach to the idea of the Good through dialectic.

Plato is conventionally taken as the first utopian. In reality, while he has certainly served as a prime stimulus to utopian social idealism, he is actually offering an antidote to the utopian spirit. The *Republic* is really a dramatic commentary on the nature and function of ideals, an experiment in pursuing an ideal radically to the bitter end. It displays what social ideals can be and do, and what they cannot. It is a dramatic exploration of the conditions of any realistic social idealism.

In the *Republic* Plato is conventionally taken as proposing the first utopia; while in reality he is offering a vaccination against utopianism. I should like not to be misunderstood—though I fear may be. This is a cardinal illustration of the Greek maxim, "Know Thyself!" And it is almost impossible for a modern to understand that maxim. Our own maxim sounds very much like it, but the tune is quite different: "See things as they are!" To us, this means,

Realize there is nothing to them. But it did not mean that to the Greek, and certainly not to Plato. To him it meant, "See things as they are, and realize all there *might be* to them," all you can make of them, if you see both what they are and what they are not.

The *Republic* is a dramatic critique of the utopian spirit, of social idealism. No one can read it, without being convinced that social idealism is about the most important and seductive thing in the world. It has made that impression for centuries, and such an impression is obviously intended by the author, by Plato. It is the greatest source of social idealism in the record of Western civilization—outside, at least, the Prophets and the Gospels. It inspires intense practical zeal. Yet it holds that zeal up and contemplates it with ironic detachment—with *nous*. Are these two attitudes incompatible? If we find them so, then I am afraid we can never really understand Plato. We can never understand the Cave Myth, with its alternation of detached vision and practical wisdom. We can never understand Socrates' contention, at the close of the *Symposium*, that comedy and tragedy are ultimately the same.

But—no reader of the *Symposium* is ever tempted to minimize the idealizing power of love, because he is there made to see the actual human love of Alcibiades for Socrates. And no man need feel that Plato is counseling him not to vote, say, a Marxian ticket, because he is urging him to see Socialists and Communists as they are. In fact, if one wanted to put the central point of the *Republic* in a very different but perhaps more contemporary language, one might say, it is just what Karl Marx had in mind when he urged that Socialism should strive to be not utopian but scientific—an advice many Marxians might still do well to heed.

One further illustration may clarify the point being in-sisted upon. Some years ago, in 1931, Bertrand Russell re-wrote the *Republic,* in Part III of his volume called *The Scientific Outlook,* entitled "The Scientific Society." What Plato called the "Perfectly Just City," Russell brought up to date by dubbing "the Scientific Society," the society con-sciously planned so that every institution will be scientifi-cally organized, and administered by scientific experts, in accordance with the best scientific techniques. Now Russell is the last man in the world to minimize the importance of science, or to try to persuade us not to be as scientific as we can. So he asks, what would a society be like, in which sci-entific efficiency were allowed free sway, and everything else subordinated to it? Russell's answer turns out to be identical, down to the last detail, with the scheme put into Socrates' mouth in the *Republic.*

There is one major difference: modern scientific orga-nization would obviously demand a world state. Hence there are in Russell's scientific society only two classes: there are no Platonic Guardian soldiers. There would, however, be no liberty, and no equality. There would be rule by an oligarchy of experts, who know what is best to do. Individuals would be ruthlessly sacrificed; Christian ethics is clearly revealed as unscientific. There would be a scientific control of reproduction, and the community of women: the family would have to disappear. Every particu-lar loyalty: of man and woman, of parents and children, even of friendship, would have to be sacrificed to an unde-viating loyalty to the State, fostered by pills and propa-ganda. There would be an education of the working class to be "docile, industrious, punctual, and thoughtless, 'co-operative,' and contented," by means of drugs and psychol-ogy; and of the governing class of experts, in "intelligence, self-command, and command over others." Yet no one would be allowed to question the value of science; all fundamentally novel ideas would be discouraged. There would be a bureaucracy of experts leading to scientific stagnation.

Thus every institution would be perfectly scientific, and every man perfectly miserable. At least, he would be, if he were not psychoanalized and fed pills to make him like it. There would be no poetry, no art, no love, no idealism, and no real science.

Now Russell is not a dramatic artist, like Plato, and so he has to state his point expressly, where Plato makes his reader "see":

The scientific society which has been sketched . . . , is, of course, not to be taken altogether as serious prophecy. It is an attempt to depict the world which would result if scientific technique were to rule unchecked. The reader will have observed that features that everyone would consider desirable are almost inextricably mingled with features that are repulsive. The reason of this is that we have been imagining a *society developed in accordance with certain ingredients of human nature* [emphasis mine] to the exclusion of all others. As ingredients they are good; as the sole driving force they are likely to be disastrous. The impulse towards scientific construction is admirable when it does not thwart any of the major impulses that give value to human life, but when it is allowed to forbid all outlet to anything but itself it becomes a form of cruel tyranny. There is, I think, a real danger lest the world should become subject to a tyranny of this sort, and it is on this account that I have not shrunk from depicting the darker features of the world that scientific manipulation unchecked might wish to create.4

4 Bertrand Russell, *The Scientific Outlook* (New York, 1931), p. 260.

This is the universal philosophy of politics, of the nature and function, of the importance and limitations, of political theorizing, embodied by Plato in the *Republic*. It is clearly as applicable to the ideal of Communism, or to whatever we are willing to call our own social ideal, as to the Greek ideal Plato makes Socrates ironically expound.

But it is impossible not to believe that Plato had a very particular application in mind. To the audience for which the *Republic* was first written, the perfect city of Socrates' ironical criticism could have had but one meaning: it was the Spartan ideal. Spartan institutions form the ground-work of the perfect city: they are perfected and elaborated by Socrates into a super-Sparta. We must remember that Sparta had defeated the Athenians in the long Peloponnesian War; and many Athenians were naturally fascinated by its harmonious and efficient military organization—it might well be the salvation of Athens to copy Sparta's successful military machine. In modern terms, many Athenians were tempted to adopt the enemy's authoritarian social organization and ideal of efficiency at all costs. The *Republic* may even have begun to take form under the Spartan occupation of Athens (404/3 B.C., when Plato was 23, and Socrates still alive); we do not know, of course, its exact date. But the situation is analogous to a Frenchman defending the ideal of French civilization against Prussian military bureaucracy under the German occupation of France during World War II.

We can well imagine Plato saying to the collaborators, All right! Let us take the Spartan ideal, and let us take it at its best, as Athenians would work it: of course, nothing so unenlightened and stupid as Sparta actually is could ever happen here. Let us take the Spartan ideal as a genuine ideal, proceed to develop its implications, and see where that ideal leads us. Of course, there would be no individual happiness, no moral responsibility; it could be made to work only by propaganda and "royal lies." There would be no art, and no poetry; scholars and scientists would all be coordinated with the Régime. Wisdom would be chained to a military machine. There would be a full eugenic program of mating, to prevent racial defilement and to improve Athenian blood. We should be left with businessmen, soldiers and bureaucrats, and Party members. Is that what you collaborators really want? Of course, we Athenians could stand a lot more sense of order and discipline and disinterested devotion to our city than we have got. But—do you really want to go Spartan? Or Nazi? the modern will add.

To the audience for whom the *Republic* was originally written, it must have been a sustained piece of Plato's dramatic irony, a magnificent defense of the Athenian ideal against the Spartan. Plato saw the genuine values of Spartan efficiency and military organization—especially for a war state, such as the perfect city definitely is. But he was hardly rooting for Sparta—not even for a super-Sparta.

There, organization takes precedence even over the life of *theōria,* of imaginative insight. The philosopher is there forced back into the cave, and is lucky if he can ever escape again. There, philosophers are good rulers because they hate the whole business, and are doing it only from a sense of duty, of "justice." There are much better philosophers in imperfect states, in actual human cities. There will be in them better art, better poetry, better life, better men—better everything but Justice or efficient organization.

XIII

The Good Life: "Later" Treatment

THE previous discussion of Plato's handling of the theme of the Good Life has been based on the dramatic or Socratic dialogues, culminating in the *Republic*. The "schoolmaster" dialogues also deal with the same theme at length. I want to point out certain things about the *Philebus,* which treats it in individual or ethical terms, and about the *Statesman* and the *Laws,* which carry on the examination of the good, rather than the perfect city.

It is worth dwelling on these so-called "later" dialogues —which we must remember may not come from the same hand as the dramatic dialogues—for several reasons. First, the average lover of Plato is less likely to read them, so there is more excuse for suggesting what is in them. And there is a great deal of philosophical interest; but the reader needs to be enticed to look for it, while he needs no such enticement with the greater dialogues.

Then, too, scholars like Burnet have warned us, "So long as readers are content to know only something of the *Republic* and the earlier dialogues, Platonism must remain a sealed book to them." This caution holds for the whole later Platonic tradition. It applies to Aristotle, whose own writings all begin in the atmosphere and views of these

later dialogues. Without a thorough knowledge of them, it
is impossible to understand and appreciate what particular
strands of Plato's thought Aristotle took over, and how he
elaborated and developed them in his own characteristic
fashion.

But the chief reason for dwelling on the later dialogues
is that it is much easier to say something about them. The
Symposium or the *Phaedo* are to be read and reread. To say
anything very significant about them, you have to be a phi
losopher and poet yourself.

The *Philebus* is about the same theme discussed in the
Protagoras: what is the Good Life for the individual man,
and is it pleasure or knowledge? But the temper is quite
different. Where the *Protagoras* is a Sophistic debate between the two positions, in which neither will give an inch,
and where the two are contrasted as sharply as possible, and
as dramatically, here it soon develops that both pleasure and
knowledge have an indispensable place in the Good Life.
The question is, what is their relative position, what kinds
of each are there, which of these kinds have a place and
which do not? The complexity of the problem overshadows
the dramatic opposition of the *Protagoras*. The outcome is
the same: in the *Protagoras,* the measurement of pleasures
brings thought and pleasure together; here pleasure, knowledge, and measurement are all found to be ingredients of
what is in the *Philebus* now called the "mixed life." John
Stuart Mill could call the closing discussion of the *Protagoras* the first statement of the Benthamite or Utilitarian
position. In the same spirit, we might call the *Philebus* the
first statement of the Aristotelian eudaemonistic position.
Both, in English, are conventionally taken as making "happiness" the end. Here in the *Philebus* "happiness" has
grown more complex than in the *Protagoras,* unless we

want to say that the complexity there is a *dramatic* complexity, while here it is an explicitly formulated and *stated* complexity.

Here too is explicitly formulated the Aristotelian doctrine of the mean, in a manner making clear its background in the Pythagorean elements in Plato's thought. The mean is a proportion between the Boundless or Indeterminate, which includes pleasure, and the Limit, which brings in thought. This Pythagorean classification makes the *Philebus* the dialogue where Plato has gone farthest in writing out his mathematical ontology: from it, together with commentators on Aristotle, are taken most of the bits of evidence for that mathematical philosophy.

The *Philebus* is typical of the later dialogues in being the discussion of other men's opinions. Aristotle tells us that the view that pleasure is the sole good is the position of Eudoxus the geometer, while the view that pleasure and pain are both bad and that only knowledge is the good was advanced by Speusippos. The young Philebus holds with Eudoxus; Socrates mediates and determines the question.

It is assumed by both sides in the discussion that "the good for man," human well-being, is "a condition and disposition (*hexis kai diathesis*) of the soul." [1] This well-being (*eudaimonia*) is an art, an achievement; the question is, what materials to use, and how to mix them properly:

Soc. As to the mixture of wisdom and pleasure (*phronēsis* and *hēdonē*) if anyone were to say that we are like craftsmen (*dēmiourgoi*), with the materials before us from which to create our work, the simile would be a good one.[2]

---

[1] *Philebus* 11 D.
[2] *Philebus* 59 D, E.

Here is the explicit statement of the problem dealt with in all the Socratic or dramatic dialogues. The elaborate method of division, with its careful classifications, is introduced to make distinctions in this complex material, as a means to determining just what materials to choose.

Socrates formulates the issue:

Philebus says that to all living beings enjoyment and pleasure and gaiety (*to chairein kai tēn hēdonēn kai terpsin*) and whatever accords with that sort of thing are a good; whereas our contention is that not these, but wisdom and thought and memory (*to phronein kai to noein kai to memnesthai*) and their kindred, right opinion and true reasonings, are better and more excellent than pleasure for all who are capable of taking part in them, and that for all those now existing or to come who can partake of them they are the most advantageous of all things.[3]

But the life of pure pleasure soon breaks down: it contains not even awareness, to say nothing of recollection or anticipation; it would be the life of an oyster. Likewise, the life of pure thought would have no feeling at all, and would hence be inhuman. So the life of both combined is to be preferred. But will this life be nearer pleasure or wisdom? and what will be the "cause" of the combination? This leads to the classification under four heads: the indeterminate, the limit, the mixture, and the cause. Now mind and wisdom (*nous kai sophia*) are the cause of the mixture, and the mixture itself is a harmony and proportion. Pleasure is a process of becoming (*genesis*), and whatever becomes, becomes for some end or good. Hence pleasure is not itself the Good, but is for the sake of the Good: it has a subordinate place in the harmony.

The Good, then, is the mixed life. Its ingredients are:

[3] *Philebus* 11 B, C.

First the eternal nature has chosen measure, moderation, fitness (*metron kai to metrion kai kairion*) and all which is to be considered similar to these. . . .

Second comes proportion, beauty, perfection, sufficiency (*tò symmetron kai kalon kai to teleon kai hikanon*)

Count mind and wisdom (*nous kai phronēsis*) as the third. . . .

And will you not put those properties fourth which we said belonged especially to the soul—sciences, arts, and true opinions (*epistēmai kai technai kai doxai orthai*) they are called? . . .

Fifth, those pleasures which we classed as painless, which we called pure pleasures of the soul itself (*hēdonai alupai kai katharai*).[4]

This "mixed life" of the *Philebus* is thus the bald prose statement of the unification of factors dramatically suggested in all the discussions of individual excellence in the Socratic dialogues. It also points directly to the "mingling" or "weaving together" of factors which will be the primary work of the Statesman in the *Statesman* dialogue and in the *Laws*. And it points to Aristotle's formulation of the problems of ethics in the *Nicomachean Ethics*. Here too Plato provided Aristotle with his starting-point.

In the *Statesman*, the protagonist is not Socrates, but a figure called the "Eleatic Stranger." And where Plato in the dramatic dialogues uses Socrates to set forth various views, which he then proceeds to comment on and develop dramatically, the Eleatic Stranger seems rather to be the mouthpiece of Plato himself, who is here speaking to us directly—and undramatically. The difference in style and in method is profound. But is there a difference of viewpoint,

[4] *Philebus* 66 A, B, C.

a difference of political philosophy, from the *Republic?* Not fundamentally—if we take the *Republic* in the sense suggested. Of course, if we forget the drama and the irony, and read the *Republic* as Socrates' campaign speech, then Plato does seem to be saying something quite different.

The characters are talking here not about the Perfect City in the sky, not about the Idea of Justice Itself, but about the actual world of men and about human cities, the world of politicians and officeholders, of compromises and intrigues, of elections and campaign promises, of mudslinging and vituperation, of Madison Avenue build-ups and undercover religious bigotry. It is the world in which the practical choice lies between the best candidates available. In that world, is the best solution to elect our outstanding philosopher "king," and tell him to take over?

The speakers start in by trying to define the Statesman. He will be a man with real knowledge of what is best to do; he will have absolute power, ruling his people like a good shepherd. That is, he will be like the philosopher-king of the *Republic.* But they feel that something is wrong. So the Stranger tells a story, a myth: There used to be a time when God himself guided and directed the world, and men. But somehow God lost control of the helm, and the world and everything in it started going backwards. Men were born out of the earth, and they were born old, and proceeded to grow younger and younger. Everything was in a parlous state. Finally, God managed to get control of the world again, but he never did regain control of men. Ever since, men have had to manage human affairs themselves: God is not equal to it.

Now, the divine shepherd, or philosopher-king, governed in the earlier Golden Age, when God was still in control of men. In those days there was no private property, no toil, no marriage, no wives and children, no State. But now men must rule, using human materials and human institutions. Men are not like a swarm of bees: they have no natural born ruler or leader.

What would such a human rule be like? It would be an art like weaving; and like all arts, it would be governed by certain standards. It would be a "weaving" or "mixing" of different human elements in the proper proportions. There are of course many class antagonisms between groups of men. But the best ruler will harmonize the interests and values of these different groups, and adjust the groups to each other, in the light of a standard of the mean. He will create a common ideal, and by means of a common education and mixed marriages, he will seek to create the best type of man. And he will bind all the groups together by common sentiments, honors, and opinions. There is much in this whole conception that suggests the older American social ideal of the melting-pot.

Throughout the whole discussion, there runs a strong sense of the value of the individual. Men should aim, not at efficient organization, or Justice, as in the *Republic,* with its war-state, but at something quite different: at Self-Control, *Sōphrosynē,* individual character. The goal should be, not specialization, as in the *Republic* war-state, but a blending. This is a human ideal, it is insisted. Above all, the ruler will avoid developing one excellence at the expense of all the rest—he should avoid developing men of pure courage, fit only for the Marines; or men of pure caution, pure moderation, fit only to be college presidents. He will seek, both in the individual citizens, and in the governing bodies of the city, a balance, a proportion, a mean. Significantly, these are all fundamental Aristotelian concepts. As in the *Philebus,* this is where Aristotle came in.

For statecraft so conceived, the important question will be whether knowledge is in control, not the number of men who govern. Will wisdom rule? Will the blending be done in the light of a knowledge of the standard, of the mean, and of the possibilities of human nature? Is the consent of the governed important? That does not really matter. Will the government be a government of laws? Laws, after all, are a bad thing: they are such a check on the wise artist. Will the captain in steering his ship, will the physician in healing the sick, be bound by inflexible rules? No, enlightened and benevolent despotism is best: for it is the rule of a man, of an artist, of wisdom, not the rule of laws and red tape.

We must remember that "law" meant to the Greeks a fixed, unalterable code, not the continuous work of a legislature; that is, it meant a written constitution, the kind of thing of which Americans have had a considerable experience. Plato is here the artist: politics is the creation of an artistic masterpiece. Plato is demanding for his ruler the flexibility of the free creative artist, planning and bringing into being a whole social organization, creating an entire culture. Here is also something of the political sense of the British: why have a written constitution? Why have a Supreme Court hampering the Statesman's fitting of new techniques and new devices to the solution of new problems? Constitutions and laws are such obstacles to doing what is best to do, to doing what an intelligent man sees the situation obviously demands.

But—those who feel these restrictions most keenly are the first to appeal to the Constitution, when some one else— actual human politicians—start doing things, and they turn out to be the wrong things. Plato sees this clearly: the rule of enlightened despotism, of the intelligent but irresponsible expert, of the philosopher-king, is, humanly speaking, intolerable and impossible. The human ruler is not wise; if unrestrained, he becomes arbitrary, a tyrant. If he—or they —are gifted and intelligent, it happens all the sooner; for the rulers become impatient at men's stupidity, and act according to their own better lights. Such a state is worst of all.

There is no ideal ruler; there are only Tories and Labourites, Republicans and Democrats. The human city is not a beehive with a superman at its head. We are back in the Golden Age once more; that is so easy in political theorizing. A god, Plato goes on, would have no need of laws: there seems to be for him no Supreme Court in Heaven. But law is far better than the arbitrary, ignorant rule of unchecked human rulers. A government of laws is not perfect; but, humanly speaking, it is the best we can hope for. In it are maladjustment, limits on creative action, ignorance. But—it suits human nature. It is the nearest human embodiment of Justice Itself.

The *Statesman* is sober, sane, and wise; but it is not exciting. There is about it a sense of the inevitability of limitation, not the free play of the imagination, as in the *Republic*. It exhibits common sense rather than intellectual imagination. The difference between the *Republic* and the *Statesman* is the difference between political discussion and practical politics: we *talk* about socialism, communism, anarchism, and the rest; but we *vote* for Republicans or Democrats.

The *Laws* dialogue exhibits the same temper as the *Statesman,* only more so. It is full of shrewd and wise observations of life, and exhibits a sense of the facts of human nature; but it has always seemed intolerable to the idealist.

It is not surprising to be told that Aristotle loved it. Its controlling theme is, "The Best is not possible." To work for it would be crass perfectionism. Of course, we must be practical and "realistic," even if it kills us—as being practical and realistic so often does. Of course, communism—the community of goods—is best; but only gods could make such communism work. Men will be peasant-proprietors. In the Perfect City, there would be no courts and no lawyers; but men will need detailed penal codes and law enforcement. There is in the *Laws* no fire, no incandescent imagination, no irony, no poetry. But there is a startling insight into human nature and human institutions.

Three elderly gentlemen, a Cretan, a Spartan, and an Athenian Stranger, meet to discuss and plan the foundation of a new colony. Through their talk runs a sense of disillusionment, of lost ideas, a tragic hardening of views. These man have grown with age cautious and conservative: they tend to view new ideas and proposals with alarm. The difference between the *Republic* and the *Laws* is like the difference between the free play of imagination in postulate systems, in the social writings of Bertrand Russell, and the moralizing of an experienced old political commentator like Walter Lippmann. The characters who speak in the *Laws* are in a sense much wiser than those in the *Republic*, but they seem burnt out. This is the wisdom of an opinionated, dogmatic old man. It is the folly of experience—so much more deadening than the enthusiastic folly of inexperience, and often so much more deadly in its results.

The three gentlemen ask, "What are the best regulations for the new colony?" We no longer hear the free creative artist remolding human nature and aflame with the ideal. Those regulations are best, it is answered, that make the best citizens, well-rounded individuals, and not mere slaves of the state. Each man should aim at the whole of excellence, not at a mere part. The highest excellence is Self-Control, *Sōphrosynē,* not Justice, efficient organization. The happiness of the individual citizens is important.[5] There should be mixture and compromise. Above all, Freedom matters. You must get men's consent to what you ask them to do, you must appeal to men's reason.

The Athenian ideal is explicitly stated and advocated: "To be good, not by external compulsion, but by inner disposition." All men should be trained both "to rule and to be ruled rightly." But even self-control by itself is worthless; and the best institutions will not work of themselves: they need good men to run them.[6]

The *Laws* opens with a magnificent argument against prohibition, and in favor of light wines. Men should pray, "O God, Lead us into temptation!" Only thus can we learn self-control. We need practice in mastering pleasures as a part of our education, not ascetic flight.[7] The laws should not regulate men's conduct too much: they should rather offer persuasive advice. They should set standards. Trivial regulation breeds only disrespect for all law. Unfortunately, the old men soon forget this wisdom.

The entire aim of the institutions of the new colony should be not war, but peace and friendly feeling, the securing of permanent friendliness. The true Statesman will not prepare for war in time of peace, but even during war he will be ceaselessly preparing for peace. Military success is no valid test of the goodness or badness of institutions: it is

---

[5] *Laws* 630 E; 631 C, D; 743 C.

[6] *Laws* 642 D, 640 E.

[7] *Laws* 640 D, E; 666 B; 672 D; 631 C, D; 635 B, C; 647 B. It is not known whether Mark Twain was reading the *Laws* just before he wrote *The Man Who Corrupted Hadleyburg.*

largely accidental, and depends on power, not on worth.[8]

This utter rejection of warfare is in marked contrast to —it is in fact the most striking difference from—the perfect city of the *Republic,* where organization, efficiency, justice, is bent to the sole aim of military power, and the efficient organization or justice of the city is to be tested by whether its institutions will be effective in war. The perfect city of the *Republic,* we have seen, is a war-state—it is the Spartan ideal.

Why this glaring contrast? The answer is clear. Sparta had fallen at Leuctra in 371 B.C. and had finally been completely overcome by the Thebans under Epaminondas at Mantinaea, in 362 B.C. The great war-state was an utter failure. Plato could now afford to say, "I told you so." His whole ironic defense of the Athenian ideal against Spartan militarism in the *Republic* was now justified before the entire world. It was a damning indictment of Spartan institutions and the Spartan ideal. They aimed at power and military efficiency alone, and they failed to get even that. Power without wisdom, says Plato now, is ignorance of the greatest of human interests. No, institutions must develop men of self-control, men of character—not mere soldiers.[9]

War is a disease, to be avoided at all costs. It is caused by commercial greed; and Plato goes on to describe something close to what we have known during the past century as "economic imperialism." The Peloponnesian War, he suggests, was really the contest between the rival commercial empires of Athens, and of Corinth in alliance with Syracuse, with Spartans as the pawns. Such imperialism is fatal! Hence everything that leads to it must be shunned.

[8] *Laws* 628 A–E; 638 A, B.
[9] *Laws* 688 C–689 C.

So the three planners propose a program of embargoes on commerce, neutrality laws, and the like.

When the three come to discuss the origin of government, they recognize that the actual laws of any city are the product of the pure chance that reigns in human affairs.[10] What we find should be perfected by human art. Get a monarch, young, intelligent, courageous, temperate, fortunate in having as his adviser a noble lawgiver. (Is this the fruit of Plato's hopes for the young Dionysius?) Thus the most efficient artistry will be possible. But—such things, the three old men agree, do not happen, "certainly not in our time." The next best form of government is some type of constitutional democracy. Once, in the days of Cronos, there were kings who governed wisely and nobly. For Cronos, who knew, "No human being is capable of having irresponsible control of all human affairs without becoming filled with pride and injustice,"[11] sent beings of a divine race, Daimons, to rule the cities of men. But where a mortal, and no god, is monarch, there is no rest from ills and toils. Hence today we ought to obey only the Divine Ruler, the Daimon who dwells within us, Reason and Law, *Nous* and *Nomos*.

Law, *Nomos,* is the wisdom of experience, wiser than any man: it is the Divine *Nous* in actual cities and states. It restrains passions, serves as a power binding men to men, and embodies the motives for good actions. Law is fundamentally a spirit to be known. Hence to every law for the new colony there should be an extended preamble, giving the reason why. These Preambles to the laws should serve as the content of the education of the young. They should

---

[10] It is to be noted that Plato now has no more use for the idea of a Divine Providence than Aristotle.

[11] I.e., "Power corrupts, and absolute power tends to corrupt absolutely." Lord Acton knew his Plato.

promote stability, respect for rational standards of conduct; and they should secure the consent of those governed. They should thus inculcate rational obedience, not mere compulsion.

The three lawgivers now proceed to plan their colony. The institutions are all to be closely regulated. For, Plato asks, "If private conduct is unregulated by law, how can we expect men to submit in public and civil life?"

Economically, the colony shall be based on private property, subject to social control. There shall be fixed and inalienable holdings in land, all equal, of which every citizen shall have one. Other capital is allowed, up to four times the value of the allotment of land, creating four economic classes according to men's wealth. Both the maximum and the minimum shall be strictly enforced. There shall be common consumption: a common table for all, as in an army.

For the citizens, there shall be allowed no trading and no handicrafts; they are to be left to the metics, the aliens. And there shall be for the citizens no toil in the fields; that will be left to slaves. Thus the citizens are to be a leisure class on a slave basis. It is noteworthy that in the *Laws,* Plato, like Aristotle, accepts the institution of slavery, without any of Aristotle's qualifications and reservations. The citizens should be freed from economic worries and activity to devote themselves to festivals and games. There shall be no money: riches and goodness will not mix. But even these economic arrangements are admitted to be an ideal pattern, which in practice will admit of compromise.

The institution of marriage is also accepted and idealized. Yet it too must be closely regulated: there is proposed a body of "Lady Watchers of the Bed," to see that enough children are produced, and not too many.

There shall be a government of laws, administered by a

group of thirty-seven magistrates, democratically elected, together with a Council, elected by manhood suffrage on an elaborate four-class system according to wealth. Thus wisdom will be mixed with liberty, and there will be a "democracy of laws," a mean between democracy and monarchy—very much like Aristotle's *Politeia* or "constitutional government."

Yet in the end, in Book XII, Plato returns to the philosopher-king and artist-ruler idea. He proposes a "Nocturnal Synod" composed of grey-beard philosophers together with young associates, who all know the true aim of the State, and the means to achieve it, and are experts in political science and the "true wisdom of the Good." This will be an advisory council meeting in secret before dawn, a kind of invisible government.

The detailed penal codes form the major portion of the *Laws* dialogue. They are on the whole marvelously wise, and exhibit a view of criminal law and punishment that strikes us as very "modern." Crime is considered to be a disease; hence the laws should aim not at retribution, but at the reform of the soul. This portion of the dialogue, we are told, became the basis of many of the Hellenistic legal codes.

Finally, in Book X there is advocated a state religion. Heresy, defined as private worship independently of the state cult, is punishable with death. There are three heresies: first, atheism, the denial of the gods; secondly, belief that the gods are indifferent to man, the denial of the Providence of the gods; and thirdly, the belief that the gods are venal, that their favors can be bought. The last heresy is the worst of all; it is the basis of "priestcraft." And Plato here displays a very Lucretian hatred of all such priestcraft; there must hence be no private cults allowed.

In all this religious legislation, Plato's motives, as always in touching on religion, are moral and political: we men must so live as though the gods were watching us. But Plato does here maintain, that men's speculative opinions are dangerous to others. Atheists who are themselves perfectly just are to be imprisoned, argued with for five years, if necessary, until they are converted to sound belief; and then, if this brainwashing has still not convinced them, they must be put to death. The spirit is certainly not Socratic; but, considering our own world, is quite "modern."

Is this the same Plato who wrote the dramatic dialogues? Yes—and No! Mostly No. The philosopher-poet is gone; the observer of men is still left. What has become of the free life of the mind, of *nous* and *theōria?* It has given way to the philosopher-king, the lawgiver. And it is a bad philosopher: philosophy becomes a religious apologetic. The *Laws* culminate, in Book X, in the full spirit of the Middle Ages at their worst, with the reign of a priesthood trained in theology, a spiritual power making religious threats, and a full-fledged Inquisition calling for the stake. The aging Plato seems to have succumbed to the curse of social idealism, which has so often begun with the flaming vision of a new day, has then encountered the obstinate stubbornness of unregenerate human nature, and has ended with the secret police.

Plato's "Ideas"

PLATO clearly felt the supreme importance of knowledge: he certainly makes his readers feel it. It is the most
important factor in the Good Life. But did Plato also have
an explicit "doctrine" of knowledge? This is a more doubtful question.

We do find, running through the dramatic dialogues, a
passionate emphasis on what is worth knowing—a distinction between different objects of knowledge, which is essentially a distinction of value, though based on a distinction
between two ways of knowing. There is a recurrent discrimination between the things known through the senses,
and the things known through mind—between things
aisthēta, and things *noēta,* things sensed and things
"noused," [1] or, in Latin, things sensible and things intelligible. Where this discrimination is made, there is the passionate conviction that the things known through *nous,* mind
intellect, which Plato calls Ideas, *ideai,* are alone really
valuable, alone objects of true knowledge, *epistēmē.* In the
dramatic dialogues there certainly is to be found a *theōria,*

---

[1] I still have a fondness for this word, ever since I first heard
it from the mouth of my teacher Wendell T. Bush.

a vision of knowledge—of what is worth knowing, of
Ideas.

But is there to be found in the dialogues—in the dramatic dialogues—any concern with knowledge itself, with
its nature and problems, as contrasted with the concern
with these objects of true knowledge? Is there any clearly
formulated theory of knowledge, in the sense of an account
or explanation of knowledge? In a word, is there to be
found in the dramatic dialogues any epistemology, in the
sense made notorious in modern philosophizing?

Now there is a deeply rooted tradition, stretching back
to Aristotle, that there is. This is the famous Platonic
"Theory of Ideas." But, if this is to be found in the dramatic dialogues, in just which one shall we look for it? It is
a hard question to answer. I remember once at an oral
examination for the Ph.D., where perhaps this "theory of
ideas" is most relevant, the candidate was asked this question. He had been going strong; but now he stopped short,
scratched his head, thought for several minutes, and finally
said, slowly, "The best statement of the Platonic doctrine of
knowledge is to be found in the sixth and ninth chapters of
Book Alpha of Aristotle's *Metaphysics.*"

Now this is of course an excellent answer. But just what
does it mean? It means, I judge, that the Head of the
Academy may have held such a theory of knowledge—such
an epistemology; but hardly the author of the dramatic dialogues. This latter contrast is not quite true. The dialogues
do mention a "theory of ideas," in the sense of a "doctrine
of knowledge," once—in the opening passage of the *Parmenides*. But it is mentioned there only to argue that it is
all mistaken. As an account, an explanation, an interpretation, a construing of the fact of knowledge, it is a
quite impossible doctrine.

This Theory of Ideas has had a long and eventful history. Judged by its power—as we must ultimately judge philosophies—it is one of the greatest philosophies in the world. It can well stand on its own foot, even if we should decide, there is no conclusive evidence that it was shared by Plato the author of dramatic dialogues. This theory is based on the distinction between things, on the one hand, and Ideas or Forms which are apart from things, on the other. Things participate in Ideas; and the mind, following the suggestions in things, can rise, by a dialectic process, to a knowledge of its proper objects, the Ideas. The only true science or *epistēmē* is thus a knowledge, not of the world, but of something quite different—of an "intelligible realm" of pure Forms or Ideas somehow apart from the world.

This Theory of Ideas has traditionally claimed to be the systematic statement of what is taught about "Ideas" in the various stories or myths told on appropriate occasions in the more dramatic dialogues. ("Ideas" are treated more technically in the *Phaedo,* the *Symposium,* and the *Republic,* Books VI and VII.) Perhaps the fullest is the myth in the *Phaedrus,* which tells how the soul of man is really deathless and eternal, and lived in heaven before it was born upon earth. It has the form of a chariot with a charioteer and two winged steeds, one noble and one base. There is a great procession of gods and souls in heaven, led by Zeus himself. They go to a feast, "passing outside and taking their place on the outer surface of the heaven, and the revolution carries them round," as on a kind of celestial merry-go-round, and they behold the things outside the heaven—the Ideas themselves.

But the region above the heaven was never worthily sung by any earthly poet, nor will it ever be. . . . For the colorless, formless, and intangible truly existing essence (*ousia ontōs ousa*), with which all true knowledge is concerned, holds this region and is visible only to *nous,* the pilot of the soul. Now the divine thinking (*theou dianoia*), since it is nurtured on *nous* and pure knowledge, and the *nous* of every soul which is capable of receiving that which befits it, rejoices on seeing Being for a time (*idousa dia chronou to on*) and by gazing upon truth is nourished and made happy until the revolution brings it again to the same place. In the revolution it beholds justice itself, self-control, and knowledge . . . that knowledge which abides where true Being is (*tēn en tō ho estin on ontos epistēmōn ousan*). . . . Such is the life of the gods.[2]

Alas, there is a fall of the soul; it forgets, grows heavy, loses its wings, and is born on earth among mortals. "The soul that has seen most of Truth comes to birth as a philosopher, a lover of beauty, or an artist, a musician, or a lover. He who has seen least becomes a tyrant." (*Phaedrus,* 248)

The earth-bound soul now beholds the earthly beauty—a beautiful boy, perhaps—and sees the heavenly Beauty shining by reflection in it. This stirs the soul's recollection of what it had gazed upon in heaven. The soul gets hot and itchy—its pinfeathers are beginning to sprout again. The soul that has forgotten heaven rushes upon the object of its love in lust; but the soul that remembers goes on to beautiful politics, then to beautiful mathematics, and philosophy, and finally, its wings fully restored, flies back to the top of the dome of heaven again.

There are other myths of reminiscence in the *Meno* and the *Phaedo.* The point is always, that knowledge is like remembering, like being reminded of something—they always make central the element of recognition in knowing—what Aristotle was to call *nous.* Are these myths or stories in Plato to be taken literally, as they have been by Platonists

[2] *Phaedrus* 247–248.

and other innocent souls? All such men overlook the point of the myths, the reason why the story is introduced.

In the *Meno,* for example, Meno reports that his teacher Gorgias held, you cannot really teach or learn anything. Socrates answers, "All right! If so, then we'll call it something else: like the Pythagoreans, we'll call it remembering. I'll tell you a story, and then I'll show you how I can 'remember' a fellow some geometry." The myth is introduced to answer Gorgias, and to show, in commenting dramatically upon his contention, that you *can* teach mathematics —*ta mathēmatika,* the "teachable things."

It is clear, Plato used the Orphic and Pythagorean belief in the pre-existence of the soul to make his points in his stories. These religious ideas are the source of his illustrations. But there is no evidence whatever that Plato himself believed, as we misleadingly say, in the pre-existence of the soul—or in its future existence, either. Plato did believe in the immortality, in the deathlessness of Soul—but that is something quite different.

The Theory of Ideas was made into a theory of Being, a metaphysics; into a theory of the world, a cosmology. The Ideas were perfect shining things existing in Heaven, as the *Phaedrus* myth had it, perfect, immutable, and all the rest. They were there as true and authentic Being. God looked at them, burning before—or perhaps in—his mind, and created the world by using them as a model. He called in the Demiurge, the Supreme Artist, to do the dirty work. God does not look at the base material world himself, and could not see it if he did: he beholds only the Ideas. God is really a Source of Divine Light, overflowing, like a fountain, and growing dimmer and dimmer as it leaves its Source. Our sensible world is dark, and shines only by light reflected from the Ideas. Man sees these decaying embers, his soul is kindled, and he mounts up to the Source of the Divine Light, the Sun of the Intelligible World.

Such a Theory of Ideas, such Platonism, is a beautiful, appealing, imaginative myth. If taken as literal fact, as we say, it is highly dubious—no more dubious, perhaps, than Christian theology taken as literal fact, and not yet subjected to a contemporary demythologizing. The Trinity—the Father, the Son-Logos, and the Holy Spirit—is another form of the same Platonistic myth. Platonism—what we call "Neo-Platonism," to distinguish it from the many other strands of thought in Plato himself, especially his detached and ironic vision—was the philosophical language in terms of which Christian theology was formulated. Taken as science, as literal truth, both are probably wide of the mark. Today we hardly confuse them with such literal, scientific truth. But they have for centuries furnished Christendom with a marvelous poetry, a genuine imaginative wisdom about man's life in the world. They are what intelligent theologians today call "mythical Truth," or "symbolic Wisdom."[3]

Identified as Platonism, the Theory of Ideas became the great tradition in Western culture. Men confronted the choice between commitment to the world of the senses, or to the intelligible realm of Ideas. Their salvation lay in forsaking the senses and fleeing to the realm of Ideas. Platonism became a religious gospel, the framework within which the Oriental religions of the Hellenistic world were rationalized, and in which Christianity grew up. It matured into the imaginative core of the Christian tradition, coming down in the West as the Augustinian philosophy of the

[3] I have some reservations and doubts myself about the propriety and clarification of using "Truth" in such a connection. But I have no doubts whatever about the symbolic "Wisdom."

Middle Ages. It was revived by the poets and artists of the Renaissance; it is deeply embedded in English poetry from Edmund Spenser to Shelley, yes, even in Yeats and T. S. Eliot. It is the philosophy embodied in Shakespeare's Sonnets. It has been the incentive to more imaginative expression and illustration than any other philosophy in the Western tradition. Every poet and artist not resolved to be realistic at all costs has turned to it.

Moreover, Platonism was the inspiration of early modern science, for which the realm of ideas became the realm of mathematics. There, felt the pioneers, Copernicus, Kepler, and even Galileo, in mathematical form and order, lies the proper object of science, even as Plato held. This Platonism has kept our science from ever wholeheartedly endorsing the materialism of moralizing poets like Lucretius; and from ever accepting empiricism in practice, whatever theory of science it may have been bullied by philosophers into agreeing to, or from every dissolving knowledge into a mass of unrelated and meaningless facts.

When taken seriously, as a literal theory of knowledge, or construing of the fact of knowledge, Platonism, or the theory of Ideas, has raised a number of persisting insoluble logical problems—problems which Plato himself, in the opening discussion in the *Parmenides,* points to as evidence that such Platonism cannot be taken seriously as a literal theory of knowledge, or epistemology.

1. What is the relation of Ideas, thus conceived, as apart from particular things, and abstract from them, to concrete objects?

2. What is the relation of Ideas, so conceived, to each other?

3. Where are Ideas to be found? What is their ontological status? What is the geography of the intelligible realm?

4. How are Ideas accessible to the human mind? How can we come to know them and to recognize them?

5. How does a knowledge of Ideas give us a knowledge of particulars?

These problems are all insoluble, if we ask them of the traditional theory of Ideas—this the long intellectual tradition in the West has made abundantly clear: no Platonist has ever been able to answer these questions.4 And Platonism, in the conventional sense, though revived again and again, by poets intoxicated with words, or by mathematicians intoxicated with dialectic, has again and again crumbled at the first touch of serious criticism. Platonism as a theory of knowledge, or as a theory of Being, a metaphysics, is myth. It is, to be sure, glorious myth, seductive myth, historically important myth. But, as a serious epistemology, or ontology, it just is not literally so.

But—if we ask these same traditional questions of the Platonic dialogues—if we take Plato's dramatic method seriously, and inquire into the nature and function of Ideas as they actually appear in the dialogues, quite simply, and with that height of sophistication that consists in brushing aside all accretions of interpretation and theory, and approaching the dialogues of Plato directly and naïvely, they can all, I judge, be given simple answers. For they then cease to be problems of knowledge to be wrestled with, and become, rather, facts about knowledge to be stated and illustrated—facts to be dramatically displayed and seen.

1. What is the relation between abstract Ideas and concrete particulars? It is the relation between the Idea of

---

4 See the account of this refutation of the theory of knowledge of Platonism through history in my *Career of Philosophy in Modern Times*, Vol. I, *From the Middle Ages to the Enlightenment* (New York, 1962); Vol. II, *From the German Enlightenment to the Age of Darwin* (New York, 1965).

Love, in the speech of Diotima in the *Symposium* (though "Love" is not technically called an "Idea" by Plato: its object, "Beauty," is), and the human love of Alcibiades for Socrates. It is the relation between the interminable discussion of Justice in the *Republic,* and the old Cephalus, who smiles as the dialogue begins, as he goes out himself to perform just acts. It is the relation between the talk about death, and the deathlessness of the soul, in the *Phaedo,* and Socrates drinking the hemlock, and in his inescapable death becoming deathless and divine.

That is, we see particulars, but talk about Ideas or universals.

2. What is the relation of Ideas to each other? (Plato deals with this question explicitly in the *Sophist* discussing the relations between Forms.) We start discussing any Idea, and then find all the others becoming involved, as in the *Republic.* Or, as in the *Symposium* and the *Phaedrus,* in the human experience of love and aspiration, we start with one particular love, and then find the love of all Ideas and all perfections involved in the end.

That is, Ideas are progressively unified in discourse, in knowledge, through discussion, through dialectic—and in experience, in love. This answer is not only illustrated again and again in the dialogues, it is explicitly stated: All Ideas are unified in the light of the Idea of the Good, of the harmony of all values.

3. Where are Ideas to be found? What is their ontological status? Are they separate from things? Or apart from things? Are they outside the Heavens in a separate "intelligible realm"? Could one possibly imagine a more irrelevant, more meaningless question than to ask about their geographical habitat, their spatial location? Or a clearer case of what Gilbert Ryle calls a "confusion of categories"?

There is no "realminess" to be found in Plato: as to realms of Being, Plato is strong for union now. It is clear that in the dialogues there is no separate realm of Ideas.

Where, then, are the Ideas to be found? The simplest and most obvious answer is, in Plato's dialogues themselves: Plato's dialogues *are* the "realm of Ideas." And this means, the Ideas are found in human discourse. Ideas have their being in discourse, in *logos:* they have a logical existence in human talk—and in the vivid emotional experience of aspiration or love. For Plato, therefore, the dialogues themselves reveal, the "realm of Ideas" is the realm of discourse and the realm of experience.

4. How are Ideas accessible to the human mind? How can mind come to recognize them? Through talk: they are clarified through discussion, through dialectic, the Greek word for "talk." This occurs when discourse is about what experience has suggested, and art has led men to see. It does not occur when men were taken for a ride by the gods before they were born.

5. How does knowledge of Ideas give knowledge of particulars? Talk, discourse, about Justice Itself does throw clearer light on just cities and just men. Talk about friendship, in the *Lysis,* does clarify human friendship—though no talk ever exhausts all that might be said about the subject of discourse: we must see, besides and before talking.

In other words, if we ask these traditional questions of the dialogues of Plato themselves, and really let the dialogues answer them, simply and directly, we get the answers Aristotle gave them, when he asked these same questions of the world.[5] This means, I judge, that if we insist

---

[5] It has been a standing question for the long line of those who in the Western tradition have tried to harmonize Plato and Aristotle, of whom perhaps Pico della Mirandola is the most famous,

on asking the Platonic dialogues for a theory of knowledge, and insist on an answer, we find in them a theory of knowledge in all its essentials identical with Aristotle's. I am afraid I have never been able myself to find any significant difference between Plato's doctrine of knowledge and Aristotle's doctrine of knowledge—except the possibly not insignificant difference, that it seems highly doubtful whether Plato had any doctrine of knowledge at all, or thought it of any value to elaborate one; whether Plato had any theory of knowledge, save the *theōria,* the vision, of what is worth knowing—i.e., the conviction that the highest object of knowledge, an Idea, is, in the last analysis, something to be seen and loved and felt.

For Aristotle, the highest object of knowledge is something to be grasped and expressed in words, in *logoi.* Aristotle's *archai* are that in terms of which things can be *said to be* what they are. Aristotle is wedded to the method of words, *logoi,* to a logical method.

For Plato, the highest object of knowledge, though words, talk, discussion, dialectic, lead us near it, is in the

---

why then did Aristotle criticize Plato's theory of knowledge? Why did he not find his own answers in Plato himself, as we have here done? The answer seems to be, because Aristotle was not a sensitive and imaginative poet-philosopher like Plato, but rather a literal-minded scientific thinker who often missed Plato's subtlety and many levels of irony and metaphor.

It is also possible that Aristotle was arguing against the interpretation of Plato's theory of knowledge adopted by his fellow-students in the Academy, and Plato's successors, Speusippos and Xenocrates, who definitely did hold to the theory of knowledge of Platonism, here being criticized. It seems to be often their views against which Aristotle's criticism is being directed, rather than any views a modern can discover through a perceptive reading of the Platonic dialogues themselves. But doubtless Platonic scholarship will never reach agreement on this fundamental point: Simmias' interpretation of Plato's dream of the swan is here very much to the point.

last analysis something to be *seen* in a picture, in an intellectual vision, a *theōria;* and is to be expressed and communicated in a story, a myth—which makes us see the point.

Platonic myths are not ways of stating what is hard to say in literal words—they are not allegories. Plato is perfectly capable of stating in precise terms what he wants to state. Plato may be, as in the present fashion, a villain and a reactionary—for us, the terms seem to be identical—but Plato is certainly not a simpleton or an incompetent—when it comes to making words do what he wants them to. Plato's myths are rather ways of making us *see* something; and of expressing and communicating what the seeing does to us. That is, the myths are ways of communicating what the artist sees and feels: myths do not state anything, they do something to us. The function of myths in the dialogues is not expressive but impressive—it is not to express truth, but to impress truth upon us, to impress the point of the story upon us.

A story does not state anything, it makes a point, when told to bring home to us and clinch the conclusion of an argument. The function of Plato's Socratic myths is to make us see the point, as with any good story—much more effectively and impressively than any bald statement of the point could possibly do.

That is, the function of Platonic myths is to provoke an emotional as well as an intellectual response, to make us feel something as well as to make us see something: in Plato's own language, to provoke *erōs* for their objects as well as *nous*—objects which the *Symposium* and the *Phaedrus* ultimately identify. That is, in the language of present-day German philosophizing, the function of Platonic myths is to provoke an existential commitment to one's ultimate concern.

Ideas are the object of that vision—*idea* is literally a

sight word, "something seen"—in the light of which things are *seen* and *felt* to be what they are. This naturally leads Plato to employ the method of the spectacle, the dramatic method.

The contrast in intellectual method between Aristotle and Plato is obvious enough, and will take one pretty far—as far as one will ever want to go in distinguishing "Platonism" from "Aristotelianism." In the end, it did, historically, generate two significantly contrasting theories of knowledge.

◀ XV ▶

Platonic Idealism

PLATONIC idealism has been not only a religious, artistic, and scientific inspiration; it has been not only a poetic intoxication with words, a childlike erection of words into things; it has been not only something that can be formulated clearly and simply into an Aristotelian doctrine of logic, if one insists on demanding a doctrine from the dialogues. Platonic idealism has been more than all these things. Men, revolted by the wrongs and injustices of a sordid and tragic human life, have found in it the promise that, despite all the imperfections of existence, somewhere perfection does have its being. So insistently have they felt the claim of the True, the Beautiful, and the Good—of *to kalon kai agathon*—that for them it has become the real thing, the only Reality; and for this vision of perfection they have lived and died.

For Platonism, or Platonic idealism, is the expression of that spirit that makes men feel, there is something more worthwhile than the squabble of rival political machines for power, and makes them forgo all chances of picking a winner, to vote for the tiny minority that is devoted to that something more worthwhile—that makes them cast a protest vote, as we say. Platonism is the expression of that spirit that makes men, even in the midst of wars and rumors of wars, yet feel certain there is a better way; and makes them proclaim their devotion to the establishment of methods of peace, no matter what the odds, or the personal cost.

Platonism is radical and revolutionary, the enemy of all comfortable philosophies of complacency, and of all cowardly and cynical philosophies of despair. Scornful of the wisdom of experience, of the weight of what has always been, it puts its faith in a rational vision of what is best.

Historically, of course, such idealism has gone farther: it has claimed that perfection is not only the proper goal of human striving and struggle in the imperfect world of men. Somewhere perfection even now has its being, it is rooted in the nature of things, and the whole dialectic of history proves that injustice must and will be overthrown, and a truly classless society will be realized on earth. Or Platonism has even been brash enough to maintain that perfection has produced imperfection; that the God of man's aspirations is not only a worthy and compelling human ideal, but is also the Creator of Heaven and earth and all that in them is, somehow through its Divine Providence controlling the forces of the weary world. Platonism has been what Santayana calls an "inverted physics." Now this is of course, we say in our wisdom, unscientific. That is, it does not seem to be justified by any facts, or verified by sufficient evidence. But it is close to the faiths by which men have lived. And it may be true.

Did Plato believe this? Was he, too, deluded by his own vision of perfection into believing that perfection already exists, and is within the grasp of men? One can only say to this, as to any such question about what Plato really believed, that the schoolmaster of the Academy may have so held. Schoolmasters are only too easily deluded.

But is this to be found in the great dramatic dialogues? Only as myth, as symbol and poetry. The *Timaeus,* where it has been most found, is explicitly stated to be all myth, and written in the "language of probability," the *eikōs logos.* In these dramatic myths in the dialogues, the important point is never whether perfection created imperfection, nor even whether the world can be made perfect by men, by human art. It is always rather, that we mortals, dwellers in an imperfect world, can nevertheless behold the perfect—and that in the light of the more perfect we can discern in imagination, we can discriminate, among the many and diverse imperfections in the midst of which we find ourselves, what is worthwile and real—what is *to ontōs on.* And this seems to be true. It appears to be even a fact. Perhaps only a literal-minded scientist might be tempted to deny it; and then he would be deluded too, far more deluded than the idealist.

Can we say, then, that man's ideals, taken as processes, as Plato takes them, and hence more precisely stated to be the idealizing power of human nature, of "the soul of man," to use Platonic language, are as much so, as much a fact, as anything else in human experience. Men *can* see, in their daily struggles, the promise of a perfection that is not yet, and that surely in their own lifetime they will never behold on earth. Nothing, points out Plato, is seen as it really is, unless it is seen as suggesting something better, its own perfecting. And the perfections of which the imperfect and transitory things are suggestions are the "real things." For Plato's vision, "The excellent becomes the permanent," as Jane Addams, that realistic idealist and Platonist, used to put it.

To say that these perfections are the "real things" is not a statement of warranted fact; it is not a scientific proposition. It is not even a metaphysical theory. It is a conviction of value. They are the real things because they are what is worthwhile, what makes life worth living—indeed, what makes its tragedies supportable.

The practical results of this conviction of value are that the imperfections of existence become intolerable. Men go out and start doing things; they cannot feel easy or rest until they do. They proceed to turn the world upside down, and create a terrible situation, and immense havoc. The world would certainly be much pleasanter and more comfortable if men never had any ideals, and were really content to take things as they come—even though it would be considerably less human. Certainly the non-Platonists— ironically, they call themselves today the "realists," stealing a good traditional Platonic term—would be much happier and less disturbed and upset. It is notoriously men with ideals who cause most of the trouble and disturbance, to themselves and to their fellows. They embrace one, and go out murdering and killing, wrecking homes and cities, forcing it at the point of the bayonet—or the bomber—on those too blind and stupid to accept it as a gift.

Look at the Communists! They beheld an ideal; they were on fire with the vision of a society founded on justice and not on organized injustice, one ordered and planned by intelligence, not wrecked by executive stupidity. They proceeded to turn Russia upside down, with an immense amount of cruelty and suffering and murder. They created terrific problems for themselves, and had to live like slaves trying to solve them. They invited their neighbors to devastating attack, and when they had acquired the strength made them accept their own ideal. They have long kept the

whole world in a turmoil of fear and envy—and all because
they conceived the ideal of a just society.[1]

This, I take it, is the real meaning of the Christian promise, "I come to bring not peace but a sword." That
promise has been fulfilled. Christianity has probably caused
more warfare and suffering than anything else in Western
history. For it brought into the world an absolutely un-
attainable ideal "Be ye perfect, even as your Father in
Heaven is perfect." This is the most dangerous counsel in
the world, to become perfect and to force perfection on
others. Its consequences are worst of all when it is proclaimed by those who are themselves honest and sincere.
We remember the Cromwells, and the Robespierres, and
the Lenins.

In our wisdom, we Americans used to say, in the now
dim past, how much happier the Russians—and the rest of
us—would be, if they only had a Warren Harding to return
them to normalcy, or perhaps a Russian Calvin Coolidge—if
they could only be prosperous and disorderly, and corrupt,
go to the movies, own cars, speculate on Wall Street, and
never have to worry about social justice. Or at least, we
used to admit grudgingly, if they could only keep their dis-
turbing ideal out of their practice, if they could only be
realistic, accept the facts of social life, take human nature
into account, work with what they found, play the game,
and act like any other nation from fairly enlightened self-
interest. And then—when they expelled Trotsky and the
rest of the Russian Platonists, and started doing just that—
we were not quite so sure.

---

[1] I pass over the unhappy results of the American attempts to
bestow the ideal of the "American way of life," "democracy," and
"freedom" on the reluctant and often recalcitrant "underdevel-
oped countries."

Now if one does not feel the insidious appeal of "idealism"—if one does not see how much better it was to have been a Communist in Russia before the first bloom was rubbed off and the Platonist Old Bolsheviks thrown out, then to be a complacent Republican businessman under Calvin Coolidge, or a banker in Eisenhower's cabinet— then I am afraid nothing can be done about it. Platonism is not for him. The only way to reach such hard hearts is to point out how often the miracle happens. The idealists do succeed in getting something done—not all they had hoped for, of course, and never quite what they had intended. But the world does hang on the words of those three great sources of idealistic crusades—Moscow, Peking, and Washington.

For Plato himself, of course, the practical result, that nothing succeeds like Platonism, is only incidental. For him the important point is, we will *know* and *see* what life is only if we see it as more than it actually is—only if we see what is imperfect in fact as perfectible in imagination. Human life is not only tolerable, it is only *intelligible,* if we idealize it. We do not understand what it really is unless we see what it *might* be.

Look at our voters. Have they actually much sense? We know, when we stop to think—especially about the other side—that most of them have not. They have no more political wisdom than you—or I. We know what motives will go into the ballots at the next election.[2] They are, we know in our disillusionment, a mob, swayed largely by passion, prejudice, and ignorant self-interest, a mob which every practical politician knows how to play upon.

But could we go through with the rather frustrating

---

[2] Any "next election"—till philosophers are kings.

business of self-government at all, if we did not see that mob as a "democracy," something to be guarded with eternal vigilance, defended as a cherished possession, ceaselessly improved, and extended to every area of human relations? Could we ever hope to understand what self-government has come to mean to those nations—there are not too many of them—who have had a long-continued experience with it?

Or look at business and the businessman. We all suspect that business efficiency is one of the biggest Platonic myths perpetrated in modern times. Nothing, it often seems to our discouragement, could be more inefficient, wasteful, estravagant, and stupid than the way business is carried on. Yet could our industrial and technological machine plod on for a day, if businessmen saw themselves as their critics say they actually are? No, they must believe in that wise, forceful, energetic, and efficient hero of mythology, whom Carlyle first dubbed the "captain of industry." What would happen to our whole economy, were there no public relations men to remind them, and the rest of us, what businessmen *might* be?

I have, of course, no particular grudge against the businessman. To continue my illustrations of Platonism, what would happen if teachers saw themselves and what they do as they actually are? Or students, even?

Do these examples all mean, then, that Platonism in this wider sense is at bottom fooling yourself? Not exactly— unless all imagination be a form of self-deception. But if one does not like anything of the sort—then one is an Aristotelian, satisfied with seeing things as they actually are. And how, for all our professions of realism, we hate that kind of thing! We Americans especially—we are normally the most confirmed idealists in the world.

Of course, my whole argument so far has been that Plato is not a Platonist in this sense at all, but an Aristotelian, and that he grew more and more so; that from the beginning he could see men through and through. And has not that been the experience of most of us? For the half-century since 1918, we have pretty much all been disillusioned idealists. That is, we were all sophisticated: we saw through it all, nobody could fool us. During the five decades since 1918 young people have been turning up their noses at what I am here calling Platonism, or idealism in this wider sense. It almost began to seem that Platonic idealism had lost its eternal appeal for youth. Everybody knew life for "just what it is." Everybody was hardboiled, in the egg. The young no longer fell in love; they thought in terms of sex-appeal. They no longer talked about the perfect union of two souls, but about erogenous areas. I sometimes suspect I have been so corrupted myself by my sophisticated students that I can no longer bring myself to seem naïve. I am even beginning to wonder whether I have not given an Aristotelian twist to all my illustrations of Platonism. I am afraid I cannot argue for it as persuasively as I once could.3

This decline of Platonic idealism long seemed a pity. For no young person can really afford not to have enjoyed the experience of idealism. It is clearly one of the great, universal human experiences. If it be missing from one's life completely, the gap cuts one off from so much. And, besides, it is highly dangerous. If you can manage to catch it

---

3 At the age of two or three years. A devoted aunt has told me that the first words I ever uttered were: "The Idea!" It was a favorite exclamation of hers; but that "mythos" was clearly sent by Apollo.

young, the chances are you will be able to develop immunity. If you cannot so manage it, you are likely to be swept off your feet by it when it really gets a hold on you. Far worse than being a disillusioned idealist is to be a cynic with illusions. The ranks of Fascist and Nazi Europe were swarming with them.

The changed temper of the sixties, beginning with the civil rights movement, has shown that idealism, like God, is not really dead, but has rather found new incarnations. Idealism is really endemic; we need not fear its demise in America. What is needed is "guideposts" lest it become too virulent, among the liberals and the radical left alike.

We have been talking, of course, about Plato's theory of Ideas. I hope we have managed to suggest, that the theory of Ideas is not merely a technical doctrine of knowledge, as it has so often been turned into, by Platonists from Aristotle down. It is rather an attitude toward life, a pilgrimage of the soul, the life of the poet and the artist, the life of the lover of perfection. The man who has truly assimilated this attitude will look on the actual world, and see in it more than is there. He will see the perfecting it suggests to the imagination—to *nous*. He will look on the processes in society about him, and idealize them, as we say. He will see that for which they exist, what they might become. Starting with any fact, he will be led on, in imagination, to discern its ideal possibilities. In the jargon of modern German Romanticized Platonism, starting with any facts of man's "existence," with any existential facts about "empirical man," he will be led by his phenomenological analysis to their ontological significance for "essential man," for what Plato would call the Idea of man, which he can then proceed to create as his own "nature." For such a man, earth will not be mere earth, earthy, but the suggestion of Heaven; and to that vision of what is of supreme value his soul will mount as to its natural home.

And when he returns to the cave again, to actual human life or human existence, practical men may despise him, and a cynical generation will scoff, accusing him, with the worldly wisdom of our best theologians, of crass perfectionism. For us today, being unrealistic has become the unforgivable sin against the Holy Ghost. But he will have a force and a power that will carry him through the discouragements and even the tragedies of living, and in the right soil, will sweep everything before it, cause ancient empires to totter, and overthrow established economic systems.

No, the theory of Ideas is not a mere doctrine of knowledge. It is a radical gospel, a revolutionary force. For it is a *theōria,* an imaginative vision, and an *erōs,* an ultimate commitment, directed towards the ideal.

Platonic Immortality

Platonic Immortality has been terribly misunderstood.
Take the *Phaedo*, which presents the picture of a man
dying, and dying in such a way that he became "deathless,"
and has ever since been a living force. It is not hard to
imagine what the Christians have done with the *Phaedo*.
Hundreds of foolish sermons have been preached, and
essays written, about it. Socrates might have taught their
authors better, and the great theologians could have carried
the process to completion. From them it is possible to learn
what it really means to be deathless and immortal. They
learned it, in the West, from Plato.

It is really astonishing how much wisdom the really
great theologians have to offer. Our generation is apt to reject all sound theology, of course—it is something medieval
and outgrown. And so on such matters as immortality we
prefer to rely on our practical common sense and our modern up-to-date "scientific" methods. So away, we say, with
all these traditional arguments about immortality. We will
go into the laboratory, we will experiment; we will turn to
extra-sensory perception. And so we bring our pathetic little
faith in the omnipotence of scientific instruments and
methods into the presence of a noble ideal. You can do so

much with such devices; why cannot you use them to conquer death?

So we resort to a spiritualistic medium, and try to get in touch with a departed friend. And when the conversation turns out disappointing, when it proves trivial or rings false, we merely suspect we have got the wrong number, and resolve to try again.

No, whatever it means to be "immortal," it cannot mean *that.* The Church was never wiser than when it set its face against all dabbling in what we call spiritualism. But we are apt to imagine, the *Phaedo* is about some such kind of future life. We ask, did Plato really believe in such a future life, in continued human personal survival after death? Again we must answer, perhaps the Scholarch of the Academy did. According to Aristotle and other more recent scholars, Plato taught in his supposed lectures an extraordinary amount of foolishness. There is plenty of foolishness even in the dialogues. But is that particular brand of folly to be found in the dialogues we still possess?

It is, I judge, difficult for any sensitive and imaginative interpretation of them to maintain. It is true, various demonstrations of the deathlessness of the soul occur, nearly always in connection with the telling of a myth, where a free, poetic employment of Pythagorean material is being used, obviously not with literal intent. The point of the myth, and presumably of the nearby argument as well, is always ethical: we mortals ought so to live that at the end of life we could face a searching Judge. But in the dialogues it is made clear again and again, the Good Life needs no external rewards and punishments. Except in the *Phaedo,* the demonstrations are always rather perfunctory, and obviously fallacious, relying on the same sophistries satirized and refuted elsewhere in the dialogues. It may be significant that the same argument is never repeated. And among scholars there is considerable agreement that Plato himself was perfectly aware they are none of them conclusive.

All the arguments presented amount to showing that it is the nature of "soul" as such to live. Since the Greek word *psyche* that we translate into the Christian tongue as *"anima"* or "soul" means literally and fundamentally "life," the power possessed by living organisms to live, with all that involves,[1] it is hardly surprising that the nature of *psyche* or "soul" should be "to live," or that it should turn out to be a logical contradiction for "life" not to be alive, to be dead. To say, in Greek, that life is deathless or immortal, is thus really a tautology.[2] Hence at best the arguments prove nothing about individual "lives"; they demonstrate only that "life" as such is deathless.

But, if Plato was completely aware of all these obvious facts—and it is hard to conceive a mind so subtle as his not being aware of them—did he nevertheless still believe in the deathlessness of the soul? He believed in immortality, yes. But we rarely stop to ask, What *kind* of immortality is he convinced of? We hit on the word, and it is so easy to conclude, he must have believed in the Apostles' Creed and the Resurrection of the Flesh—or perhaps in some conception of immortality like those of intelligent modernist theologians. The resurrection of the flesh, incidentally, is a belief in fundamental opposition to the Platonic doctrine of the immortality of the soul, however we understand Plato: such "resurrection" would have shocked St. Paul beyond measure, who regarded putting off the flesh as the essence of salva-

---

[1] As Aristotle abundantly shows in his historical survey of Greek conceptions of *psyche,* in Book I, chs. 3–5, of the *De Anima.*

[2] This is obviously another case of what Gilbert Ryle calls a "confusion of categories."

tion. To the orthodox Christian tradition, which has always accepted the doctrine of the Resurrection of the Flesh advocated by Ignatius of Antioch, belief in the "immortality of the soul" has always been, if taken literally, a cardinal heresy.

What, then, was Plato's conception of immortality? In most passages, as in the *Symposium,* the yearning for deathlessness is a longing to "create in the beautiful." In one way only, it is held, can mortal nature become immortal, by *generation:* generation of the body, thus partaking of immortality in one's children and descendants; or generation of the soul, thus procuring a glory and renown immortally renewed in the memory of mankind. But Plato's conviction of the deathlessness of the soul goes deeper than racial continuity or fame. Hence we ask, did Plato "believe in" a future life?

Whatever the opinions of the historical Socrates may have been, it is very difficult to believe that the author of the *Phaedo* held such a view. Here Socrates is about to die. He is trying to offer comfort to his friends by showing them that he is unmoved by death, because death cannot touch him. Why can it not? Because he knows he is going to Heaven? Of course not. What would Socrates possibly do in Heaven? All the interesting people to talk to, all the philosophers, the lovers of Wisdom, are in Hades. You do not have to take my word for it—or even Plato's. Ask Dante: he had been there and knew.

Why is Socrates, both in the *Apology* and the *Phaedo,* so confident of his own deathlessness? Because of the arguments and demonstrations Plato puts into his mouth? Because of the argument from opposites, from reminiscence, that the soul is not a mere harmony of the body, that it is simple? It is clear, Socrates is trying to give his friends what they most want, consolation. He is helping to convince them of that of which they are only too eager to be convinced. The arguments are not to be taken literally: they are all myths and parables. Clearly they are the ground, neither of the conviction of Socrates, nor of the conviction Plato's *Phaedo* impresses on the reader. No, Socrates is sure of immortality, not because he is going to Heaven: he has already *seen* Heaven, the Platonic Heaven that is so real a part, not of death, but of human life and experience. Socrates is deathless, not because knowledge is like remembering, and not because the soul is simple, but because Socrates has *lived* like Socrates, and is *dying* like Socrates. Plato makes us *see* that, inescapably: he has made generation after generation *see* it, so impressively that Socrates is alive today.

The final argument, we may, I trust, judge that Plato wants us to take seriously, if not literally: the argument that the soul "participates" in the Ideal. And it suggests the kind of deathlessness Plato is convinced of—the dialogue makes us *see*, dramatically, just what it means. There are two kinds of thing: the things that "exist," that come into being and pass away; and the things that "are," divine, and irrelevant to time, like the objects of mathematics, and hence eternal—things like Justice, Wisdom, Goodness, and Beauty. The latter are the real things, for the sake of which what exists comes into being. But the ends of human existence do not themselves exist; they *are*. And the soul of man can become *like* them: ideal, divine, irrelevant to temporal events, and non-existent. The soul can participate in the Ideal, the eternal, the non-existent.

Human bodies endowed with life can attain a quality of living, a quality of soul, to which birth and death seem irrelevant episodes: a quality of living or soul intelligible in

terms, not of the physical instrument of living, the body
and its structure, its growth and decay; but of living's time-
less and eternal ends. The existence of human bodies, for a
brief interval in time and space, seems like a transitory and
passing illustration of something which *is* in a wholly
different way. The significance of that illustration is to be
sought, not in the body on which it depends for its existence, but in the vision of the Ideal it achieves. It is not by
having died, but by having so lived, that the soul of man
puts on deathlessness. There are moments of supreme experience, of vision and insight, in which the soul reveals its
total incommensurability with the body which sustains it,
and without which it cannot exist: in the presence of a
Shakespearean sonnet, in hearing Mozart's G minor quin-
tet, in the perfect sympathy of friendship, in the piercing
ecstasy of love. *That* is true immortality! To know the Divine, to become one with the Perfect—what could continued personal survival possibly offer, compared with *that*? A
future life is clearly irrelevant to such immortality.

This conception has entered the religious tradition in
the West as "Life Eternal." All the great poets, theologians,
and mystics have felt that a future life, the many vulgar
pictures of the Hereafter, are irrelevant to such ideal experience. "This is Life Eternal," we read in Holy Writ, in the
words of the Platonic Fourth Gospel. What is? Is it to
twang harps? No, "This is Life Eternal, to know Thee the
only true God." To behold Truth, to gaze on Beauty bare,
to participate in True Being.

But in modern times we have forgotten all that. For a
century and more men have had a new and up-to-date
model of immortality. They have felt that the essential
sting of death lies in its sundering of all human earthly ties
and relationships; and they have proclaimed this "cruel, un-

just, unreasonable." So men have looked forward to meeting once more those they have loved in the Hereafter. They have felt a longing for a purely personal survival to be slightly discreditable. Moderns have made immortality a social matter, as they have made so much else.

Of course, even the literal Heaven of traditional religion was not precisely a place whose chief function was to consummate unrealized earthly romances, and to promote family reunions. It is rather surprising, in fact, that anyone familiar with the actual functioning of the Christian tradition could ever speak of a "longing" or of a "hope" for personal survival, or could ever have concocted our popular myth that men once forsook action in the world to dream of a good time coming. The Hereafter has not been a flight, an escape from the ills of life. It has been the one fact that, struggle as men might, was inescapable. When they have dreamed in the past, Christians have dreamed, not of Heaven, but rather of Hell. No wonder they have dreamed as little as possible about the Hereafter, and have tried to put it out of their lives. In the religious tradition death has meant not the serene entry of the soul into never-ending bliss, but the dread facing of an Omniscent Scrutiny—alone. "It is an awful thing to fall into the hands of the Living God."

No matter! Our literal-minded moderns have changed all that. They look forward to a congenial reunion of loved ones. We turn to Sir Oliver Lodge, the eminent physicist.[3]

[3] Sir Oliver Lodge, *Raymond, or Life and Death* (London, 1916), an account of spiritualistic communications with his son, killed in World War I. Even fifty years later, so responsible a man as Bishop James A. Pike continued to furnish accounts of his communications with his own son, who had also died. *The Other Side* (New York, 1968).

He tells us how his son woke up in Heaven, took out a celestial cigarette and lit the fag, and then went to a celestial breakfast with Aunt Mary, who was looking very well in her new astral body.

Such ideas, seriously and literally maintained, are tragic. No, immortality cannot be a future existence, but is rather a deathless quality of soul, something attainable here and now, in living human experience, if anywhere. For the Greek, immortality was a quality of being. *Athanatos* is an attribute of the gods: they are always "deathless and divine." Justice is deathless, Beauty is deathless, and the soul of man can put on such deathlessness.

Such a conception of immortality—Platonic immortality —makes the poor meager little Heavens of the older popular imagination seem pitifully ridiculous. Consider what that imagination in past centuries did with the idea of a future life, and embodied in its hymns. The saved gather in white robes and with harps, about the celestial throne, lifting their voices in never-ending song. The great poets have done better with an essentially impossible task. Dante is very clear on Hell: he has plenty of materials to work with there. Hell is just like earth. But when he finally gets to Heaven, he can only describe points of pure light in unceasing motion, while the spectators discuss theology. One may doubt whether men want to be points of light. But—to know God: that is another matter.

No one, I judge, can read Plato perceptively, and fail to emerge with the conviction that the notion of a future life, of a hereafter, is a tragic delusion. It is so, not because it is "unscientific," not true. It may be true; when our time comes, we may quite possibly all wake up and find ourselves dead. One may hope this is not so, and not merely because, since one has not precisely lived like Socrates, one may have a strong suspicion of where one would find one-self when the awakening came. And not because such "pie in the sky when we die" has been the opiate of the people, and has set them dreaming instead of revolutionizing the world. Even the strongest souls need dreams, and secular revolutionaries—as the *Republic* long ago made clear—are the greatest dreamers of all.

No, the notion of a future life, however the imagination may try to depict it, is such a pathetic, foolish, unworthy ideal. It is so pettily human, springing from the baser, not the nobler of the two steeds that together with *nous* form the soul of man. Fortunately, for all the theories of the priests who have used the belief to spur men on in their efforts, in their lives men not religious professionals have rarely taken it very seriously. Its only possible value lies in the chance it might promise of attaining real immortality, the only form of immortality worthwhile. And men can find that here and now—like Socrates, who, though he too was mortal, as all men are mortal, and though he died the most famous death in secular history, was nevertheless deathless, and *is* deathless. If one cannot find deathlessness here on earth, why should one hope to find it elsewhere? 4

---

4 In commenting on Platonic Idealism in the wider sense, the reader was warned that Plato is quite capable of turning the sober-est of men into a crusader. Woodbridge helped—see *The Son of Apollo* (Boston, 1929), ch. 6, "Death"; and Bush; as well as Santayana in *Reason in Religion* (New York, 1905), ch. 13, "The Belief in a Future Life," ch. 14, "Ideal Immortality."

◄ XVII ►

Plato's "Later" Philosophy

A COMMENTATOR on Plato the dramatic artist-philosopher, might well like to stop at this point. But, according to the legend, Plato himself did not. He founded an Academy, taught for some twenty years, and during that time wrote little, occupying himself with immature students and with other schools of thought, the opinions of other men. Finally, he had to express himself; and when he did, he found that something had happened. He found himself writing "later dialogues," not mature dialogues. If we accept the nineteenth-century legend that these productions are later in time, something has certainly happened. Plato the dramatist is gone—the Plato that makes us see *theōria,* a vision of life. There is left a figure remarkably like Aristotle, though hardly so imposing or valuable.

These "later" dialogues contain long, prosy, pointless exercises in division, barren and monotonous stretches of logic-chopping. Could the author of the *Republic* and the *Symposium,* we ask, possibly have written these futile exercises? Anybody could! Then, we must add, any Greek; and finally, any Greek who had gotten the point of what the dramatic Plato was trying to make us see.

Whether they were written literally later or not, whether

they were written by Plato, or by Aristotle, or by somebody else, they are certainly different from the dramatic dialogues that bear Plato's name. They all have certain marked characteristics in common. First, there is in them all an atmosphere of controversy, echoes of other long-forgotten opinions. It is hard to discover what the arguing is all about. It is like picking up a modern philosophical review. All this naturally delights the scholar: what do all the allusions mean? Think of the dissertations you can write about the problems! It is hard to write an article about the *Symposium.*

Then again, these dialogues are all dogmatic rather than dramatic. They present a pedagogue expounding his theories, not an artist presenting *theōria;* and he is not so good a teacher as Socrates is. Socrates is not the spokesman, save in the *Philebus,* but there appears rather an "Eleatic Stranger." These dialogues argue for a conclusion; they do not try to make us "see." They are no longer narrated, with sly comments. Their dramatic form consists largely in interruptions of "Yes, stranger," "No, stranger." This is something scholars can understand: there is no irony, no literary art, no imaginative sweep, little not obvious on the surface. This is refreshing and comforting to all who would like to set Plato's "doctrine" down in black and white; it is reassuring to those without much imagination.

Were they written for college students, freshmen in the Academy? Were they written for the imperceptive Athenians, who could not get the point unless it was labeled? with, perhaps, premonitions of future professors of Greek?

The style, that is, is markedly different from that of the Socratic dialogues. But it is not necessary to deny Plato's authorship because of the views they contain. They display not so much a different doctrine, as a bald literal statement of the positions implied in the dramatic clash of opinions, the confrontation of talk with fact, that marks the dramatic dialogues. The unity of Plato's thought is easy to maintain; the unity of his art and method would be much harder. But they are toned down. The enthusiasm is gone: there is no passionate devotion to knowledge, no "love," no *erōs*, no aspiration. Rather is there a mere pointing to the obvious importance of knowing, and to the dangers of a one-sided intellectualism: remember, there are others things also.

Throughout there runs a criticism of other men's theories: in the *Theaetetus,* the *Sophist,* the *Parmenides,* the *Philebus.* Who advanced them? Are these the views of Aristippus and the Cyrenaics? of Antisthenes and the Cynics? of the rather Eleatic Megarians? Or do they reflect discussions in the Academy itself? But these other men are known largely through Plato alone, and he does not tell.

There is great interest in various theories of knowledge, an interest that fails to appear in the dramatic dialogues at all. There, the concern is with what is worth knowing. Here, it lies in, what is knowledge itself? What are its status and problems? In general, the artistic and ethical interest has been supplanted by a logical and metaphysical interest.

This can all be summed up by saying, these later dialogues are all very Aristotelian. So much so, that they might have been written by the young Aristotle, especially by the Platonistic Aristotle to whom Werner Jaeger has called our attention—he is in fundamental agreement with their thought. Just as the *Statesman* and the *Laws* are very close to Aristotle's *Politics,* and the *Philebus* to his *Ethics,* so are the treatment of logic and knowledge in the *Theaetetus* and the *Sophist* close to the *Posterior Analytics.* We can only ask, did Aristotle get all his ideas from Plato? [1] He is supposed to have been studying with Plato at the time these dialogues are supposed to have been written. Did Aristotle, perhaps, even write some or part of them? He may well have: we know he wrote dialogues like them.

Now, running through the dramatic dialogues is an implicit conception of the nature of knowledge, stated by Socrates in terms of simple, homely illustrations, drawn from the arts and crafts. To know a thing is to know its function, what it can do, what it is good for. This functional conception of knowledge is perhaps most clearly stated in the opening of the *Cratylus:*

Socrates. What has the carpenter in view when he makes a shuttle? Is it not something the nature of which is to weave?

Hermogenes. Certainly.

Socrates. Well, then, if the shuttle breaks while he is making it, will he make another with his mind fixed on that which is broken or on that form (*to eidos*) with reference to which he was making the one which he broke?

Hermogenes. On that form, in my opinion.

Socrates. Then we should very properly call that the shuttle itself?

Hermogenes. Yes, I think so.

[1] Friedrich Solmsen would almost say yes. Cf. his unpublished paper, read at the Philadelphia, 1964, meeting of the American Philosophical Association, Eastern Division, "Plato and Aristotle; Continuity of Problems: Change of Emphasis." See also his "Platonic Influences in the Formation of Aristotle's Physical System," in eds. I. Düring and G. E. L. Owen, *Aristotle and Plato in Mid-Fourth Century* (Göteborg, 1960), pp. 213–35; his "Antecedents of Aristotle's Psychology and Scale of Being," in *American Journal of Philology,* LXXXI (1955), 148–64; his "Nature as Craftsman," *Journal of the History of Ideas* XXIV (1963); and his definitive *Aristotle's System of the Physical World* (Ithaca, 1960).

Socrates. Then, whenever he has to make a shuttle for a light or a thick garment, or for one of linen or of wool or of any kind whatsoever, all of them must contain the form (*eidos*) of shuttle, and in each of his products he must embody the nature which is naturally best for each?

Hermogenes. Yes.

Socrates. And the same applies to all other instruments. The artisan must discover the instrument naturally fitted for each purpose and must embody that in the material out of which he makes the instrument, not in accordance with his own will, but in accordance with its nature. He must, it appears, know how to embody in the iron the borer fitted by nature for special use.

Hermogenes. Certainly.

Socrates. And he must embody in the wood the shuttle fitted by nature for each kind of weaving.

Hermogenes. True.

Socrates. For each kind of shuttle is, it appears, fitted by nature for its particular kind of weaving, and the like is true of other instruments. . . .

Socrates. Now who is likely to know whether the proper form of shuttle is embodied in any piece of wood? The carpenter who made it, or the weaver who is to use it?

Hermogenes. Probably the one who is to use it, Socrates.

Socrates. Then who is to use the work of the lyre-maker? Is not he the man who would know best how to superintend the making of the lyre and would also know whether it is well made or not when it is finished?

Hermogenes. Certainly.

Socrates. Who is he?

Hermogenes. The lyre-player.

Socrates. And who would know best about the work of the ship-builder?

Hermogenes. The navigator.

Socrates. And who can best superintend the work of the

lawgiver and judge of it when it is finished, both here and in foreign countries? The user, is it not?

Hermogenes. Yes.[2]

To know, then, is to know a thing's function, its use, its value, its possibilities. To know a shuttle is to know how to weave; to know a ship is to know how to navigate. Generalizing, to know man is to know what man is good for, the Good Life. To know Courage or Justice is to know its function in the Good Life. Knowledge is of ends, functions, "good fors": it is functional and teleological. The highest knowledge is of the highest ends of life. To know these ends or "Ideas" is to know their function in the complete harmony of ends, in the Good towards which all things aim. To see the Good is "to see the best in existence." This is Plato's conception of knowledge, a thoroughly functional point of view, developed by Socrates out of the know-how of the craftsman, the artist. What is the know-how for living well? This is the Socratic search.

Here, in the non-dramatic or schoolmaster dialogues, the concern is with what knowledge is not—with the criticism of other theories. The *Parmenides* opens with the criticism of a "theory of ideas,"[3] a doctrine about knowledge, made out of Plato's distinction of value in what is to be known. By whom was the theory elaborated? By the Megarians, who seem to have talked that way? By Plato's own disciples, the "Platonists" Aristotle talks about, when he is speaking about "we Platonists"?

The discussion begins with the question, What are "Ideas" or "forms"? What is their status? Now if we take

[2] *Cratylus* 389 A–390 C.
[3] *Parmenides* 126–136.

literally the metaphors and myths expressive of the experience of *erōs,* aspiration, we arrive at absurd results. Are
Ideas real things, physical objects, with quantity and dimen-
sions? How then could particular things "partake" of them?
One object cannot partake of another. If the Ideas are "in"
things, how could one object be "in" many objects? If they
are rather "apart from" objects, then they are merely more
things to know. We should then need to know the "idea"
embracing both particular objects and the idea-object, and
so on: we should be in an infinite regress.

Well, then, are Ideas in the mind as "thoughts," *noē-
mata?* This suggestion is "irrational." For Ideas are not
knowledge, parts of knowing, but rather *what* we know
when we are knowing; our thoughts are *of* them. This
view would mean that "everything is made of thoughts."
Interestingly, Plato here impatiently brushes aside the view
we call subjective idealism.

Are Ideas then "in nature, as patterns," *paradeigmata?*
Are they things off in the sky, as in the poetic myths? This
is the popular interpretation. But then again they would be
particular things, and could hardly explain knowledge,
which is not of particular things, but of "all of a kind." So
we would need a further Idea to include the particulars and
the pattern—we would be caught in the regress again.

Above all—and this is offered as the greatest objection to
the Theory of Ideas—if Ideas were real things off in the
sky, they would have nothing to do with knowledge of the
world: they would be quite irrelevant to human knowledge, would have no validity for, would throw no light on,
human affairs. When we want to know navigation, we
want to know how to steer a boat, not something else in the
sky; when we want to know courage, we want to know
how to be excellent in an appropriate way. Any "intelligible

realm" that is not a part, an aspect, of the actual world, is unknowable and futile. Knowledge must be directed, not to a separate intelligible realm, but to the intelligible aspect of *this* world.

Yet—the discussion continues—"Anyone who denies the existence of 'forms' of things, *eidē,* and does not assume a form, an *eidos,* of each individual thing, a form that always remains the same, will utterly destroy the power of talking, *to dialegesthai."* Forms are the conditions of intelligible discourse.

The implications of this acute discussion are, first, that Ideas cannot be "apart from" things, but must be "in" them, as their intelligible aspect; and secondly, that Ideas cannot be "things," but must be the ends or functions of things.

Parmenides asks the young Socrates, Are there Ideas of the Just, the Beautiful, the Good? The reply is, By all means! Are there Ideas of man, or fire, or water? Socrates is rather doubtful. Are there Ideas of mud, hair, dirt, and such worthless things? Certainly not; that would be absurd. Yet Socrates remains a little troubled: "Perhaps what is true of one thing is true of all." In other words, as a *logical* theory, if Ideas are the "forms" of things, then they must be logical universals, and in that case there will have to be ideas of every class. But then they will be located in discourse, they will have a logical status. If Ideas are the ends, possibilities, or uses of things, then there will obviously be no Idea of what has no use or function.

In other words, the clear implication of this whole opening discussion in the *Parmenides* is Aristotle's doctrine of knowledge: "ideas" are forms or universals in discourse, or final causes in processes by nature or by art. Plato has clearly anticipated every one of Aristotle's objections to the "theory of ideas" as the theory of knowledge of the Platonists.

The *Parmenides* dialogue goes on to refute the doctrine of the One, which seems to be Megarian: it is self-contradictory and unintelligible. It is refuted by its own weapon, the Eleatic dialectic. Implied is the claim that Plato is the true follower of Parmenides. This might suggest that the "theory of ideas" so severely castigated is also Megarian. But no two students have ever interpreted the central argument of the *Parmenides* the same way; and this suggests that Plato intended that effect: that was just the kind of philosopher Parmenides was.

The *Theaetetus* offers criticism of a number of theories of knowledge. We have not the slightest idea just who held them. In the dialogue they are associated with the names of Protagoras, Heraclitus, and Parmenides. But our knowledge of those men's theories of knowledge comes largely from the *Theaetetus* itself, and here, in the dialogue, a number of obviously differing and incompatible interpretations of their views are offered; and it is made very clear that the views set forth are *not* what these great men of an earlier age actually meant. Whose views, then, are really being examined? The Cynics? The Cyrenaics? The Pythagoreans? The Schools of Megara and Elis? in other words, Plato's contemporaries, and not the great figures of the preceding generation? Or are they, perhaps, views of students in the Academy (if Plato had an Academy, and if there were students in it)? We can only read the voluminous scholarly literature, and scratch our heads, resolving, perhaps, to concoct a new theory.

The conclusion to the discussion is formally negative: the characters have not been able to state any conclusive answer to the opening question, What is Knowledge really? But they have disposed of a number of impossible answers. The position implied in the successive criticisms is remarkably like Aristotle's. Did Aristotle perhaps write the *Theaetetus?* There is no mention—certainly no explicit mention—of "Ideas" or "Forms." Instead, the dialogue gives an Aristotelian table of predicables. There is the puzzling circumstance, that though Aristotle says the Ideas formed the substance of Plato's later teachings, no reference to them appears in those writings which since the nineteenth century we have decided to call later dialogues.4 "Forms," *eidē,* do of course appear in the *Sophist* and the *Timaeus.*

At the outset of the *Theaetetus,* the question is asked abruptly, What is Knowledge, *epistēmē?* The first answer runs, Knowledge is *aisthēsis,* sensation. This answer is identified with the view of Protagoras, and is taken to imply a picture of What Is like that of Heraclitus, in which Being is motion, becoming, activity. There is developed a view of a world of events in relation, of interactions and functional occurrences, of processes taking place. Everything in this world is "Motion," which is a cooperation between active and passive motions, issuing in new motions, new becomings or events. In this world of motions, sensation will be just such a correlative interaction or cooperation between two motions: it will itself be an event or motion. In seeing, for instance, the motion of "sight" from the eye meets the motion of "whiteness" from the wall; the meeting generates a new event, the eye becomes a seeing eye, and the wall becomes white, but it is the same event. We note that here Aristotle's theory of sensing is clearly stated in detail. Did Plato work it out for him?

This so-called position of Protagoras is developed very

---

4 But see the conclusions of Gilbert Ryle, that Plato in his "later" dialogues had passed beyond and largely abandoned his Theory of "Ideas" or of "Forms," cited in Chapter XX, note 1.

sympathetically. All things, according to it, arise by the intercourse of motions with each other. Nothing exists as "always the same," "itself by itself," *haplōs,* apart from its relations to other motions, but everything is always coming-into-being *for* something else. There is no Being that just *is,* but everything is a "becoming-for." This holds even for universals like "man." There is clearly stated what we moderns should call an objective relativism.

But there are difficulties. How then about dreams and illusions? Are such sensings then knowledge, and true? How can we distinguish between dreaming and waking? merely by the length of time spent?

The answer is, here are two different events, cooperations between different motions. All sensations are true *for* that particular cooperation. The sensations of Socrates well and Socrates ill, of Socrates dreaming and Socrates awake, are all different, but all *valid*—for each is knowledge of a different event. What is is always the specific event. Hence sensation or knowledge of what is, as the same event, is always specific too. Being *is* becoming, and is always *for* or *in relation to* or *of* some other motion. The becoming that is sensation is always an *event-for-me,* always a part of *my* Being. Hence for me my sensation is always true.

There are difficulties. Then a pig's sensing will be true? Yes—for the pig. Why did Protagoras argue and teach, if every man's sensations are always true for him? Then there is the existence of what may be called "objects of ignorance," like hearing a foreign language spoken, getting the sensations clearly, but *understanding* nothing. You have the sensations, but they convey no meaning, bring no knowledge, which seems something more.

At this point there is undertaken a defense of Protagoras. That is not what he really meant. He held, opinions are not "true" or "false," but "better" or "worse." The true is really the good. And there *are* standards of value, of the goodness or healthiness of an opinion, of its normality.

But this lands us in worse difficulties. We can turn the tables easily on Protagoras. Most men believe in a fixed, impersonal truth. If the true is the good, the normal, then majority opinion will always be right. Protagoras will thus be committed to democracy in knowledge, as he is in his political views.

Besides, knowledge is not of sensations, but of what *future* sensations will be. Truth is a matter of prediction and verification, of knowing what other sensations will be had under given circumstances; and here *skill* clearly counts. There *are fixed relations* between sensations, so that what will give most men the sensations they value is a *structure* of sensations to be discovered. It is the *intelligent man* who can discover this structure who is the "measure of all things," not any old man. Here Plato is developing a full functional or instrumentalist theory of knowledge.

Moreover, if the Heraclitean doctrine, that all things are in motion, even sensations, is true, then we have nothing to count upon, and no statements will be possible.

It is clear, knowledge is not just having sensations: it is an intellectual perceiving of their *relations,* a *reasoning* about sensations, a *comparison* of sensations, a *reflection* on sensations. And it can be improved by proper education, whereas mere sensing cannot.

This is Aristotle's view: that knowledge is not mere sensing, but a perception of universals, meanings, implicit in sensations. And Plato builds up an Aristotelian list of common attributes or categories. The soul views directly Being, Non-Being, Likeness, Identity, Plurality, Good, Beautiful. These are not perceived through the sense-organs, like the sensations of sight, hearing, or the like. So the characters make a fresh start, agreeing that

knowledge is not sensation: they offer the second definition: Knowledge is true opinion, *alēthēs doxa*. It is significant, "opinion" is now admitted as a candidate for "knowledge," if rightly understood, and not dismissed as a dis-
tinctly lower form of knowledge, as in the *Republic*. Is
Plato more *empirical?* He is certainly more Aristotelian.
There follows a long discussion of how false opinion is possible, not answered till the *Sophist:* how can we be said
both to know and not to know? The opinions seem to get
interchanged. For the soul is like a wax tablet, on which
impressions are made. These impressions get erased, confused, blurred. Aristotle took over the figure, as did John
Locke with his soul as a *tabula rasa,* with momentous consequences for modern epistemology. It starts with the
Theaetetus. Knowledge, in fact, is like a large bird-cage, in
which the birds in the cage are flying around. They are indeed in our "possession" (*ktēsis*), but we do not "have
them in hand" (*echein*). We often pull the wrong bird
out of the cage: that is false opinion. Here is Aristotle's distinction between actual and potential knowledge: the latter
we possess when we are asleep, but we have actual knowledge only when we are awake and exercising it.

There is difficulty even here. True opinion is not enough
for genuine knowledge, *epistēmē.* For we can be persuaded
by rhetoric—we moderns would say, propaganda—*that* a
thing is so, without knowing *why* it is so. This suggests
Aristotle: to have science, *epistēmē,* we must know not
only the "fact that", *to hoti,* but also the "reason why," *to
dioti.*

So a third definition is proposed: knowledge is true
opinion with the reason why, with *logos,* "*meta logou alēthēs doxa."* This is Aristotle's "Knowledge of the reasoned
fact." But what is this *logos,* this "reason why"? Several

suggestions prove unacceptable. It is not making explicit, for that is implied in every true opinion. It is not analysis into elements, and there follows a long discussion of what we call reductive analysis: such reductive analysis is possible without arriving at any real knowledge. Nor is it a mere combining of names, mere dialectic. And it is not definition, which is indeed necessary for any true opinion, but adds nothing.

This "reason why" or *logos* is actually just what we mean by knowledge or science, *epistēmē*. What can it be? There is implied, when the dialogue breaks off, the development of a theory of reasoning, of what was to be called the "syllogism." We should expect the next step to be an Aristotelian analysis of *apodeixis*, "demonstration."

The *Sophist* purports to be a continuation of the *Theaetetus*, but, judged by all the stylistic tests, it is much later. In it Plato is developing a theory of logic to explain the *logos*, the "reason why," that must be added to "true opinion" to make it "knowledge." The Sophists spoken of and criticized are clearly not the great teachers of the Periclean Age, but somebody else. Just who are they? Are they the later followers of the Eleatics, the dialecticians of the Schools of Megara and Elis, who got all tangled up in words, and who form the background for the meticulous clarification that Aristotle undertakes in Books Zeta and Eta of the *Metaphysics,* which clearly presuppose much confusion among the Greeks as to the precise relations between words and things?

There is now undertaken a serious grappling with the problem of the meaning of "Non-Being," *to mē on.* The Sophist is one who gives false judgments: he says things are what they are not. How on earth can he do it? How can a

thing "not be"? How can a Sophist say what "is not"? Indeed, what does it mean "to be" anything? This is the central problem from which Aristotle's First Philosophy starts,
the context within which his "ontology," or "metaphysics"
—neither term is due to Aristotle himself—has its origin
and relevance.5 It is clear, the ghost of Father Parmenides
was still abroad, and Greeks were still worried by the implications of talking, of the relations of words to things, of
discourse, *logos,* to its subject matter—the problems in
which Books Zeta and Eta of the *Metaphysics* almost bog
down.

The difficulty lies in the Eleatic dogma, *to mē on ouk
esti,* "Non-Being is not." But falsehood is at least a significant opinion: it means something. How can falsehood refer
to what is non-existent? To say a thing which "is not"
seems to put that saying into the class of those things which
"are not"; and this is a "null class": there are no such
things, and no such class. In some sense, then, it seems as
though "Non-Being" *is,* and "Being" *is not.*

"Being," in fact, is just as hard to understand as "Non-
Being." There are many theories of Being: of "what it
means 'to be' anything." This is a statement of the problem
of Aristotle's First Philosophy, the context within which it
appears as a genuine problem. Plato proceeds to consider
it.

The first theory of Being is that of Parmenides, who
says: "What is, is One," and "What is not, is not." But on
analysis these dogmas are discovered to involve a host of

<hr/>

5 "Metaphysics" as the term for Aristotle's First Philosophy comes
from his editor Andronikos of Rhodes, and means "the writings
that come after those on *Physics*" in the order of Andronikos' edition. "Ontology" was invented by Christian Wolff in the eighteenth
century, in contrast to "epistemology," which Wolff also coined.

contradictions. How can this "One" have a name, "Being," different from it? or how can it have another name, "One"? If "what is" is really "One," you cannot *say* anything about it, you can only point, or gulp. No talking or thinking would then seem to be possible. Yet the Greeks obviously talked.

Again, for Parmenides, the "One" which *is* clearly has parts: he says: "All are equally distant from the center." But a unified whole which has parts is clearly different from the "One Itself." In fact, there is a *gigantomachia*, a "Battle of Giants," because of this disagreement about What Is.

The second theory of Being is that of the partisans of body, the materialists. This is the only reference to the Atomists and Democritus in the dialogues, and neither his name nor that of the school is mentioned. These men hold, "to be" means "to be body," *sōma,* something visible and tangible. But they admit there is such a thing as a "living body," a *sōma empsychon,* a body endowed with *psyche,* life. And one life is just, another unjust, one wise, another foolish, etc. And the materialists agree, Justice and Wisdom are themselves not bodies: hence they admit that some Being is non-bodily.

What, then, do what is bodily and what is non-bodily both alike possess, that leads us to say they both *are?* The answer given states what, one judges, must be the starting-point of any sound ontology or theory of Being:

Eleatic Stranger. I suggest that everything which possesses any *power* (*dynamis*) of any kind, either to produce a change in anything of any nature or to be affected even in the least degree by the slightest cause, though it be only on one occasion, every such thing *really is* (*pan touto ontōs einai*). For I set up as a definition to define the "things that are" (*ta onta*) that they are nothing else than "power" (*dynamis*). . . .

We set up as a satisfactory sort of definition of the "things that are" (*ta onta*) the presence of the power to act or be acted upon in even the slightest degree (*hē tou paschein ē dran kai pros to smikrotaton dynamis*).⁶

The third theory of Being is that of "The Friends of the Forms," *hoi tōn eidōn philoi*. Presumably these are the Pythagoreans, though they are not so mentioned. They say, " 'To be' means 'to be a Form.' " But there *is* such a thing as *knowing*, else there could be no knowledge of the Forms. And knowing is an activity, a process, a *kinēsis;* while what is known, sameness of character, or Form, is not an activity, a *kinēsis,* but is at rest, *stasis.*

We have now found three classes, Activity, Rest, and Being. These classes mingle with each other, so that we can say, "Activity *is* Being," "Rest *is* Being," But "Activity *is not* Rest"; so some classes mingle, while others do not. There must be an art of the correct mingling of classes, an art of what came to be called logic, of what you can say and what you cannot say. For the mingling takes place in *logos,* in discourse or talk. "Is" and "is not" have a meaning only in talk, in *logos.* "To be" unites what is said with that about which it is said, it unites what in Latin came to be called "predicate" with "subject"—while "to be not" separates them. Neither in itself implies either existence or non-existence. "Activity *is* Being," and "Activity is *other than* Rest." In fact, everything that "is" something *"is not"* all the other things it is not. So "to be" something involves "not being" all the others—in Latin, involves a host of negative determinations. To say, "Grass *is* green," implies, "Grass *is not* red, yellow, or blue."

⁶ *Sophist* 247 D, E; 248 C.

Hence Non-Being *is,* for "to be not" does not mean, "not to be at all," not to exist. It means, "to be other than," "to be different from." Non-Being, *to mē on,* thus turns out to be really a determinate class of Being, "being other than." This is that aspect of anything by which it is distinguished from other things.

We are now, says Plato, in a position to answer our original question, "How can false opinion *be?*" "False opinion" is opinion that is "other than" what is. It is clearly a wrong mingling of classes. And it asks for the formulation of an art of right mingling of classes. And thus the *Sophist* ends with the demand for an Aristotelian organon or tool of Analytics—what came to be called logic.

Thus the puzzles of Parmenides, Zeno, Melissos, and the Megarians about words, about what you can say and what you cannot say, about predication, were solved by Plato's developing a theory of logical distinctions, obviously a crying need in that Greek intellectual atmosphere.

⸙ XVIII ⸙

Plato's Mathematical Cosmology:
His "Unwritten Philosophy"

THE "later" Plato was interested not only in the nature of knowledge and logic; he was concerned also with
the foundations of mathematics, and with a mathematical
philosophy of nature, or cosmology. We encounter the surprising statement of Aristotle: "Plato in most respects
agreed with the Pythagoreans." He made a few changes:
Ideas or Forms are all numbers; and "The numbers are the
cause of Being in everything else." [1] This view is not in the
dialogues at all—it is in Aristotle: and it is supplemented by
remarks in his commentators. And in Aristotle himself it is
mixed up with his criticisms of the "Platonists" who taught
in the Academy after Plato's death, and who clearly did re-
lapse into Pythagorean views. To be sure, certain of the
"later dialogues," notably the *Philebus* and the *Timaeus,* do
suggest a concern with, and a background of, a theory of
mathematics and a mathematical theory of Being.

These Aristotelian references, together with the suggestions in the *Philebus* and the *Timaeus,* have been exploited

[1] See evidence in O. Toeplitz, *Quellen und Studien zur Geschichte der Mathematik, Astronomie, und Physik* (1929), Part B,
i.1, p. 19.

238

and worked over by much recent Platonic scholarship, beginning with Léon Robin's *La Théorie Platonicienne des Idées et des Nombres d'après Aristote* (1908), and John Burnet's *Greek Philosophy, Part I: Thales to Plato* (1914). This scholarship has concerned itself largely with trying to reconstruct the philosophy Plato is supposed to have taught, but would never put into writing. It is a fascinating game— and an interesting, if insoluble, problem.[2]

None of the scholars in English—Burnet, Taylor, Ross, Whitehead, Demos—has been too successful at this game. The most successful seem to have been certain historians of Greek mathematics writing in German, O. Toeplitz and S. Luria,[3] who have shown how Aristotle's remarks make sense if Plato is viewed against the background of the development of Greek mathematics, as dealing with the crucial problems of the mathematical science of that time.

Plato took mathematics very seriously: it was the one real science he could find in the Greece of his day.[4] It was the great bulwark, if not the actual basis, of his cardinal distinction between Being and Becoming. The mathematical side of his thinking is to be understood only in the con-

[2] On this theme, see Harold Cherniss, *Aristotle's Criticism of Plato and the Academy* (Baltimore, 1944); W. D. Ross, *Plato's Theory of Ideas* (Oxford, 1951; 2d ed., 1953); H. J. Kraemer, *Arete bei Platon und Aristoteles* (Abhandlungen der Heidelberger Akademie der Wissenschaften, 1959); K. Gayser, *Platons ungeschriebene Philosophie* (Stuttgart, 1963).

[3] Toeplitz, pp. 3–33. See F. S. C. Northrop, "The Mathematical Background and Content of Greek Philosophy," in *Philosophical Essays for Alfred North Whitehead* (Boston, 1936), pp. 1–40. See also S. Luria, "Die Infinitesimal Theorie der Antiken Atomisten," *Quellen und Studien, etc.,* Part B., Vol. II, pp. 106–85; H. Hasse and H. Scholz, *Die Grundlägenkrisis der Griechischen Mathematik* (Berlin, 1928), especially Supplement, pp. 34–72.

[4] The medical school of Hippocrates made little impression on Plato, though it of course formed the background of Aristotle.

text of the contemporary problems and their solutions in Greek mathematics. Plato's philosophy of mathematics is interesting; but it is of importance chiefly in the history of Greek mathematics. For Plato's mathematical philosophy did not enter into the later Platonic tradition. The problems to which it was an answer were forgotten, and the mathematical side of the *Timaeus* was misunderstood. For Plato's pupil, Eudoxus, discovered the General Theory of Proportions, which forms Book V of the compilation we know as "Euclid," and became the basis of subsequent Greek mathematics. Eudoxus solved the problem of incommensurability; and he solved it in such a way as to make impossible not only Plato's theory of the foundations of mathematics, but also any reduction of geometry to arithmetic, of the continuous to the discrete—to make impossible any form of atomism, whether that of Democritus, or that of Plato's "Ideal Numbers." Aristotle realized this scientific fact: "Democritus and Plato are forced to affirm what mathematics has since denied." [5] Thereafter, Greek mathematics made any type of atomism "unscientific."

Eudoxus' discovery, by emphasizing the irreducible and infinitely divisible continuum of nature, made quality prior to quantity, as the only basis of differentiation. It forced Aristotle to develop his qualitative physics and logic. Hence it was knowledge rather than ignorance of the mathematics of his day that supported Aristotle in all his characteristic positions. In other words, Aristotle was a better mathematician than Plato—at least, a better Greek mathematician—because he came after and not before Eudoxus. Plato's mathematics was dismissed as a half-way house on the road to Eudoxus. So it is no great loss that Plato's philosophy of

[5] *De Generatione et Corruptione* 325b25; *De Caelo* 303a20; 306 a27.

mathematics was not written out, but only very sketchily reported by Aristotle.

Aristotle tells us Plato taught:

1. Numbers are distinct from sensible things; they are objects of *nous*.

2. Besides sensible objects, and Ideas or Forms, there is an "intermediate class," *ta mathēmatika*, eternal and unchanging. But of them there are "many alike," while Ideas are all unique.

3. There are "Ideal Numbers," which, unlike ordinary or mathematical numbers, are "unaddible"; that is, they are not aggregates. These Ideal Numbers are identical with the Ideas or Forms themselves.

4. The Ideas are the "causes" of everything else. Hence the number series is derived from the "One"—which is not a number but an Idea—by participation of the "great-and-small," the "indeterminate two" or dyad.[6]

What does this mean? The history of Greek mathematics throws light on the problems to which these views were an answer. The Pythagoreans early discovered numerical harmony and "proportion," or "ratio," *logos*. This convinced them that numerical relations could be found everywhere. The science of the observed continuous extension of things, geometry, could thus be reduced to the science of numbers and their ratios, arithmetic.

The discovery of incommensurable magnitudes came hence as a great shock to the Pythagoreans: here there was no numerical ratio or *logos*. Henceforth, men must deal with two kinds of magnitude: those with numerical ratios, the "rational" magnitudes; and those without ratio, and

---

[6] See W. D. Ross, *Plato's Theory of Ideas* (Oxford, 1953), ch. 10, "Aristotle's Account of Plato's Earlier Doctrine"; ch. 15, "The Ideas and the Ideal Numbers."

hence "irrational," the objects of science and *nous,* and the objects of the senses. The rational magnitudes form the "real world" of individual units or numbers, with exact ratios; the "irrational" magnitudes, the "world of the senses," with its infinite divisibility, incommensurability, and absence of ratios.

Democritus, who had an elaborate atomistic theory of mathematics, recognized this distinction between the two classes of magnitudes as that between the "real world" of rational atoms or "Ideas," [7] which are numerical units, and the "bastard" continuum of the senses. The same distinction appears in Plato as that between "the class of the Limit, . . . which by introducing number makes opposites commensurable and proportional," and "the class of the Unlimited," the indeterminate continuum, divisible without limit, the "more-or-less," the "indeterminate magnitude" or dyad.

What was needed was a theory of mathematics that could embrace both these kinds of magnitude, the commensurable and the incommensurable. Now the moderns gained a unified theory of geometry and arithmetic by generalizing the notion of number, introducing "irrational numbers." The Greeks accomplished the same unification by generalizing the notion of ratio or proportion, introducing "non-numerical ratios." They thus made ratio more fundamental than number, which the Greeks always limited to the so-called natural numbers. This unification was accomplished by Eudoxus, in his General Theory of Proportions or ratios, which embraced both commensurable and incommensurable magnitudes.

This is the context of Plato's problem in his philosophy

---

[7] The word "Idea" seems to have been invented by Democritus as the name for his indivisibles or "atoms." See Luria, pp. 106–85.

of mathematics. How did he try to solve it? I shall here report a fairly plausible interpretation of the evidence, for what it may be worth; this is an illustration of such speculation when it is more fruitful. I should hate to have to set forth an instance of such speculation at its most dubious.

Plato's unaddible Ideal Numbers, more basic than mathematical numbers, and identical with Ideas or Forms, which generate the mathematical numbers, are really *ultimate ratios* or *logoi*. Unfortunately, Plato put them on an atomic basis: he made them the ratios of the sides of the ultimate triangles he took as the constitutive elements of the world. That is, Plato denied infinite divisibility, a view made impossible soon thereafter by Eudoxus' more adequate Theory of Ratios.

Theaetetus, Plato's pupil, and inventor of solid geometry, had demonstrated that there are only five regular solids, which he correlated with the five elements of the sense world. But these elements—earth, air, fire, and water (the fifth was the whole cosmos)—pass into each other, and hence are clearly not ultimate. So the regular solids cannot be ultimate elements either. The *Timaeus*, pushing this mathematical atomism, analyzes the solids into four "elemental" or "atomic" triangles. These ultimate triangles are the "elemental" *mathēmatika* or "intermediaries" Aristotle mentions, the "many alike." [8] These triangles are combined to produce the solids or sense elements we experience. Solid geometry thus gave a comprehensive mathematical theory of the Cosmos. The triangles served as atomic elements, joined in the regular solids as molecules. Now the sides of the elemental triangles are incommensurable, and are definable only in terms of ratios or *logoi*, the ultimate

[8] *Metaphysics* I 987b15, 992b15.

Ideas not expressible in terms of mathematical numbers.

This was Plato's way of making the ratios of incommensurables more basic than numbers. These ultimate ratios or Ideas, when they "mix" with the "more-or-less," or "indeterminate magnitude," generate the atomic triangles, which are thus "mixed," "intermediate," *ta mathēmatika*. Then the triangles "cut the boundless" again, giving rise to the mathematical number series, in the "mixed world" of "the mathematicals."

The ultimate ratios, because they are Ideas generating the mathematical numbers, Plato called "Ideal Numbers," though they are really ratios. Because they are all interrelated, as a whole he called them *"the One,"* the system of ultimate ratios—of Forms. Plato thus used irrationals—that is, non-numerical ratios—to define the rational or natural numbers.

Plato is thus made to appear as the first to generalize the notion of ratio—to bring commensurable and incommensurable magnitudes into a common theory. On this interpretation, the "Idea" of fire, e.g., is not a general term or universal for sensed fire. It is rather the proportion of ratios or Ideal Numbers defining the *tetrahedron,* the "mathematical" of sensed fire: that is, it is the formal structure or formula of sensed fire—its equation, a modern might put it. In just the same sense, for Spinoza the "idea" of the circle is "$a^2 + b^2 = R^2$." Plato shared the same mathematical vision of the world as Spinoza, based on the same unification of numbers and geometry. In Spinoza's case, this unification was effected in Descartes' analytic geometry. Plato would have understood Spinoza's vision.

According to legend and rumor, all this elaborate mathematical cosmology was set forth in Plato's famous "Lecture on the Good," which he never, never would write out. It is reported in the Aristotelian commentators: Plato held

that "The *Archai* of all things are the One and Indeterminate Magnitude, or the 'more-or-less.' "9 He was setting
forth a mathematical theory. But more: "Many attended
the lecture under the impression that they would obtain
some of the human goods, such as riches, health, power, or
above all a wonderful blissfulness. But when the exposition
began with mathematics, numbers, geometry, and astronomy, and the thesis: 'The class of the Limit taken as One is
the Good,' the surprise became general. A part lost interest
in the subject, the others criticized him." 10

This identification of "the Good" with "the One," as the
first principles of mathematics, is not in the dialogues at all.
What could it mean? I could start with the conviction that
is there: "What gives knowledge is Good," and deliver a
pretty fair "Lecture on the Good" myself, bringing in: "If a
man is to be happy and blessed," he must go on from the
study of arithmetic, geometry, solid geometry, to astronomy, "for then will be revealed a single bond of Nature
binding all these together." But I shall refrain. We have
gotten far enough away from the dialogues as it is. I shall
leave the "Lecture on the Good" to Whitehead, who has
written it out.11

We can only set the "approach to the Good through
Mathematics" side by side with the "approach to the Good
through Discourse" and the "approach through Love," as
the schoolmaster's addition to the work and insight of the
artist. At least, there is suggested the same process of unification, toward a unified "science of the Good."

In certain other passages, Aristotle seems to say, not that

9 See Toeplitz' excellent marshaling of the sources, I, 19.

10 See *Ibid.*, pp. 18–27; quotation from p. 13.

11 "Mathematics and the Good," in Paul A. Schilpp, ed., *The
Philosophy of Alfred North Whitehead* (Evanston, 1941), pp. 666–
81.

Plato identified Ideas with the ultimate ratios of mathematics, but that he assigned numbers to all Ideas. Aristotle tells: In his "Lectures on Philosophy," Plato said, *"Nous* is One, Knowledge is Two, Opinion is Three, Sensation Four. Justice is Ten." Had Plato succumbed completely to Pythagoreanism? In any event, it is no wonder Aristotle complained: "Philosophy has become mathematics for our present-day thinkers, though they profess that mathematics is only to be studied as a means to some other end." [12]

[12] *Metaphysics* I 992a30.

Plato's Ethical Cosmology:
The Timaeus

D ID Plato teach what Santayana has called an "inverted physics," that the Good is the scientific cause of the world? Did he do so in any other sense than the purely mathematical sense attributed to him by Aristotle and his commentators, in which "the Good" is the name for the ultimate system of ratios at the basis of the mathematical structure of the world—its formal cause or equation, as it were? This would make Plato's "Idea of the Good" very much like Spinoza's "God or Nature," and would suggest a similar mathematical vision of the cosmos.

The *Timaeus* has been so read; and it has been read more widely and more continuously than any other of Plato's writings. It has been clearly the most influential of all the dialogues, the only one never "lost" in the West, the only one read in Latin, in an incomplete version translated by Cicero and Chalcidius, throughout the Middle Ages until the fifteenth century. The *Timaeus* is what "Plato" meant in the Western tradition, till the Renaissance, and what he meant for many even till the nineteenth century. It has been the source of the whole Western current of rational theology, of the "Great Chain of Being" idea. Hence the *Timaeus* is of tremendous historical importance for the whole culture of the Western world.

The entire dialogue takes the form of a long myth or story, put into the mouth of a Pythagorean cosmologist. That is, the *Timaeus* myth is drawn from the same sources as all the other materials Plato uses in his imaginative stories. At first, only Aristotle took it literally—he would! The *Timaeus* is a magnificent creation myth. It describes how God made the world. But of course for Plato no creation in time ever took place. Hence this account is obviously not intended to be taken literally; it is offered as "a likely story," as *eikōs logos.* The tradition held, for Plato cosmology is an appropriate subject matter for myth, not for science, since it deals with Becoming, not with Being.

Timaeus of Locris, a Pythagorean astronomer, describes the creation of the world, in what is called "the likely language" of probability—or poetry. He does so with eloquent, moving, and exalted passages. The world is the work of *Nous,* fashioned by the supreme *Dēmiourgos,* the Supreme Craftsman, the Supreme Artist or Maker, *Poiētēs.*

Now God is good, so he had to make the world as like himself as possible, good and perfect.

Let us now state for what reason Becoming and this universe were framed by him who framed them. He was good; and in the good no jealousy in any matter can ever arise. So, being devoid of jealousy, he desired that all things should be, so far as possible, like unto himself. That this is the supremely valid principle of Becoming and of the order of the world, we shall most surely be right to accept from men of intelligence. Desiring, then, that all things should be good and, so far as might be, nothing imperfect, the god took over all that is visible, and seeing that it was not at rest but in a state of discordant and unordered motion, he brought it from disorder into order, deeming that order was in every way better.

Now it was not, nor can it ever be, permitted that the work of the Supremely Good should be anything but that which is best. Taking thought, therefore, he found that among things that are by nature visible, no work that is without *nous* will ever be better than one that has *nous*, when each is taken as a whole, and moreover that *nous* cannot be present in anything apart from life (*psychē*). In virtue of this reasoning, when he framed the universe, he fashioned *nous* within life and life within body, to the end that the work he accomplished might be by nature most excellent and most good. Thus then we must declare that according to the likely account (*kata logon ton eikota*) this world came into existence through the god's providence, in very truth a living creature (*zōon empsychon*) endowed with life and *nous*.[1]

God created a rational, intelligible order out of formlessness, out of "chaos." It was not a creation *ex nihilo*, but rather a Greek ordering, a "making out of." Hence the world has made a rational, living being, or *empsychon*, with a World *Psychē*, a World "Life," round and smooth. In making this World Life, the Supreme Craftsman and Artist took some of that Being "that is ever in the Same state," and some of that Being "that is divisible and 'becomes' in bodies," and mixed them together into a third form of Being composed of both. Likewise he fashioned a compound of "the Same" that is indivisible and of "the Same" that is divisible in bodies, and another compound of "the Other" that is indivisible and of "the Other" that is divisible. Then he took these two compounds of "the Same" and "the Other," and mixed them together into Being, following a complicated Pythagorean mathematical formula. He made the threefold mixture into a long band, slit it down the middle, bent the two halves around to form the circles of the Zodiac and the Celestial Equator.

[1] *Timaeus* 29 E–30 C.

Then the Craftsman made Time, "a moving likeness of eternity."

When the Father who had begotten it saw it in motion and alive, a thing of joy to the eternal gods, he too rejoiced, and being well pleased he took thought to make it yet more like its pattern. So as that pattern is the Living Being forever existent (*zōon aidion on*), he sought to make this universe, so far as he could, of a like kind. But inasmuch as the nature of the Living Creature was eternal, and this character it was impossible to confer in full completeness upon what is generated, he took thought to make, as it were, a moving likeness of eternity; and as he set in order the heaven, of that eternity that abides in unity he made an eternal likeness, moving according to number, even that which we have named Time. . . . Time, which imitates eternity and circles round according to number.[2]

The Craftsman made the planets and their motions, and the stars, and the heavenly race of gods who indwell them as their *psychai*. He addressed these created gods, the planets and the stars, and bade them in turn fashion the three kinds of mortal creatures:

The winged kind which traverses the air, all that dwells in the water, and all that goes on foot on the dry land. . . .

There are yet left mortal creatures of three kinds that have not yet been brought into being. If these be not born, the heaven will be imperfect; for it will not contain within itself all the kinds of living being, as it must if it is to be perfect and complete [the Great Chain of Being idea]. But if I myself gave them birth and life, they would be made equal unto gods. In order then that mortal things may exist, and that this World-all may be truly all, do ye turn yourselves according to your own nature to the work of fashioning these living crea-

[2] *Timaeus* 37 C, D, E.

tures, imitating my power in generating you. Now so much of them as it is proper to call "deathless," the part we call divine which rules supreme in those who are fain to follow justice always and yourselves, that part, having sown it as seed and made a beginning, I will hand over to you. For the rest, do you, weaving together the mortal with the immortal, thereby fashion and generate living beings; bring them to birth, feed them, and cause them to grow; and when they fail receive them back again.[3]

So the Craftsman left the generation of man to the created gods, he himself supplying the immortal part of the soul, which he made out of what was left over from the mixture of "the Same" and "the Other" and Being out of which he had already made the World "Soul" or Life. In their work of creation, the created gods—the stars and planets—acted always for the best: they were guided by final causes or ends. They made the liver for prophecy, the hair to give shade against the heat of the sun, the eyes in front, to see where one was going, and not in the back, where one could see only where one had been. The "soul" was given a seat in the head, lest it be disturbed by the emotions in the lower part of the body.

But in this work of artistic creation, *Nous* was limited by the materials it had to work with, limited by Necessity, which resists *Nous* and is not wholly amenable to its persuasion.

Now our foregoing discourse has set forth the works wrought by the craftsmanship of *Nous;* but we must also furnish an account of what comes into being through Necessity (*di' anangkēs*). For in truth this cosmos was generated as a compound, from the combination of Necessity and *Nous. Nous*

---

[3] *Timaeus* 40 A; 41 B, C, D.

overruled Necessity by persuading her to guide the greater part of the things that become toward what is best. In that way and on that principle this universe was fashioned in the beginning by the victory of reasonable persuasion over Necessity. Wherefore if we are really to tell how it came into being on this principle, we must bring in also the Errant Cause—in what way its nature is to cause motion.4

The world is obviously imperfect, it contains evil. *Nous* is not completely free: it needs materials to work with, but is limited by them. There follows a long analysis of these materials, with which *Nous* has to work, based, as has already been pointed out, on Theaetetus' discovery of the five regular solids, compounded out of elementary triangles. Thus Fire is pyramids, tetrahedra, since it is sharp and cuts; earth is cubes, capable of forming a compact mass, etc. This is a mathematical atomism, Pythagorean and not Democritean in background; and as such, proved enormously influential down through the seventeenth century. It made possible and stimulated the development of a mathematical science of nature, and a mechanistic biology.

Now, Timaeus goes on, there must be something— "some Form"—"in which" the stream of fluctuating qualities of experience, earth air, fire, and water, make their transient appearance, like fleeting images in a mirror, and in which these geometrical structures underlying them are embodied. This Form is "the Receptacle," *hē hypodochē,* or "Place," which is, "as it were, the nurse of all Becoming." This Form is later called "Space," *Chōra,* which is everlasting and not admitting of destruction, providing a situation for all things that come into being.

Now the argument seems to compel us to try to bring to light and state in words a Form difficult and obscure. What

4 Timaeus 47 E–48 A.

nature must we then conceive it to possess, and what part does it play? This above all: that it should be the Receptacle (*hē hypodochē*) and as it were the nurse of all Becoming. . . .

It must be called always the same, for it never departs at all from its own character; it is always receiving all things, and nowhere and in nowise does it assume any shape that is like any of the things that enter it. Its nature is to be there as a moulding-stuff for everything, being changed and diversified by the things that enter it; through their presence it appears different at different times. The things that enter and depart are copies of the eternal things, being stamped from them in a fashion marvelous and hard to describe. . . .

For the present then we must conceive three kinds of thing: that *which* Becomes, that *in which* it Becomes, and that *from which* what Becomes is copied and produced. Indeed, we may fittingly compare the Recipient to the Mother, that *From Which* it is received to the Father, and the Nature that arises between them to the Offspring. Furthermore, we must observe that if the stamped copy is to assume diverse appearances of all sorts, that in which the impress comes to be situated cannot have been duly made ready unless it is in itself free from all those characters it is to receive from elsewhere. For if it were like any one of the things that come in upon it, then when things of a contrary or entirely different nature came, in receiving them it would reproduce them badly, through obtruding its own features alongside. Hence that which is to receive in itself all Kinds must be devoid of all forms: just like the base which the makers of scented ointments skilfully contrive to start with: they make the liquids that are to receive the scents as odorless as possible . . . ; Wherefore the Mother and Receptacle of what has come to be visible and otherwise sensible must not be called earth or air or fire or water, not any of their compounds or components; rather, if we describe her as a Form invisible and without character, all-receptive, and partaking in some very puzzling way of the intelligible, we shall describe her truly. . . .

This third Kind is Space (*Chōra*), which is everlasting and admits not of destruction; providing a situation for all things that come into being, but itself apprehended without the senses by a sort of bastard reasoning, and hardly an object of belief. This indeed is what we look upon as in a dream and say that it is somehow necessary that anything that is must needs be in some place (*topos*) and occupy some space (*chōra*), and that what is not somewhere on earth or in Heaven is nothing.5

This "Receptacle" is a notion close to Aristotle's generalized "First Matter" or *prōtē hylē*. But it is identified by Whitehead, who grew wildly enthusiastic over the *Timaeus,* with the "Space-Time" of modern physical theory. Whitehead was followed in this by A. E. Taylor in his large commentary. Historically, it is the ancestor of the notion of "Space" as an empty and receptive container, maintained throughout the long Platonic tradition—in Newton's "Absolute Space," for instance. This is the "Platonic" notion of Space. Just so is the Time which is a "moving likeness of Eternity," moving and circling around according to number, and in its movement "measured by number," the ancestor of that notion of Time which itself "flows and moves," and is measured by the "motion" of the stars— Newton's "Absolute Time"—this is the notion of Time always maintained by the Platonistic tradition: it is the "Platonic" notion of Time. These are the conceptions of Space and Time consecrated for classical modern physics by Isaac Newton, made eternal "Forms of Sensibility" by Kant, and since abandoned for the more relativistic conceptions of Aristotle and Leibniz.

What is the meaning of this *Timaeus* myth? Just what is Plato's point? Traditionally the myth has been taken as a cosmology, a theory of Nature, and as such has had a long and fruitful history, down to Whitehead in our own day. It is taken by Whitehead as a perfect example of "the philoso-

5 *Timaeus* 49 A, B; 50 B, C; 50 C, D, E, 51 A; 52 B.

phy of Nature," in contrast to "natural science," i.e., as a statement of the fundamental notions which any science of nature must illustrate with its own particular and determinate conceptions—a statement of the notions underlying *any* mathematical physics.

Whatever else it may be, the *Timaeus* myth is certainly not science, though down through the ages it has served as a tremendous stimulus to scientific speculation. Whatever else it may suggest, it is clearly a superb myth, made, like its companion myth of Atlantis in the *Critias*, out of Orphic and Pythagorean symbols.

The Divine *Nous* or Mind, a harmonious order, in mathematical expression, is immersed in obstinate and recalcitrant materials. The excellence of the world consists in resembling *Nous* as much as possible. The human *nous* is part of the cosmic, World *Nous*. Hence men should strive to become as like as possible to the Good, by participating in the Reason of things. The *Timaeus* myth is thus very close to Aristotle's theology, as expressed in Book Lambda of the *Metaphysics*—the Unmoved Mover is a form of the same myth, rationalized in its meaning and in the argument for it, though not in its language, which remains Plato's "likely language" of poetry and symbol.

The point of the myth can be stated: the striving for Perfection is the source of all order in the world, and in man's life; it is hampered by imperfect but existent "facts." The "Idea of the Good" means an intelligible, rational order, itself indifferent to that striving towards it. This is what Arthur O. Lovejoy called "Self-Sufficing Perfection," like that of Aristotle's Unmoved Mover. To this idea, the *Timaeus* adds the idea of what Lovejoy called "Self-Transcending Fecundity." The point is, the possibility, within natural limits, of approaching Perfection. The myth is a superb statement of the prime Platonic conviction: the world is perfectible, and he who sees the possibility in *the-ōria* must strive to perfect it and thus perfect himself.

As regards the most sovereign form of life in us, *nous,* we must conceive that heaven has given it to each man as a guiding daemon—that part which we say dwells in the summit of our body and lifts us from earth toward our kindred in the heavens, like a plant whose roots are not in the earth but on high. And we speak most truly; for it is to the heavens, whence the soul first came to birth, that the divine part of us attaches our head or root and keeps the whole body upright.

Whoso then indulges in lusts or contentions and spends all his pains upon them, must of necessity be filled with thoughts that are wholly mortal, and so far as that is possible he cannot fall short of becoming mortal altogether, since he has nourished the growth of his mortal part. But if his heart has been set on the love of learning and true wisdom, and he has exercised that part of himself above all, he is surely bound to have thoughts immortal and divine, if he shall lay hold upon the truth, nor can he fail to possess immortality in the fullest measure that human nature admits: and inasmuch as he is forever tending his divine part and duly magnifying that guardian daemon who dwells with him in good estate, he must needs possess supreme well-being. Now there is but one way of caring for anything, namely, to give it the nourishment and exercise proper to it. The motions akin to the divine part in us are the thoughts and revolutions of the universe. These therefore every man should follow, and correcting those revolutions in the head that were deranged at birth, by learning to know the harmonies and revolutions of the world, he should bring the part that thinks, in accordance with its original nature, into the likeness of that which thought discerns, and thereby attain finally to that goal of life which the gods set before mankind as best, both for this present time and for the time to come.[6]

[6] *Timaeus* 90 A, B, C, D.

Epilogue: Plato and the Tradition
of "Platonism"

IN this volume Plato has been approached and read as an intelligent, educated modern reader, familiar with the Greek background of the Western philosophical tradition in modern times, would approach, read, and understand the dialogues. Such a reader would be accustomed to come at literary masterpieces with some sense of the discernment and discrimination they demand, and with some skill in applying to them a perceptive and imaginative interpretation of their riches of ambiguity and irony.

Such a reader would have the critical acumen to realize that the dramatic, Socratic dialogues, including the *Republic*, cannot be read and understood in just the same way in which we would want to, and would indeed have to, read and understand Aristotle's *Physics* or *Ethics*, or Kant's *Critiques*. The dramatic dialogues cannot be adequately considered as straightforward, philosophical treatises, in which every scrap of discussion is to be viewed as the literal expression of their author's views. Plato's own philosophy— the "conclusions" of the author of the dialogues—cannot be justly identified with the opinions put into the mouth of Socrates, which the latter is then made to expound. Nor can we pull portions of the long discussion out of their dramatic context and setting, and then label those selected portions as Plato's views on a given theme, as many eminent scholars who have edited volumes of selections from Plato have often done. The Sixth and Seventh Books of the *Republic,* for example, can hardly be taken as setting forth Plato's own theory of knowledge in its entirety. This would be to forget the place of that discussion in a long and extremely ironical treatment of "Justice Itself"—and in a treatment of those Athenians who approached Justice in such simplicity and innocence. It would leave unintelligible the sharp criticism of a theory of Ideas as a theory of knowledge that appears prominently in the opening section of the *Parmenides.*

To be sure, Plato usually finds congenial the views he puts into the mouth of his central character, Socrates. In a few cases, like the *Protagoras,* in which his sympathies seem to lie rather with the ideas of Protagoras the Sophist than with the malicious teasing of Protagoras indulged in by Socrates, Plato seems to be using Socrates for his own dramatic purposes rather than agreeing with him. But this does not mean that Socrates is ever the mere mouthpiece of the author's own views—of Plato's own philosophy. That philosophy is presented as much richer than the statements Socrates makes.

Thus Socrates is often made to expound what a later tradition came to call a philosophy of "Platonism." That "Platonism" Plato himself views very sympathetically, it is true. Yet by all his dramatic devices, by the very carefully planned structure of the dialogue as a whole—Plato is a consummate hand at such skill—by his confrontation of Socrates with other characters of differing views, by his many layers of Platonic irony, by his revealing myths, introduced to clinch his central point, Plato presents that "Platonism" to the reader's gaze, holds it up, exhibits it in its dramatic context, with all its ironical implications, and critically evaluates it, by a kind of criticism which Hegel called "dialectical," and which we moderns usually call "contextual."

It is not here being denied that "Platonism" is a central strand in the Socratic dialogues.[1] It is there far too deeply

[1] The position taken here on Plato's "Platonism," that is, what is more technically known as his "Theory of Forms," differs somewhat from that recently maintained by Gilbert Ryle. Both the writer and Ryle consider this "Platonism," or the "Theory of Forms," as an important strand in Plato's total philosophy, but as by no means the whole of it, or its very substance. It is here maintained that even in the Socratic dialogues of Plato's "middle" period, the Theory of Forms was put by Plato in its context in human experience by the dramatic methods Plato used in those dialogues. Ryle takes this "Platonism" or Theory of Forms as *absent* from the earlier dialogues, which he considers purely "eristic": "It is in the dialogues immediately succeeding the last of the dialectical dialogues that we *first hear* of the famous Theory of Forms. Here for the first time we find Plato putting forward a positive philosophical doctrine." Ryle, article "Plato," in *Encyclopedia of Philosophy*, ed. Paul Edwards (New York, 1967), VI, 320. Ryle takes this "Platonism" also as *absent* or at least minimized in the so-called "later" dialogues. That is, we ourselves are here maintaining the *unity* of Plato's thought, though by no means any unity of his method and scheme of exposition. Ryle emphasizes rather what he calls "Plato's progress" in getting beyond the Theory of Forms in the later dialogues.

Ryle himself writes: "Historians of thought and commentators are apt to speak as if the Theory of Forms was the whole of Plato's thinking. It was indeed of great importance, but it has to be remembered not only that the theory is unthought of in the elenctic dialogues [the early ones] and is either ignored or criticized in the late dialogues; but also that during the very heyday of the theory, from the *Symposium* to the *Timaeus*, the page space given to the theory is only a small fraction of all that Plato uses. In the *Phaedo*, which seems to have been the source of most of Aristotle's ideas of the theory, the theory is employed as providing only one interwoven to make any such contention plausible. But the core at least of such Platonism is an equally central strand in the thought of the sober and unimaginative Aristotle. In his writings it underlies the layer of what we moderns are apt to consider the distinctively Aristotelian strain in Aristotle. The point emphasized in interpreting Plato's philosophy in this present volume might well be put in these terms. Whereas Aristotle introduces his own contextual criticism of the Platonism he took over from Plato and retained, through the explicit statement of the results of viewing that Platonism in its broader context in human experience, Plato himself brings in his own version of contextual criticism, of what we are calling Aristotelianism, rather through the dramatic interplay of character and confrontation, assisted by the employment of all the dramatic devices he knew so skillfully how to use. This addition of Aristotelianism to Platonism, this expression of contextual criticism, is a viewing of the Ideal in the context of what Aristotle calls the world of Nature we actually see. The difference between the two thinkers is that Aristotle is quite explicit in stating in words the results of supplementing the vision of the Ideal with "what we see," *orōmen*. Plato through his drama makes us actually *see* it. Aristotle is wedded to his own method of using literal words, to a logical method. Plato, it is here contended, is emphasizing, in the Socratic dialogues at least, his own dramatic method. Aristotle is the logician of the Life of Reason, Plato is the dramatist of that life. But both are equally philosophers.

What the literal-minded Aristotle is criticizing in the

---

or two among several disparate reasons for believing in the immortality of the soul. In six of the ten books of the *Republic* nothing is said about the Forms. *'Platonism' was never the whole of Plato's thought and for much of his life was not even a part of it"* (p. 321; emphasis mine).

many criticisms of the Platonism he finds in the dialogues, is really this *method* of Plato's. He rejects Plato's refusal to put into explicit words what Plato the dramatist prefers to make us see, through his consummate literary skill. And Aristotle is in one sense right in criticizing Plato's method: his words can make much more precise what we see in the world of man and nature about us. That is, after all, what words are good for. But there have always been those who have received more philosophic suggestion and stimulus from Plato, the dramatist who makes us see, and makes us think still farther.

Aristotle, we are told, was studying with Plato during the time Plato was writing not dramatic but later dialogues. In these Plato was much more explicit in putting his own views into words.[2] In them he largely forsakes his earlier dramatic method for a logical method much closer to Aristotle's own. Thus, if we accept the chronology, Plato himself grew more and more explicitly Aristotelian in method. And Aristotle, in his many criticisms of the Platonism without stated context of the early Socratic dialogues, was actually defending the later against the earlier Plato.[3]

The later tradition stemming from Plato came to concentrate on Plato's Platonism,[4] and failed, since it at first

[2] Compare the *Philebus* with the earlier Socratic treatment of the *aretai*, in the *Charmides*, the *Lysis*, the *Protagoras*, or the *Republic*. Or compare the *Statesman* with the *Republic*, to say nothing of the *Laws*.

[3] And it may be he was defending Plato himself against the exclusive emphasis on the strand of Platonism of his immediate successors in the Academy, Speusippos and Xenocrates, Aristotle's fellow-students, who do seem to have taken the Platonism of Plato in pretty pure form, without supplying, as Plato's own dramatic skill did, an Aristotelian context for it.

[4] See A. E. Taylor, *Platonism and its Influence* (New York, 1924). The classic study is Heinrich von Stein, *Geschichte des Platonismus* (Göttingen, 1862–75).

emphasized religious vision, and later the vision of a mathematical realm, to see and give due weight also to Plato's Aristotelianism or contextualism. That is why German scholars of the Romantic era, able to approach Plato once more with imagination, invented the term "Neo-Platonism" [5] to distinguish this rather single-minded concentration on the "Platonism" of Plato from the much more extensive riches of insight exhibited in the Platonic dialogues themselves. There were thus left two different traditions that appealed to Plato; to them, as Whitehead put it, subsequent philosophic thinking in the West has been largely a series of footnotes. There was first what we may call the Platonic tradition, deriving from a direct and perceptive reading of the dialogues themselves. And there was secondly what we may denominate the Platonistic tradition, stemming from Plotinus' analysis and systematization of the strand of Platonism to be found, indeed, in Plato's writings.

Both Platonism and Neo-Platonism have been of immense philosophical significance. The latter has undoubtedly been the more influential in the West. It appeals to and supports strong intellectual impulses, while the former calls for more critical acumen, and firsthand appreciation of the dialogues themselves in all their complexity and ironic subtlety. Yet again and again men brought up in the Platonistic tradition have turned to the dialogues and read them afresh. With a certain shock they have rediscovered Plato, whose own philosophy is so much broader than his strain of Platonism on which the tradition had concentrated. In every tradition to which men have been committed, a re-

[5] Popularized by Hegel and by Zeller, it appeared first in English in 1831.

newed examination of the text of the original gospel is sure to bring a further revelation.

This is hardly the place in which to try to set forth the fascinating record of the later history of either the Platonic or the Platonistic traditions. One final word may, however, be in order. Most recent writing in English on Plato stands in what has here been distinguished as the Platonistic tradition. It has tended to construe Plato's philosophy in something of the systematic and literal minded spirit that Plotinus brought to his interpretation, even when it breaks from the details of that version. The present little volume has tried to focus on what, to repeated reading and reflection, the dialogues themselves reveal, with all their wealth of irony and of dramatic suggestiveness. It has endeavored to see and share that vision of human life and its setting which the dramatist of the Life of Reason is trying to make the reader for whom he was actually writing see. It attempts to get behind the long Platonistic tradition and approach, and to recapture that *theoria* Plato was presenting to his audience of sophisticated and perceptive Athenians— to his lay audience of intellectuals. The dialogues hold the mirror up to such readers, and reveal to them what they themselves are. Even today, they can still reveal us to ourselves. If we will but read them closely and attentively, we shall find in them the humanity of man.

Plato the man may elude most attempts to discover what he himself as a citizen of ancient Athens may have been like, and what he actually felt and did during his lifetime. But Plato the philosopher-poet surely reveals himself in the Socratic dialogues as the dramatist of the Life of Reason.

INDEX

Abelard, 45
Academy, 1, 11, 22-23
Acton, Lord, 184n.
Addams, Jane, 203
Aegina, 22
Aeschines, 25
Aeschylus, 3
Aesthetic experience, philosophy of,
    140-41
Agathon, 107, 129-31
Age of Anxiety, 45; of Reason, 45
Akmē, 10
Alcibiades, 49, 91, 118, 121, 129,
    167, 196
Alexandrian period, 37
Alleyne, S. F., 14
America, 150
American constitution, 179
Americans, 147
Analytics, 237
Anarchism, 180
Anaxagoras, 63, 123
Anaximander, 62
Anaximines, 62
Andronikos of Rhodes, 234n.
Annikeris, 22
Anthesteria, 58
Antigone, 143
Antigone, 46, 48
Antiphon, 90
Antisthenes, 157, 222
Anytus, 105, 112 ff.
Aphrodites, the two, 130
Apollo, 208n.; birthday of, 18
Apollodorus, 10-11
Apology, 214
Apostles' Creed, 213
Archelaus of Macedon, 117
Archimedes, 50, 66
Archytas, 26

Aretai in Plato, 154-55
Aretē, 21, 84; in Plato, 152-53,
    155-56
Aristippus, 25, 222
Aristocles (Plato's name), 18
Aristodemus, 26, 130
Aristophanes, 98, 130-31
Aristotelianism, 207-8
Aristotle, 4, 11, 23, 26, 31, 33,
    38, 123, 135, 141, 143-45, 158,
    165, 172-74, 200, 212-13, 221-
    23, 227, 229, 231-34, 238, 241,
    243, 245-46, 254, 255, 257;
    criticism of Theory of Ideas,
    197 9¥n.; debt to Plato, 222-23
Art, 42; in Plato, 145n.
Artistic attitude in Greece, 146-47
Artistic experience, philosophy of,
    135, 140-41, 146-47
Asceticism, ethics of, 151
Athanasius, 44
Atheism, 186-87
Athenaeus, 26
Athenian ideal, 165, 171, 182-83
Athens, 81
Atlantis, myth of, 255
Atomism, 235, 240, 242n.
Atomism, Plato's mathematical,
    243-44, 252
Audience of Plato, 103, 120-21
Augustine, St., 44, 136
Augustinian Platonism, 136, 193

Bacon, Francis, 4, 6
Balfour, A. J., 89
Barth, Karl, 44
"Battle of Giants," 235
Beautiful, the, 231
Being, 231; problem of, in Sophist,

Being (*Continued*)
234-37; definition of, in *Sophist,*
235-36; in *Timaeus,* 249
Benn, A. W., 83
Benthamite position, 173
Bias of Priene, 70
Birdcage, in *Theaetetus,* 232
Boas, George, 9
Bolsheviks, 206
Bradley, F. H., 78
British political sense, 179
Buchanan, Emerson, 28
Buddhism, 156
Burke, Edmund, 82
Burnet, John, 15-16, 30, 66, 69,
74, 94, 172, 239
Bush, Wendell T., 188, 219n.

Callicles, 90-91, 115, 118-20, 124
Calvin, John, 15, 44
Capitalism, American liberal, 149
Cardini, M. T., 64n.
Carlyle, Thomas, 207
Cave Myth, in *Republic,* 167
Cephalus, 196
Chalcidius, 247
Charmides, 17
Charmides, 154, 261n.
Cherniss, Harold, 9, 11, 23, 239n.
Chōra (space), 253-54
Christian Church, 149, 212
Christianity, 147, 156, 193, 205,
217
Christian theology, 122, 136, 193
Chronology of dialogues, 34-35
Cicero, 247
Cleisthenes, 82
Clement of Alexandria, 44
Communism, 149, 170, 180
Communists, 167; as idealists, 204-
6
Coolidge, Calvin, 205-6
Control, 50-51
Copernicus, 66, 194
Cornford, F. M., 57-58
Cratylus, 13, 19
Cratylus, 127, 223-25

Critias, 17
Critias, 255
Criticism, contextual, 259-60
Cromwell, O., 205
Cronos, 184
Cynics, 157
Cyrenaics, 222

Daimons, 184
Dante, 136, 148, 214, 218
Dates of Plato's life, 10
De Anima, 213n.
Definitions, 87, 105, 110
Delphic oracle, 100
Demeter, 59
Demiurge (*Dēmiourgos*), 192, 248-
49
Democracy and the Good Life, 157-
58
Democracy of laws, 184, 186
Democrats, 180
Democritus, 63, 69, 80, 124, 235,
240, 242, 252
Demonstration, 233
Demos, Raphael, 16, 239
Descartes, 137, 244
Dewey, John, 45, 48, 54, 73, 133,
135-36
Dialectic, 3-4
Dialektikos, autos ho (the Absolute
Talker), 2
Diasia, 58
Diels, Hermann, 69, 74
Diogenes the Cynic, 21
Diogenes Laertius, 6, 11, 27, 30, 88
Dion, 21, 23, 25-26, 124
Dionysian cult, 60-62, 65, 73
Dionysius the Elder, 21, 23-26
Dionysius the Younger, 24-25, 28
Dionysus, 60, 67, 184; festival of,
42
Diotima, 116, 129, 131-32
Döring, August, 95
Doxa (opinion), 4
Duns Scotus, 45
Düring, I., 223n.
Durkheim, Émile, 57

Dyad, indeterminate, 241-42, 244-45

Early Greek Philosophy, 39-40, 57, 62-79, 80-81
Ecstasy, 60
Edelstein, Ludwig, 9, 28
Education, 2-3, 25; Greek, 83, 87-88; Plato's philosophy of, 158-60
Edwards, Paul, 7, 83, 97, 259
Einstein, Albert, 124, 137
Eisenhower, D. D., 266
Eleatic school, 56, 78-79, 86; Megarians, 222; dialectic, 228; dogma, 234
Eleatic Stranger, 221, 235-36; in Statesman, 176-77
Eleusinian mysteries, 59
Eliot, T. S., 194
Empedocles, 63, 111
Epaminondas, 183
Epicharmus, 19
Epimetheus, 107
Epinomis, 32
Epistēmē (true knowledge), 4
Epistemology, 125-26, 141, 189
Epistles, Platonic, 8 ff., 10, 23, 28
Er, myth of, 156, 163-65
Erasmus, Desiderius, 96
Erōs (love), 62, 139n., 143, 199
Eryximachus, 130
Ethics, Christian, 168
Ethics, Nicomachean, 51, 53, 176, 222
Euclid, 134, 240
Euclides of Megara, 20
Eudoxus, 174, 240, 242-43
Euripides, 3, 41, 57, 143
Euthydemus, 127
Euthyphro, 59, 154
Existentialism, 51
Existential knowledge, 139n., 154, 199

Faguet, Émile, 124-25
False opinion, 234, 237

Fascism, 209
Fate (moira), 58
Faust, 127
Festivals, Athenian, 58
Ficino, Marsilio, 18
Forms, in Sophist, 229, 236; in Timaeus, 229
Forms, Friends of, theory of Being, in Sophist, 236
Frank, Erich, 64
Freedom and consent, 179, 181-82, 184-85
Frege, G., 138
French civilization, 170
Freud, S., 57
Freudianism, 122
Friedländer, Paul, 14
Friendship, Idea of, in Lysis, 144-45
Future life, 212-14, 218-19

Galileo, 137, 194
Galton, Sir Francis, 4
Gayser, K., 239n.
Geometry, 66
German philosophy, 199
Gigon, O., 95
Glaucon, 90
Gods, 88; in Timaeus, 250-51
Goethe, Johann Wolfgang von, 127
Good, Idea of the, 139, 153, 156, 163, 166, 231, 255-56
Good, Lecture on the, 244-45
Good Life, 45, 46, 49, 115-16, 120-21, 137, 147, 172-73, 188, 225; Greek view of, 151-53; in Plato, 153-58; in Philebus, 173-76
Goodwin, Alfred, 14
Gorgias of Leontini, 87, 110-13, 115, 131; on teaching, in Meno, 110-13
Gorgias, 104, 115-21, 157, 192
Gospels, 167
Great Chain of Being, 247, 250
Greece, historic, 36; of the documents, 36-40
Greek civilization, 146
Greeks and Hebrews, contrast, 44

Greek tools of reflection, 40
Grote, George, 27, 83
Guardian soldiers, in *Republic,* 168
Guthrie, W. K. C., 64, 69, 74

Hamartia (sin) in Plato, 152
Hamlet, 101
Harding, Warren G., 205
Harrison, Jane, 57
Hasse, H., 239n.
H-bombs, 154
Hebrews, 44, 147
Hedonism, ethics of, 151
Hegel, Georg Wilhelm Friedrich, 45, 72, 79, 98, 259, 262
Heidegger, M., 45
Hekataios, 70
Helladics, 57
Hellenism, triumph of, 43
Hellenistic civilization, 37
Heraclitus, 19, 63, 67-74, 228-29; position, in *Theaetetus,* 229, 231
Hereafter, the, 217-18
Heresy, in *Laws,* 186-87
Hermes, 108
Hermogenes, 223-25
Hero of Alexandria, 50
Hesiod, 13, 37, 70
Hippias, 81, 90, 104, 110
Hippias Major, 90
Hippias Minor, 90
Hippocrates, 55, 62, 84, 104-5, 158, 239n.
Homer, 13, 37, 71
Humanism and humility, tempers of, 44-47
Hybris, sin of, 59-60
Hypodochē, hē (the Receptacle), 252-54

Ibsen, Henrik, 129
ICBMs, 154
Ictinus, 152
Ideal, the, 142-43
Idealism, Platonic, 201-10, 219n.
Idealism, social, Plato on, 166-67
Ideal numbers, 240-41, 243

Ideal state, 2
Ideals, nature of, 203-4, 206, 209
Ideas, in Plato, 62, 65, 142, 188, 193, 195-200, 209; in *Parmenides,* 225-28; as logical universals, 227
Identity, 231
Ignatius of Antioch, 214
Immortality, Platonic, 214-16, 218-19
Immortality of soul, 192; in Plato, 211 ff.; modern conceptions of, 213, 216-17; as goal of *Timaeus,* 256
Imperialism, economic, 183
Incommensurability, 240-44
Infinity, 42
Injustice, in *Gorgias,* 117-18, 120
Intellectual, the talker, 2, 4-5
Intelligence, 46-49, 51
Intelligibility, 78-79
Ion, 126
Irrationalism, 51
Irrational numbers, 241-42, 244
Isocrates, 7, 25

Jaeger, Werner, 39, 222
Jesus of Nazareth, 93, 126
Job, 43-44
Joël, Karl, 95
John, St., the Evangelist, 136
Jowett, Benjamin, 2, 84, 91
Judaism, 156
Judgment, Last, 62, 64
Jung, Carl, 57
Justice, as principle of organization, 154-56, 161, 163
Justice: in *Republic,* 161-63, 165-66, 196; in *Statesman,* 177-78, 180; in *Laws,* 182

Kant, I., 124, 254, 257
Kepler, J., 66, 137, 194
Kierkegaard, S., 44
Kings, philosophers as, 2, 148, 162, 177, 179-80, 184, 186
Kinsey, A. C., 128

Kipling, age of, 81
Kirk, G. S., 69, 74
Knowledge, functional conception of, 138-39, 147, 153; in *Cratylus*, 223-25; in *Parmenides*, 227-28
Knowledge, Plato's interest in, in Socratic dialogues, 137-43, 153
Knowledge, Plato's interest in nature of, in later dialogues, 222, 228-33; in *Theaetetus:* knowledge as sensation, 229-31; as true opinion, 232-33; as true opinion with reason why, 232-33
"Know Thyself," 166
Kraemer, H. J., 239n.
Kranz, Walther, 69
Kristeller, P. O., 145

Labourites, 180
Laches, 154-55
Lady Watchers of the Bed, in *Laws*, 185
Language, Greek, 56
Lassalle, Ferdinand, 73
"Later" dialogues, Ryle on, 259n.
"Later" dialogues, traits of, 172-73, 176-77, 180-81, 220-23, 261
Law: in *Laws*, 184-86; in *Statesman*, 179-80
Laws, 29, 126, 165, 172, 176, 180-87, 222, 261
Lecture on the Good, 244-45; in Whitehead, 245
Legalism, ethics of, 151
Leibniz, Gottfried Wilhelm von, 254
Lenin, Nikolai, 205
Letters of Plato, 8, 9, 27-29; Seventh Letter, 9-10, 28-29
Leuctra, battle of, 183
Life (*psyche*), World, in *Timaeus*, 249
Life as human achievement, 41-42, 59
Life Eternal, 216
Life of Reason, 141

Likely language, in *Timaeus*, 248, 255
Likeness, 231
Limit, class of, 242
Lincoln, Abraham, 148; myth of, 98
Lippmann, Walter, 181
Living creatures, creation of, 250-51
Locke, John, 232
Lodge, Sir Oliver, 217
Logic, 79
Logic, art of, suggested in *Theaetetus* and *Sophist*, 233, 236-37
Logical Positivists, 133
Logos, 69, 140
Love (*erōs*), 3, 127-32
Lovejoy, Arthur O., 255
Lucretius, 186, 194
Luria, S., 239, 242n.
Lutoslawski, W., 34-35, 39
Lysis, 30, 144, 151, 261n.

Machiavelli, N., 92
Madison Avenue, 177
Maine, Sir Henry Sumner, 38
Malebranche, N., 136
Man, creation of, 251
Mann, Thomas, 127
Mantinaea, battle of, 183
Marathon, 37
Marriage, institution of, in *Laws*, 185
Marx, Karl, 167
Materialists, theory of Being, in *Sophist*, 235
Materials, need for in Good Life, 156
Mathematical theory of Being, Plato's, 238-40, 247; in *Philebus*, 174-76
"Mathematicals," 241, 243-44
Mathematics, Aristotle and, 240, 246; Greek, 239-43; Democritus' philosophy of, 242
Mathematics, Plato's philosophy of, 24-41, 243-45

Mathēmatika, ta (teachable things), 114-15, 159-60

McKeon, Richard P., 40

Mean, doctrine of the, in *Philebus,* 174; in *Statesman,* 178

Megarians, 222, 225, 228, 233, 237

Melissos, 237

Menexenus, 46

Meno, 87, 104, 110-15, 191-92

Meredith, George, 73

Metaphysics, Plato's, 234-35

Metaphysics, 39, 42, 189, 234n.

Metempsychosis, 65

Methexis (participation), 62, 65

Method of Aristotle, logical, 144, 198, 200

Method of Plato, dramatic, in Socratic dialogues, 144-45, 195, 197-200, 257-61, 263

Method of Plato, logical, in later dialogues, 261, 261n.

Middle Ages, spirit of, 187

Mill, John Stuart, 90, 109, 124, 173

Mixed life, in *Philebus,* 156, 173-76

Moira (fate), 58

Mondolfo, R., 69

Morality human, 59

Moscow, 206

Mozart, W. A., 216

Murray, Sir Gilbert, 30, 37, 57

Music, 66

Mysteries, 56-59, 81

Mysticism, 79

Myths, 56, 58, 62; function of, in Plato, 199-200, 203; of Last Judgment, 212; *Timaeus* as, 248, 254-56; point of, 255-56

Natorp, Paul, 16, 137

Nature (*physis*), 42, 68-69, 73, 79; and art, 42; and law, 86, 88, 90, 110; Law of, in *Gorgias,* 119

Nazis, 171, 209

Necessity, in *Timaeus,* 251-52

Neo-Platonism, 193, 262-63

Neo-Pythagoreanism, 64-65

Newton, Isaac, 137, 254

Nietzsche, Friedrich Wilhelm, 61, 156

Nietzschean ideas of Callicles, in *Gorgias,* 91, 115

Nocturnal synod, in *Laws,* 186

Non-Being, 231, 233-34, 236-37

Northrop, F. S. C., 239n.

Nous, 48-49, 51-54, 63, 65, 78; as imaginative vision, 1; and *theōria,* 134, 139, 141, 143; in *Timaeus,* 248-49, 251-52, 255-56

Numbers, 66-67; and Ideas, 238, 241, 246; Ideal, 240, 243; as ultimate ratios, 243-44

Ockham, William of, 45

Odysseus, 164

Oedipus the King, 152

Olympian gods, 56-59, 61, 81

One, the, 244-45; as the Good, 245

Openness of mind, Greek, 40-41

Oriental religions, 193

Origen, 44

Orpheus, 66

Orphism, 57, 61-62, 64, 73, 79, 192; tradition, 65; mythology, 163; beliefs, 192

Osiris, 60

Owen, G. E. L., 223n.

Oxford Union, 82

Parmenides, 56, 63, 68, 74-79, 227-28, 234-35, 237; theory of Being, in *Sophist,* 234-35

Parmenides, 39, 74, 189, 194, 222, 225, 227-28, 258

Parthenon, 143, 152

Participation (*methexis*), 62, 65

Pascal, Blaise, 44

Pater, Walter, 140

Paul, Saint, 44, 213

Pausanias, 130

Peano, G., 138

Peisistratus, 61

Index

Peking, 206
Peloponnesian war, 46, 170, 183
Perfect city: in *Statesman*, 177; in *Laws*, 181
Perfect city, in *Republic*, 162, 165; possibility, 162; desirability, 162-63; 171
Perfection, striving for, 255
Pericles, 45, 88, 113; Funeral Oration, 46, 52
Perry, R. B., 73
Persian wars, 82
Phaedo, 14, 120, 123, 127, 157, 173, 190-91, 196, 211-15, 259
Phaedrus, in *Symposium*, 130
Phaedrus, 155, 190-92, 196, 199; myth, 155, 196
Pheidias, 152
Philebus, 67, 138, 156, 172-76, 178, 221-22, 238, 261n.
Phrygian rites, 60
Physis (nature), 68-69, 79; and *technē* (art), 42
Pico della Mirandola, 197
Pike, Bishop James A., 217n.
Place (*topos*), 252
Plato: the historic, 1, 6-17; as poet, 3, 19, 38, 52-54, 102, 127, 257; romance of his life, 7, 17-27; method of writing life of, 11-14; modern lives of, 14-17; reported travels, 20 ff.; no systematic doctrine, 122-23; as artist-philosopher, 122, 127, 133-36; not metaphysician, 123; dream of Swan, 123, 198; and truth, 123-24, 144-45; not logician, 124-25, 137-38; not epistemologist, 125-26, 141; not social reformer, 126
Platonic Academy in Florence, 18
Platonic corpus of writings, 30-35
Platonic *Epistles*, 8 ff.
Platonic idealism, 208, 219n.
Platonic myths, 199
"Platonism," 63-65, 126, 133, 141, 143, 150, 190-94, 198n., 202,

205-9, 258-63; in Aristotle, 260; history of, 261-63
Platonists, school of, 7, 238
Pleasure, in *Philebus*, 173-76
Plotinus, 139, 262-63
Plumptre, E. H., 47
Plurality, 231
Poetry, in Plato, 145n., 150
Polis (city-state), concerns of, 81-82
Politics, Greek, 52, 55
Politics, Plato's philosophy of, 147, 149-50
Politics, of Aristotle, 53, 222
Pollis, 22
Polus of Agrigentum, 115, 117-18
Popper, Karl, 149
Posterior Analytics, 222
Predicables, in *Theaetetus*, 229, 231
Priestcraft, 186
Principia Mathematica, of Whitehead and Russell, 138
Privileged class, 157
Prodicus, 85, 87; in *Protagoras*, 104 ff., 110
Prohibition, 182
Prometheus, 47-48, 107
Property, private, in *Laws*, 185
Prophets, Hebrew, 167
Proportions, Eudoxus' theory of, 240, 242-43
Protagoras, 85, 87 ff., 148-49, 154, 55, 159-60, 162, 173, 228-31
Protagoras, 39, 104-10, 127, 148, 258, 261n.; political art, in, 104-6, 108-9; the two logoi, in, 106-7, 109; myth of Prometheus and Epimetheus, 107; art of measuring pleasure, in, 109-10
Protagoras' position, in *Theaetetus*, 229-31
Providence, 184, 186
Prussia, 149; military bureaucracy, 170
Psychē (life), 213; *Psychē*, World (World Life), 249
Psychology, Greek, 50-51

Purification, 60, 62, 65
Pythagoras, 63-65, 70
Pythagoreanism, 62-67, 74-75, 192, 246, 249, 252; mythology, 163; element in Plato, 174, 212, 238, 240
Pythagoreans, 63, 65, 160, 192, 238, 241

Randall, J. H., Jr., 51n., 195n.; dream of, 136
Ratios, 241-44
Raven, J. E., 69, 74
Reason, Life of, 3, 5, 53, 263
Receptacle (*hé hypodochē*), 252-54
Religion, Greek, 52, 55-57
Religion, state, in *Laws*, 186-87
Reminiscence, doctrine of, 62, 64
Reminiscence, myth of: in *Meno*, 112, 191-92; in *Phaedo*, 191; in *Phaedrus*, 190-91
Renaissance, 136, 159, 194
Republic, 23-24, 28-29, 54, 66, 124, 126-27, 129, 138, 145, 148, 150, 153, 156, 161, 163-68, 170-72, 177-78, 180-81, 183, 190, 196, 219-20, 232, 257-58, 260n., 261n.
Republic of Protagoras, 88, 104, 148, 162
Resurrection of flesh, 213-14
Rhetoric, 84, 87, 116-17
Ritter, Constantin, 14, 35, 39
Robespierre, Maximilien, 205
Robin, Léon, 239
Robinson Crusoe ideal, 90
Roman Empire, 149
Romans, 147
Romanticism, 136, 139, 152; ethics of, 91, 115, 152
Ross, W. D. (Sir David), 239, 241n.
Russell, Bertrand, 79, 137-38, 168-69, 181
Russia, 204-6
Ryle, Gilbert, 7, 9-11, 23, 25, 28, 83, 97, 196, 213n., 229n., 259

Sabozios, 60
Santayana, George, 24, 28, 48, 53-54, 56, 133, 140-41, 202, 219n., 247
Schelling, Friedrich Wilhelm Joseph von, 196
Schilpp, Paul A., 245
Schneider, H. W., 129
Scholz, H., 239n.
Schopenhauer, Arthur, 143
Schwärmerei, religious, 139
Science, Greek, 19, 49-53; Hellenistic, 50
Science, in Plato, 138, 145n., 159-60
Scientific society, Bertrand Russell on, 168-69
Self-control (*sōphrosynē*), 21, 178, 182-83
Sensation as knowledge, 229-31
Sense perception, in *Protagoras*, 89
Sextus Empiricus, 89
Shakespeare, William, 6, 15, 101, 194, 216
Shaw, G. B., 39, 95
Shelley, Percy Bysshe, 194
Shepherd, myth of divine, in *Statesman*, 177-78
Shorey, Paul, 15, 164
Simmias, interpretation of Plato's dream, 123
Simonides, 107
Sisyphus, 42
Slavery, in *Laws*, 185
Social classes, Greek, 41
Social contract theory, Glaucon's, in *Republic*, 90
Socialism, 180
Socialists, 167
Socrates, 4, 19, 39, 93-102, 144; Plato's meeting with, 19; dream of, 26; historical, 93-95, 101; apologies for, 95-96; personality, 96-98, 102; teaching of, in Plato, 98-102, 257-58; on teaching, in *Meno*, 112-14
Solid geometry, 243

Index

Solmsen, F., 223
Son of Apollo, 134, 219n.
Sophist, 79-81, 124, 196, 222, 229, 232-37
Sophists, 42, 55-56, 80-92, 159; in Sophist, 233-34
Sophocles, 3, 46, 129, 152
Sophron, 19
Sophroniskos, 93
Sōphrosynē (self-control), 21, 178, 182-83
Soul (psychē), 60
Space (chōra), 253-54
Space, absolute, in Newton, 254
Sparta, defeat of, 29
Spartan ideal, Plato on, 170-71, 183
Spartan state, 149
Spenser, Edmund, 194
Speusippos, 18, 174, 198n., 261n.
Spinoza, Baruch, 44, 134, 244, 247
Spiritualism, 211-12, 217-18
Sprague, Rosamond K., 124
Statesman, 29, 172, 176-80, 182, 222, 261n.
Stein, Heinrich von, 261n.
Stoics, 69
Strife, 71-72
"Success" (aretē), 84, 105
Swan of Apollo, 19
Symposium, 127 32, 139, 167, 173, 190, 196, 199, 214, 220-21, 259
Syracuse, Plato's first visit to, 21-22; second visit, 9, 23-25; third visit, 26

Tarán, Leonardo, 74
Taylor, A. E., 10, 15-16, 31-32, 94-95, 116, 138-39, 239, 254, 261n.
Teleion, to (completeness), 42
Teleology in creation, in Timaeus, 248-49, 251
Thales, 62
Theaetetus, 89, 124, 222, 228-33
Theōria as imaginative vision, 1-3, 49, 53, 263
Theōria (vision) of knowledge and

Ideas, 188-89, 198-200, 203, 206, 210, 220-21; in education, 158; of the Good, 256
"Theory of Ideas": history of, 189-90, 192-95, 210; problems of, 194-97; in Parmenides, 226-28; Ryle on, 259n.
Theory of knowledge, in Plato, 188-89, 198-99
Thesmophoria, 58
Thomas Aquinas, St., 16, 45
Thracian rites, 60
Thrasyllus, 30, 33
Thrasymachus, 91
Thucydides, 8, 46, 52, 82, 92
Thymos (spiritedness), 155
Tillich, Paul, 45, 51, 139
Timaeus, 64, 67, 138, 203, 229, 238, 240, 243, 247-56, 259; history of, 247-48, 254-55
Timaeus of Locris, 64, 248
Time (chronos), in Timaeus, 250, 254
Time, absolute, in Newton, 254
Toeplitz, O., 238n., 239n., 245n.
Tories, 180
Tragedy, 43-44
Triangles, ultimate, in Timaeus, 243-44
Trinity, doctrine of, 44, 193
Trollope, Anthony, 82
Trotsky, Leon, 205
True opinion as knowledge, 232-33
Twain, Mark, 182n.

Ueberweg-Praechter, 95
Unity of Plato's thought, 221-22, 259n.
Unknowable, the, 43
Unmoved Mover of Aristotle, 255
Untersteiner, Mario, 74
Unwritten philosophy of Plato, 239, 244
Utilitarian position, 173
Utopian spirit, 166-67

Wallas, Graham, 152
War, character of, 18; in *Republic,* 170, 178, 183; rejected in *Laws,* 182-83
Ward, Mrs. Humphry, 82
Washington, D.C., 200
Wax tablet, in *Theaetetus,* 232
Weaving as art of statesman, in *Statesman,* 178-79
Welfare state, 149
Wheelwright, Philip, 69
Whitehead, A. N., 16, 45, 136, 138, 239, 245, 254, 262
Wilamowitz-Moellendorff, U. von, 14
Wild, John, 16
Wise Men (*Sophoi*), the Seven, 46
Wolff, Christian, 234n.

Woodbridge, F. J. E., 18, 27-28, 31, 99, 134, 219n.
World War I, 217

Xanthippe, 101
Ilenourataj ajθ.., ιίι
Xenophanes, 70, 74, 79
Xenophon, 7, 11, 20, 33, 93-95, 98
Xerxes, 119

Yankees, 50
Yeats, W. B., 194

Zagreus, 60
Zeller, Eduard, 12, 14, 262
Zeno the Eleatic, 87, 89, 237
Zeus, 107-8, 131